OPERATION RETROSPECT

A SOLDIER'S JOURNAL IN A VETERAN'S REUNION

PAUL ENDRIS

Copyright © 2019 Paul Endris
ISBN-10: 0-9600377-0-5
ISBN-13: 978-0-9600377-0-4
Rifle and pen graphic by Shaun Loveless
Map illustrated by Gregof
Cover by Facundo Cureses
Font designed by Eduardo Recife, available at misprintedtype.com

Visit OperationRetrospect.com
for exclusive content relating to this book.

The story in this book reflects the author's recollection of events. It, by no means, speaks for all veterans. The author recreated the dialogue from memory. Some journal entries were edited for clarity.

The views expressed in this book are the author's alone and do not reflect the official policy or position of the Department of the Army, Department of Defense, or the U.S. Government.

FOREWORD

As you will read in *Operation Retrospect*, individual experiences in a combat environment create incredible, unbreakable and indescribable bonds by those standing side by side. Experiences shared by those fighting the Global War on Terror in Iraq, Afghanistan, Somalia, Syria or any of the other locations where we are decisively engaged truly captures the strength of our all-volunteer fighting force.

With 1% of the American population serving at any given time, their willingness to fight for the 99% further speaks to their resilience, selfless service and courage as well as to that of their families and loved ones. However, one of the greatest challenges for this 1% is to effectively communicate what it meant to serve their nation and humanity as a whole in the Global War on Terror. We do not have a civilian-military divide in our nation today; that was a burden the Vietnam Veteran generation experienced, what we have today is a misunderstanding. The only way to address this is through effective communication and engagement on a national level.

The GWOT Memorial Foundation leads the efforts to build the National GWOT Memorial in our nation's capital to commemorate and honor the members of the Armed Forces who served in support of our nation's longest war, especially those who gave the ultimate sacrifice. Consistent with its mission, the Foundation will recognize and salute the service and sacrifices of all who served in defense of the nation in this conflict, as well as their families and friends.

I ask that you stand with me. We share a sacred duty to honor all those who have selflessly served in our nation's longest war... a charge we do not take lightly... a charge we will remain loyal to... a charge we will keep.

Gracias and Godspeed,

Michael R Rodriguez

Michael "Rod" Rodriguez
President and Chief Executive Officer
GWOT Memorial Foundation

OPERATION
RETROSPECT

DEDICATION

To my wife and other military spouses and families;
we may carry rucksacks,
but you carry a nation.

To the men of Comanche Company and other veterans;
while the sounds of guns have faded,
your service remains thunderous.

To Zayas and Weir,
two souls among the 6,970 and counting;
your extraordinary sacrifice of tomorrow
empowers us to live a life worth living today.

MAP OF OUR AREA OF OPERATIONS

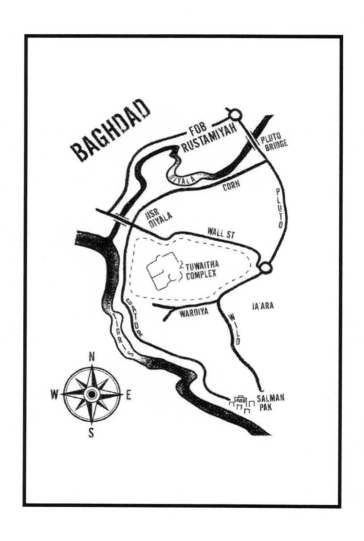

1.

WE HAVE A RENDEZVOUS WITH DESTINY

December 31, 2015 –

*D*ing. For me, it started with text messages one year in the making. "Happy New Year, Paul," my phone read. Jeff had for some time made a habit of sending me a message to ring in the first day of January. Yet, there were more than a few words in that message. The phone chimed again: "10 years!" There it was.

Son of a gun, I thought. *Has it been ten years*? I put the phone on my lap and looked across the living room. Kat, my wife, sat in our comfy armchair tired from another holiday trip to visit family. I scanned the walls filled with happy snapshots and photographs of our life—pictures from our wedding, some family vacations in the mountains, milestones we'd been fortunate to accomplish, and other typical indications of a life lived since I last saw Jeff. It was evident by glancing around our modest home, we were lucky.

Remembering my favorite poem also displayed in a frame, 'Desiderata' by Max Ehrmann, I thought to myself how the only noise and haste we knew was quietly sleeping upstairs. *Remember what peace there may be in silence*, it read. We were ordinary but undoubtedly fortunate. As my mind focused on the history the walls contained, a particular chapter was hidden from the picture frames and decorations.

I texted my shock. "Unreal, a decade."

"Who's that?" Kat asked without looking up. The New Year's Eve ball dropping pre-show continued on the television that neither of us were watching. While people had already packed New York City's Times Square hours earlier, we enjoyed the coziness of our warm and comfortable home. Happy 2016.

"Jeff texted me," I told her. She nibbled some chips and salsa she had hastily assembled after putting our nearly two-year-old son to bed while watching me collect the remnants of his destruction. Toys were routinely discarded in a whirlwind of sunny energy that eventually succumbed to feisty tiredness, but we took great joy in that golden hour where it was just us—Kat and me. Not yet knowing she carried our next whirlwind inside her belly, she propped her feet on the footrest and let out a deep sigh only expectant mothers can do. This was our average life. It was mundane and beautiful beyond measure.

I looked over at her. "We returned just over ten years ago."

"Wow," she stated flatly. "Time is flying."

"I wonder how everyone is doing."

"Ask them," Kat suggested.

"Eh, I'm not sure I have everyone's numbers." I searched for an excuse. Texting and talking on the phone were not my forte.

"You should try," Kat offered while crunching a tortilla chip.

Ding. My cell phone sounded again. "Down for a reunion this year?" Jeff texted. I smiled and relayed the message to my wife as I melted into the couch.

"A rendezvous it is!" I tapped back to Jeff. I glanced to my wife, knowing I had agreed without her consent. Homes have burnt to the ground for less.

"Deal." My phone dinged. Jeff agreed.

"Babe." I cleared my throat. "What would you say to making a trip to meet with these dudes this year?"

"Sure." She was hanging on by a thread from falling fast asleep. The holiday season had gotten to her, and she felt charitable enough to agree to the decision without debate. She was tired and willing to say yes to anything if it meant she could rest. But she understood something I did not. Something special exists between two people who have not seen one another for a decade and messaged one another on the holidays. Jeff and I had a bond. It was undeniable.

We had joined the Army around the same time but from entirely different backgrounds. He radiated from comfortable, sunny Florida and I sprouted from a flat farming town in Illinois. Our fates were set years before our New Year's Eve messaging. We had graduated infantry training at Fort Benning and reported to the 101st Airborne Division while they were transitioning from the initial invasion of Iraq back to garrison life in early 2004. After months of bouncing between regiments as the Army reorganized, we soon found ourselves as roommates and members of a reconnaissance company for the 4th Brigade—the legendary Currahees of the 506th Infantry Regiment.

"How do we want to go about this?" Jeff inquired digitally.

"I'm not sure."

But with an easy roll call, the troops were mustered. Kat and I were loading the truck and leaving our home outside Omaha for a long drive to Nashville to connect with some brothers-in-arms from another life a few short months later.

"Got everything?" Kat asked as she threw her bag into the rear seat. I carried a cardboard diaper box with memorabilia I figured might interest the guys. Printed news articles of our exploits, including a story about our midnight crossing of the Tigris River in rubber zodiac boats, trinkets from the war like the infamous CIA playing cards, and certificates of the memorial stones we fundraised to dedicate to the 101st Airborne Division museum were piled high. I threw the diaper box in the truck and climbed into the driver's seat. I shifted into reverse to ease out of the driveway but paused.

"I gotta get it," I said to myself.

"Get what?" Kat asked.

"The journal." I climbed out and sprinted into the house. I rushed to the bookcase and, buried under a stack of textbooks from my old college days, I unearthed a document that was dear to me. I had spent a year working on it, many times after long periods of being awake. Then, upon my return from combat and finding time for quiet reflection, I expanded upon my recollection. A decade later, it contained memories silenced. Many only existed on aging paper. I grabbed it, wiped off the dust, and returned to my waiting wife.

"You got it?" Her rhetorical question hinted at a follow-up inquiry. *Are you ready to share it?*

I threw it in the diaper box and backed the vehicle out of the driveway. Hitting Interstate 29 and eleven hours of drive time between the two cities, Kat soon remarked of the changes in our lives since I had returned from war.

"Gosh, so much has changed," she mused.

"We are in a good place," I said. "So many things have happened."

"School."

"Yup."

"Got married." Kat reached for my hand over the console. I accepted her offer and squeezed her hand. We had known each other in high school but had spent years apart after I enlisted. Following my return from Iraq, I would escape Fort Campbell as many weekends as I could to make the long drive to her college campus. Those drives were significant. Hours and hours on the road silent in contemplation were worth it, and we were wed a short three years later after I left the service.

"Had one kid, one on the way."

I knew these were great things. We were lucky and aware of our blessings, but my thoughts were somewhere else. Visions flashed through my mind of two soldiers I knew in another life: Zayas and Weir. It didn't seem fair to have as much abundance as we'd enjoyed. They did not get to hang pictures on their walls of family vacations. They did not get to see their families grow. They did not get to continue to write their story. Their legacy was established, and it was one of service and sacrifice, not of age and accomplishment.

"Everyone is busy living life." It was the only thing I could offer. I released Kat's hand. She turned her head and surveyed the countryside. The green leaves of the passing trees and cows placidly munching grasses were more interesting than my reluctant conversation. We passed Saint Louis, meandered through southern Illinois, and galloped towards the Bluegrass State. Miles passed and sunflower seeds were split and songs blasted over the radio and memories from another life became closer.

"How many are coming?" Kat asked, hoping to revitalize the conversation.

"I'd expect around 20 to 30." We had quite the response when I pitched the idea to the guys. It was like our fellow veterans had been waiting for somebody to bring it up but no one wanted to say anything. Collectively, we chose Nashville due to its proximity to Fort Campbell, our former duty station, and the fact it had a welcoming Veterans of Foreign Wars post. Many of us were members of the supportive veteran service organization.

"I'm sure your Army buddies appreciate you and Jeff organizing this thing." Kat knew how much had gone into planning the rendezvous and was coaching me up. She was supportive of all of my efforts but also knew when to call out my ridiculousness. "But don't act like you needed an excuse to throw a party."

I gave her a half-smile. "Well, I appreciate all of them that made this a priority." Many of the veterans had to take rainchecks due to finances, work obligations, and the like. Some of them were even deployed, still hacking it out overseas. "I had my reservations whether this would even come together."

"I never—" She yawned. "I never doubted it," Kat said. She was again fighting off the pregnancy slumber.

"Why don't you close your eyes? Get some rest."

She relented. "If you say so."

As the sun edged towards the horizon, Kat snuggled into the passenger's seat for another nap before we reached our destination—a hotel on the northeast side of the city we'd booked for the reunion, not far from the airport. The city had changed considerably since our time at Campbell, but I wasn't concerned with the transformation of the downtown scene. I was only interested in how much we all had changed since leaving years earlier. I scanned the edges of the road and sipped a cheap gas station coffee.

This is going to be a hell of a ride, I thought. I was excited to revisit our experiences together. I also knew to look back involved coming to terms with some truths and events that I had purposely left behind in a forgotten journal written by a man a few years younger—a man who wanted to connect the entries, hoping to use those experiences to plot a course for a future. My life hadn't slowed enough for me to consider how those events shaped the road ahead. I turned down the radio. The retreating sun's light danced through the thick leafy trees and lit the Ohio River, bouncing off the slow waters that cut through centuries-old bedrock. Nashville was not far. Neither was the war.

Self-reflection sometimes happens in the muddiest of puddles, sometimes on the longest of drives, sometimes in the silence of memories. We drove on in a hushed calm. There was little traffic. Three Iraqi men were advancing towards our four-member team's position along a canal filled with brown stagnant

6

water and reed grass that sprouted from the murky soup. The moon illuminated the terrain and painted the figures carrying weapons an iridescent lunar shade of steel. The road flexed over the soft rolling hills of Kentucky.

I had received an update over the radio regarding the armed men maneuvering on us, so we made a J-shaped jog to conceal ourselves behind the tall grass near a canal. I gripped the steering wheel. Through my night vision, past a hole in the reeds, I focused on the assault rifles. The moonlight bounced off their AK-47 magazines like the sun off a car window. They were getting closer. I could hear them talking. I was several body lengths from my nearest buddy and devising any sort of plan became impossible. I looked to my left: Wright. I glanced to my right: Tyler. We knew the rules, we had the training, we understood the objective. They were closing in on us. I passed an eighteen-wheeler.

"If they so much as fart in the wrong direction—waste them," I had radioed earlier to our sister sniper team at the location we hoped to rendezvous only a few hundred meters to our rear. "Radio silent."

A faint beep. "Copy." I picked a different song. These three men had trailed us guided by the night's bounty of illumination. The dirty stone glow of moonlight washed us in chalk-like dust as we moved alongside the smooth water of a dozen ponds and interconnected drainage ditches. In minutes, a small irrigation canal separated these four men holding weapons from another three men also carrying semi-automatic rifles. It wasn't far now.

One team knew of the other's location; the other three were unaware. One group was a United States Army sniper team; the others consisted of three AK-47-wielding males of military age. One soldier had called his buddy team to help kill the trackers; another Kalashnikov-armed man made a cell phone call to an unknown entity only minutes ago. My pulse was elevated and my senses sharpened. Slowly, I aimed my rifle at the center mass of the middle member of the trio. Controlled breathing, as I had been trained, became a deliberate effort. I scanned my rearview mirror.

Keep cool, I thought to myself. The drive continued. If those weapons rose above waist level, the otherwise pleasant night's silence would be interrupted by the crackling din of a hellacious volley with a few extra trigger pulls thrown in for good measure. Even with the Americans' distinct advantages, it was an exceptionally precarious situation resulting from pure uncertainty and insufficient situational awareness—the status quo of any battlefield. Here we were, a textbook example of what this war demanded. The thought crossed my mind as a rage took hold deep inside me.

How did we get here?

With a nod to say go, it was time to spring out of the reed grass concealing us. I groaned and gritted my teeth as I jumped to my feet. "Son of a..." We pulled into the hotel parking lot. We had made it to Nashville.

The fog of war is a phenomenon that is accounted for in every training scenario or exercise military leaders undergo to sharpen their combat prowess. However, the term does not merely encompass the pandemonium and confusion that develops during war that ages military leaders prematurely. It also describes how one interprets combat experiences. For many, the ambiguity involved in warfighting continues after the cacophony of rifle and machine-gun fire subsides. The smoke settles and the questions arise. What happened?

I came home asking precisely that, and it only took me a decade before I drew any conclusion about my time in Iraq. Of course, as if undertaking some sort of military operation to capture answers, I relied on the same set of brothers I fought alongside in 2006. Armed with a reluctantly shared journal from that year to cut through the fog, we sought to answer the age-old question of what war meant to the warfighter.

Arguably, outside of the invasion or the 2007 surge, the year the journal was written encompassed some of the most dynamic and consequential times of the Iraq War. Some of the more ferocious, singular battles have been recorded for the chronicles of military legend, but many of the lesser known experiences of the conflict have faded from our collective memory, particularly from the year we were there. During this time, I was patrolling the streets and outskirt neighborhoods of Southeast Baghdad from a Forward Operating Base called Rustamiyah and writing quick notes to myself about what I saw, what I did, or how I felt.

Our unit arrived in the country days after the first parliamentary elections the nation conducted under its new constitution. Even with that monumental achievement, the majority of Iraqis wanted the United States to leave their country and most favored attacking American troops. Our squadron leadership dutifully espoused the prevailing wisdom from the highest levels of government that we would depart with a functioning Iraqi security apparatus in place by the year's end. We were determined to do so.

However, sectarian violence increased significantly across the country to dramatic levels in 2006. The Al-Askari Mosque bombing in Samarra at the beginning of the year was hugely offensive to Shiites across the country and they launched a retribution campaign of violence on their neighbors and Sunni rivals. By the end of the following month, morgue officials stated that between 30 and 40 bodies were found on the streets of Baghdad daily.

As the country edged toward civil war, undisputed successes for the coalition were sparse. The tyrant Abu Musab Al-Zarqawi was killed in July 2006, ending the notorious Jordanian-born

9

militant's instigation of mass bloodshed. Despite his death, the seeds he had planted soon flourished. Violence peaked the same month with the Iraqi government claiming over 3,000 civilians were killed around the country in a single summer month. All through this time, I continued to write journal entries that painted a decidedly unique story.

The story of Comanche Company during Operation Iraqi Freedom typifies the experiences of your average infantrymen, both during the fighting and after it's over. Some entries in the journal border mundanity, while others speak to the speed at which contact with the enemy can escalate. Other no-value entries have been removed from the retelling of these events entirely. All, however, highlight the difficulties of the times and give context to the broader geopolitical issues and history involved with the conflict. Still, the deployment was challenging but not extraordinarily so—it can get worse and it has for many others.

The verisimilitude of conversations from our reunion speaks to the reasoning and rationalization of returning veterans who understood this. Our unit was supremely lucky in the grand scheme of things, and we caught a lot of breaks in terms of living conditions, access to supplies, and general hardship. There were areas in the country that saw exponentially more violence and some areas that were even lost to the insurgency. Such is the nature of war. Things are not equal. However, compared to the area just across the Tigris River, our sector had its own challenges.

Our company's area of responsibility was massive. One small reconnaissance infantry company covered an area that took 30 minutes to drive with the flow of traffic, or an hour if proceeding tactically, from its northern tip to its southern. The area was called Madaein. We were headquartered adjacent to the Iraqi Military Academy and Al-Rasheed Airfield. Forward

Operating Base Rustamiyah was not far from the intersection of the Diyala and Tigris Rivers.

From the FOB, we launched patrols along a main thoroughfare and entry into South Baghdad called Route Pluto, undoubtedly named after the dwarf planet, not the cartoon dog. It had a surface that would not be out of place in the cosmos. So many IEDs, or improvised explosive devices, had gone off here that soldiers accepted it as a matter of routine, and craters dotted every kilometer of the two-lane highway.

The route swung by a dilapidated neighborhood called Jisr Diyala and an old, derelict nuclear research complex. The district was a launching point for crime and insurgency into Baghdad proper. It was also a hive for the Jaish Al-Mahdi or Mahdi Army—the Shiite paramilitary group aligned with the young but prominent Shia cleric, Muqtada Al-Sadr. The militia was well versed in politics and its members were capable murderers.

On top of that, foreign fighters and insurgents traveled throughout our area of operation to smuggle weapons into the city or hunker down to prepare for their next operation. We, too, used the area to our advantage. Next door to Jisr Diyala, or JD for short, was the Tuwaitha Nuclear Research Facility surrounded by a 50-meter earthen berm and high fences with towers well-suited for observation posts and staging areas for coalition forces. Combined, JD and Tuwaitha created a scene ripe for conflict.

Further south, the company was also responsible for patrolling another two-lane highway past a village called Wardiya, which led to Salman Pak, a Baathist stronghold and former vacation retreat under Saddam Hussein's government. This location featured a resort that shadowed the Tigris River to the west. It had been converted into an Iraqi Public Order Brigade headquarters complete with a Baath party star fountain as the centerpiece. The water feature was bullet-ridden and filled with brown sludge—it was a stunning representation of what the country had become.

All this territory was to be secured by a reconnaissance infantry company of 90 souls responsible for 180 square miles. That's 2 square miles per soldier, a tall order considering our AO had an estimated population nearing a million people. During our operations in Iraq, Comanche Company—1st Squadron, 61st Cavalry, 506th Infantry Regiment, 101st Airborne Division— dealt with geography that dictated a change in employment.

Our company was the infantry portion of a concept the Army envisioned called a Reconnaissance, Surveillance, Target Acquisition unit. In other words, our squadron would act as the eyes and ears of the Brigade Combat Team. We, as tasking dictated, were divided into small reconnaissance teams trained to penetrate ahead of conventional infantry companies to report on whatever we found. It was a capability better suited for a Cold War Great Force showdown. However, flexibility is critical, and our mission changed to match the requirements of the war against an insurgency—albeit somewhat grudgingly.

Despite all this transformation, one thing held constant— the soldier. There was nothing extraordinary about these American soldiers. They came from ordinary places in Florida or New Jersey, cities like Seattle or small towns in the middle of the Midwest called Monticello. Most were from lower income families or comfortable middle class at best. Few were from privileged wealth. They were warriors not from lives of satin, but of cotton, not of privilege, but poverty. All were dreamers serving in the long line of silent sentinels defending our nation.

They were more than dreamers, however. They were doers. Before the ink dried on high school diplomas, many raised their right hands and took oaths to take their place in a legacy of honor and tradition of duty. They were volunteers. Yet, most were youths enamored with a romantic sense of war, wishing with an oblivious vigor for the opportunity to prove themselves.

I was no different. People have sometimes asked why I joined the military knowing that the nation was engaged in conflict, and I don't have a good answer for them. I was drawn to the service at a young age. As a kid, I had watched movies about World War Two and Vietnam, setting the VCR to record on Memorial Day movie marathons. My grandparents served in both the Army and Marine Corps, and my older brother enlisted years before I did. I had seen the transformation he had undergone and wanted to test myself too. Additionally, fighting terrorism was a worthwhile struggle regardless of the Powerball odds that a terrorist attack would occur in our cornfields. Plus, there was free college, which was a deal for any kid like me staring life in the face. Growing up, I had made so many choices based on less than sound reasoning, but if there was a principal motive to my decision to join the Army, it was that I felt duty-bound to answer my nation's call.

I'd like to say it was the ultimate act of fervent patriotism, although I did and do believe the United States of America is the greatest country on the planet. But there was another element— I didn't have much going on. I tended to win consolation prizes in most things, usually a runner-up in life. Always a safety when it came time for homecoming dates. Never first pick at dodgeball. I was an average, middle-of-the-road kid. It's not like I had a lot to lose in the eighteen-year-old sense of the world. I was immature and bullet-proof and lacked a more seasoned confidence like so many others joining the ranks. But like them, in the greed of life, our youth was surrendered for a chance at significance.

In truth, my brothers in battle enlisted for so many reasons. It was rarely one single thing that propelled them to sign on the line and ship off to boot camp, hoping to find out what they are made of. And they did. Training complete, they made their way to units across the Army chosen at random by a sleepy clerk assigning bodies by need. They were a new tribe of warriors

13

bound together by chance, connected by a devotion to the team foreign to most. These were ordinary individuals willing to do extraordinary things. These were the Comanches.

Still, the constant of the soldier was one thing, but how the Comanches got around was another. The company relied on the shoestring express mode of transportation as soldiers have for ages. Light infantry does one thing—it walks, and it walks a lot. Given the extensive area for which we were responsible, covering it on foot was not feasible, although we still found ourselves walking a great deal. On arriving in Iraq, we soon found ourselves driving retroactively up-armored, Gulf War-aged, Highly Mobile Multi-Purpose Wheeled Vehicles (HMMWVs), pronounced 'humvees', through narrow alleyways and streets of Iraqi neighborhoods.

The trucks were rough-running and had already seen several years of service. A few of us had some training driving these monstrous rolling targets, myself included, but many guys' first experiences driving them were overseas in combat zones. The changed added to the growing pains required of our deployment.

That is not to say, though, that HMMWVs were unwelcomed. Driving could be fun when you part the seas along busy Iraqi roads, but you no longer had the ability to shoot back when you were squeezed into seats not designed for the massive amount of gear and body armor we wore. To me, if you were going to be relegated to a position in the HMMWV, being in the gun turret was much more satisfying. When you rammed home the bolt of a machine gun, it was sometimes hard not to smile. It was more dangerous, or so I thought, and with the bravado aside, it meant shouldering the weight of a difficult fight.

Regardless of the way of the gun, the fight required us to close with and destroy the enemy. The value of dexterity being dismounted provided can't be overstated, not to mention the inherent ability to mix with the Iraqi populace face-to-face, rather than traveling in a metal can of death. Nevertheless, whether driving, gunning, or dismounting, we each had difficult calls to make that decided the outcome of life—both ours and the enemy's.

Though we may machine-gun, blast, bomb, melt the sands of Iraq to a sheet of glass, hurl the might of the most magnificent military force to march the Earth upon the enemy, the unnatural conditions demanded of counterinsurgency necessitated a finesse. It was a delicate dance of lethality levied upon our youth both duties of politician and patrolman, detective and destroyer, judge and jury. This endeavor required an adaption. You needed to hand out aid with one hand and return fire with another. Our skills were those honed by rigorous training grounded in decades of conventional thought on combat: find them, fix them, and kill them. In this, we excelled. It gave order to the chaos, but in a game where only one side wore a uniform, it was incongruent with our objectives. We maintained the law of armed conflict, but molded rules of engagement, or ROE, to meet the reality of our mission.

A multitude of strict limits were put in place to force our adaptation to this actuality. Positive identification was paramount. Targets had to be those of legitimate military nature. Don't fire into areas where civilians coalesced unless that area was being used for a military purpose. Minimize collateral damage. Use force proportional to the provocation. Escalate in steps but don't disregard your inherent right to self-defense. The list went on. The rules were fair but maintained a degree of decision-making at the most junior levels.

We were the ones to win the conflict—the beat cops patrolling neighborhoods on the regular, not SWAT team equivalents pursuing individuals in audacious midnight raids. Although the targeted strikes by Special Operation Forces were part of it and it can't be denied they played a decisive role in the capitulation of many high-level combatants, the objectives of the fight were incumbent upon the average soldier. Indeed, the majority of the fighting was conducted with traditional combat arms, young soldiers trained as hammers and who loved looking for nails. This was the situation and the conditions we faced upon arriving in our little corner of Baghdad in late 2005, awaiting the Iraqi New Year. The challenges were plenty, the consequences absolute, and the outcomes unknown. It was war, and it was real.

May 28, 2016 –

Searching the parking lot for a spot, we found one a little way from the entrance to the hotel tucked under a limb missing its leaves. The hotel was nothing special. It had ten floors, and the exterior looked as if it hadn't been updated in a few decades. It had a bar and a restaurant attached, so we were satisfied. I shifted into park and the truck inched forward.

"We made it." Kat was relieved. "I need to use the restroom."

"Maybe go inside to do that?" I joked. "I'll meet you in the room. Wanna check us in?"

"Okay." Kat grabbed our bag and scooted off to the lobby. I liked how she packed. Most women with her fashion sense would not dare to leave without a full wardrobe's worth of clothes, but not her. She knew how to make space count. She was organized in all things, and that kept me on track the many times I was out of sorts.

I jumped out of the truck and did a little dip in the knees. My joints crackled like embers in a campfire.

"Whew. Glad that's done," I said to no one in particular. I walked around to the bed of the truck and opened the tailgate. I shuffled stuff from the bed into the cab, so we could lock it away to deter sticky hands. I plopped the cooler into the front seat.

Maybe I oughta buckle it up for good measure, I thought. It has never taken much to amuse me. I circled around and grabbed a couple of folding chairs to lock them up next. I opened the truck's door with a couple of fingers and slid the chairs into the back. The diaper box caught my eye. There it was—the journal I hadn't flipped open for quite some time. I picked it up and flipped through the text. *Maybe I should leave this here?* I wondered. *Why am I so hesitant to share this thing?*

Ding. "Room 523." Kat texted. I finished securing our reunion gear and threw the journal in with the other memorabilia. Without shame, I lifted the box that a month ago had contained little underwear designed for the least appealing aspect of child-rearing and marched off to the hotel entrance. Rounding a few cars and navigating my way to the lobby, I entered a room full of busy travelers and tourists. I scanned the activity of the hotel as I was accustomed to doing and searched for my wife. I reasoned she must have made her way to the room. A sign pointed towards the elevator, which was tucked around a corner. I weaved through the hotel guests sporting the diaper box luggage to catch a lift to the fifth floor.

I rounded the corner right as the elevator door was closing. "Hold it, please!" I galloped in. The lone occupant, a rough-looking man with a beard to his belly with a chain wallet swinging across his thigh, stuck his flannel-clad arm out blocking the door from closing. "Thanks. Mind hitting five?"

"Yes, sir!" the man bellowed. "You didn't use to be such an asshole, Paul." The number five was already illuminated.

My eyebrows rose. I turned, half-facing the man. Eyebrows lowered. Eyes narrowed. "Holy shit. Notaro?" The elevator door closed.

"Yeah, you son of a gun!" Notaro was one of the finest non-commissioned officers of the company. His reputation was legendary. He was crazy, but he was disciplined. He was smart, but he was crude. He could connect with the soldiers but also offer direct feedback that was often painful but necessary. He had spent the years before our deployment training Rangers in Georgia, and his training background was paramount to our deployment preparation. He would dish out push-ups in multiples of fifty for the sorts of offenses young soldiers make but also opened his home to those same soldiers on the holidays when they didn't have anywhere to go. You just could never call him by his first name.

"Damn man, I didn't even recognize you!" My mouth didn't close but stayed frozen in a shocked sort of smile.

"I threw away my razors."

"I couldn't tell." Most of us had dreamt of one day growing a beard that would make any Viking envious. Notaro was living that dream. "I'd shake your hand, but..." I lifted the diaper box.

"Screw it, man. You don't know where these hands have been," Notaro joked. The number two button turned a worn shade of yellow. Three more floors to go. "Damn, diapers?" He peered into the box. "What you got in there?"

"Ah, some stuff I thought we'd look at."

"What's that thing on top? A book?"

"A journal."

"No shit."

"No shit," I echoed. "Every patrol I ever went on."

"No shit?" Notaro's eyes opened wide. "Let me take a peak."

"Eh." I turned towards the door. "I didn't think you could read." Third floor.

"C'mon." He reached for the pages I had compiled years before. "I read at a fifth-grade level."

"I don't know where those hands have been." I ripped the cardboard diaper box from his reach. A sense of familiarity washed over me. The fourth floor came and went. My smile remained.

18

"Getting smarter over the years!" He slapped his knee, laughing, and shook a finger at me. Number five flashed and the door slid open. "But damn, man, you look like you haven't aged a bit!"

"It's like we just left," I said and stepped out of the elevator.

November 17, 2005 –

I came into work to not return this year. I left my mother outside the gate to Fort Campbell. My younger brother drove me into the squadron, and the ten or so guys departing early were there. The rest of the company had been released to prepare and spend time with their families. That evening we loaded our gear onto the bus and drove to the airfield. There, we waited late into the evening on a plane that was delayed in Baltimore. Talked to the colonel and sergeant major. They pumped us up as leaders do. The time came and we boarded the chartered airliner. Next stop, Kuwait.

November 18, 2005 –

We touched down in Kuwait City, took a bus to our staging area—a dusty place called Camp Virginia. I was so jet lagged I wasn't sure if I was tired or dreaming. We secured our stuff and assembled cots in a long, white semi-circle tent. We had arrived at camp around 11, went to sleep at 3a.m. I'm a world away.

November 28, 2005 –

Thanksgiving wasn't bad and not long after the holiday, the rest of the company arrived. We helped secure the additional company gear for the team. The tent went from 10 dudes to packed full. We traveled into the desert to zero our rifles and melt in the sun in the name of acclimatization. Oddly enough, the temperatures weren't terrible. We will spend the next few days continuing our ventures out into the desert surrounded by Kuwaiti Bedouins roaming amongst their camel and goat herds. It's like a scene straight from Lawrence of Arabia—I can hear the melody now.

December 15, 2005 –

It's my 21st birthday. I didn't tell anyone to avoid the traditional whooping or pink belly. Davis, Fogle, and I played a game of Monopoly at the Morale, Welfare, and Recreation Center. We even finished. I joked about making it another year. On the television, they had footage of Iraq's first parliamentary election today. Maybe this whole thing will be over before my 22nd birthday.

Your twenty-first birthday is one of the big ones and I, and thousands of other service members, spent that time in the desert or worse. Despite this travesty, I was not on patrol or pulling guard or dodging bullets. Playing Monopoly with some great people is not a terrible way to turn twenty-one.

I may not have had the opportunity to buy my first beer or hit a bar for a night of blurry memories as is typical of Americans at this age, but I was able to relax and socialize with some of my closest friends. They were like family. Every year on my birthday, I part with more of the things of youth, but I remain thankful. That sentiment took root there, in that tent, where I played a board game instead of undertaking the standard rite of passage.

I remember thinking that this war would only delay the birthday celebration while also morbidly questioning the next one. Dark humor is a necessary skill required for keeping your sanity in an otherwise insane environment. You joke about things that make people in other circles cringe, but I have since viewed it as a coping mechanism for those dealing with anxiety and dread. Back then, I would not have admitted to any fear, but I was ignorant of the reality of the conditions to which I would soon be exposed.

Fear is duplicitous. On the one hand, you do not want to be so engrossed with it that it cripples control over your actions, but it is already rooted in the deepest crevices of your psyche. I did not want to let anyone down. I was fearful of how I'd react under fire, and that fear was a strong motivator to come to terms with my own existence. I turned twenty-one thinking that I might die, but at least they wouldn't call me chickenshit.

Mortality aside, on the same day I was allowed to purchase booze by law, thousands of Iraqi nationals dipped their fingers in purple ink to cast a vote ushering in a democratic government in the form of a 275-member council of representatives. As I sat in the relative Park Place of a tent in the Kuwaiti desert playing a board game with friends, citizens of a nation optimistic at the chance for a functioning elected political system risked murderous reprisal to have their voices heard.

The results were the establishment of a shaky government led by an unreliable candidate soon replaced by US-favored Nouri al-Maliki four months later. Maliki was popular and could unite Iraqis, which at the time, was fundamental to governance, but he had a questionable past. In addition to the leadership turmoil, al-Maliki was closely tied to the political party of Muqtada al-Sadr, the leader of the Jaish al-Mahdi, or Mahdi Army, the militant force reportedly strengthening in our area of operations. Regardless, Maliki was the man in which we had to place our trust to unite the country, organize its resources, and secure its provinces. He had as much experience with politics as I had with combat.

December 17, 2005 –

It's time to head north. Our section went first again. We boarded the bus and drove 45 minutes to some airfield. We had to keep the curtains shut to conceal troop movements. I wasn't sure a curtain was going to keep anyone from knowing we're in town. I'm volunteered for detail. We stacked the bags and rucksacks on crates for the C-130. The thing was a mound taller than any man in the company. It was evidence we carried a lot of gear to combat. After that, the soldiers relaxed in a tent until the leaders called us forward.

It was time. We drove unto the airfield to the awaiting airplane. It was somewhere around 2100 hours. An Air Force kid gave us a spiel regarding the aircraft and safety. I couldn't hear a damn thing, so I stuck in earplugs. Lights went out. Davis' rifle smacked my knee 100 times. Lights came on. Ramps fell to the Earth. We ran out, guided by another Air Force kid who steered us away and loaded a group of reporters onto the same aircraft.

Within minutes, they were gone. Quite the operation. We hung out at Baghdad International Airport and worked out a ride to FOB Rustamiyah. I stood listening to the small arms fire from the direction of Baghdad and watched tracers fly into the air. A CH-47 helicopter landed. We snatched our stuff from a massive heap of gear and ran to the Chinook. It was a nightmare of an 800-meter sprint carrying all our stuff from the pallets.

We flew to Rustamiyah buried under another mountain of equipment. We landed and dug our way out before sprinting clear. Birds left. All was quiet. 2315 hours. My first smell of Rustamiyah and it smelled of human excrement tinged with a scent of burning plastic. Trucks came to pick us up, and we drove to squadron headquarters. We unloaded and took our stuff to a room designated by the executive officer. Sleep.

I can remember the eerie glow of the camp as we arrived in the middle of the night. It was calm, like a kind of graveyard, and I remember one young soldier standing outside his hooch, our new commandeered living quarters, watching the trucks rumble through loaded with his replacements.

Dressed in flip-flops and his physical training shorts, he neither smiled nor frowned as his relief arrived. It's a golden rule in the Army to look like a tough guy to strangers or even your fellow soldiers. The vibe resembles a prison to the uninitiated. It is a puzzling concept to me, but at that moment, despite his tough guy demeanor, I felt as if I was looking at my future self.

Herded into our new home, we pulled our gear off the truck and carried it to our assigned rooms. A non-commissioned officer came to speak to our section leaders and orient us to the compound. I stood to listen. I knew I had much to learn, and I wasn't above looking like a fool and asking questions. Our NCOs gleaned all the information they could about the compound—indirect fire actions, chow hall hours, phones, and if Rustamiyah always smelled like an outhouse.

The section leaders stood stoic and stern, taking in all the information. Staff Sergeants Wright and DeLay were polar opposites but got along well. Wright was tall, lean, and good at soldiering. He could shoot, run, and ruck march with the best of them. More cerebral and of a heartier constitution, DeLay was a sage among young sinners. He'd give life advice where he could and listen to complaints to help where he might.

Our team was also lucky enough to have a six-and-a-half-foot tree of a man named Tyler who sometimes lacked a filter when he smelled bullshit. We had Davis—an intelligent, balding sniper who was comfortable not being the loudest in the room, but if he had a better idea, he voiced it in the best way. Fogle rounded out the team. He was smart and quiet, which suited his skinny build and gaunt features well. The man we'd tease about having hollow bones like a bird would wait until he got around his inner circle to take flight.

I joined the team late in the game. Our leadership wanted to beef up our manpower from the traditional two-man sniper duo to a three-man element for additional security. I wasn't much of a sniper in comparison. I failed initially, but got a second chance and trained hard to eventually secure a spot in the sniper section. I had been a designated marksman in first platoon previously and knew my way around a radio so I had some skills to offer. It was humbling to be surrounded by soldiers with twice the ability.

Together, we explored the camp, learning as much as we could. Like the other Comanches, we had grown close through the last eighteen months of piercing cold, rainy days in the field that readied us for this moment. Because of those hard days, we found the forward operating base blessed with a guilty comfort.

It was undeniable that FOB Rustamiyah was a palace; a palace that smelled like a sewer, but a palace nonetheless. Formerly, it was part of an Iraqi Military Academy complex, and we garrisoned a series of three cinder block buildings riddled with mortar and rocket blasts. We had a few personnel to a small room that contained two wall lockers and two bunks with actual mattresses. We had a fixed latrine, complete with American style toilets, and most of them even worked.

After the invasion, contracting money had flowed into the war zone, improving it to a degree of luxury that would make any grunt feel guilty. Frankly, our training had prepared us for far worse. We weren't sleeping in holes. We had hot food. We had showers. It was a palace, and we sheepishly smiled as we investigated our new digs. I was thankful then, just as I am thankful now.

December 19, 2005 –

Enjoyed a nice little mortar attack. Sirens went off and we gave a count to the section leader. "All accounted for." The rest of the company landed minutes after the indirect fire. Sirens sounded the ALL CLEAR signal, and we coalesced outside the command post to greet the rest of the team. What a welcome to the show.

The upside of being the advance party is the experience is fresh. The sights, sounds, and smells are new. The bad side is that there are no shortages of tasks and few people to lend a hand. You have to assemble the company's equipment, you have to find your way around, and you have to figure out procedures. Nobody is going to show you, especially not the regular joes who you are replacing. I found that they took a bit of joy in watching newbies figure these things out.

When we went on patrol, though, the unit we were relieving changed gears, took us by the hand, and showed us around the neighborhoods. With pride and warped nostalgia, they wanted to show us where significant actions had occurred, where their victories had taken place, and sometimes where their defeats had happened. Our company was advantaged to receive full participation from the leadership in the changeover—what the Army called relief in place, transition of authority. Other units simply packed their bags and wished you good luck.

Clearly, it would take some time to figure out the lay of the land, familiarize ourselves with the local area, and iron out our initial combat operations. We were a different breed than those we were tapping out. Being light infantry, we had trained to patrol on foot and carried our equipment to the fight on our backs. We replaced an armored cavalry unit who rode around in heavily armored M2 Bradley Fighting Vehicles and fortress-like M1 Abrams tanks. They packed serious firepower.

Many of them were veterans of the invasion, where they had raced across the desert in a sandy blitzkrieg, destabilizing any counter-efforts Saddam's troops could muster. Now, this conflict called for stabilizing the grounds they had so dynamically seized. It required an assumption of risk rooted in the bravery of average American service members who soon found themselves in a transforming fight. That was us. Comanche Company, our tribe of untested joes but experienced NCOs, was exposed to this evolving reality. There was a question we openly answered but secretly debated: *Were we ready?*

2.

OUR STRENGTH AND COURAGE

May 28, 2016 –

"Look who's here!" Kat called out. I spilled from the elevator into the hallway, leaving Notaro to continue to his room to drop off his gym bag. I spotted Kat holding the door to 523 open and gave a quick nod to thank her for her assistance.

"Paul!" I heard a familiar voice. "Get your ass in here!"

I laughed and put my shoulder in the door to free Kat, who spun into the room. I nudged the door open, asking, "What's going on in here?"

"Just rode in," Jeff answered, "and bumped into your wife in the hallway."

"Well, how the hell are you?" I dropped the diaper box into the open closet that contained an ironing board, a few hangers, and a safe. I wrapped Jeff in a welcoming hug and a pat on the back. "I ran into Notaro in the elevator."

"You kidding me?"

"Nope, he's here."

"The gang is supposed to be meeting in the bar downstairs soon," Jeff said. "I can't wait to see everyone!"

"Well, let's get you guys a drink," Kat suggested.

"Perfect." Jeff and I agreed.

"Now, get out. I gotta use the restroom." Kat shooed us out into the hall.

"I can't wait to see who else is here," Jeff said, eyeing the hallway for his wife, Kara.

Ding. "Apparently Fogle." I had just received a message from my former teammate.

"Yeah? So far, we've got messages from Doc Winsor, Burns, Oliver, Sorbello, Schmidt, and Mannino. Doc Wicker will be in tomorrow, so will some other guys." Jeff scrolled through his phone. "Looking like a good turnout so far."

"It's a start," I commented.

"There you are!" Kara rounded the corner, spotting Jeff. "You must be Paul!" She smiled and extended her hand, closing the distance.

"I am."

"I've heard so much about you," she stated. I panicked and disregarded the handshake for a gentle, awkward hug. I had always been better at goodbyes than hellos. More pleasantries were exchanged until Kat exited the room to join us, displaying the skill of practiced grace before leading the charge to the lounge. We walked together towards the elevator and the five-floor journey. We arrived in the lobby, and a flurry of people were checking in and walking towards the restaurant and bar. We joined the march.

"Hey, you!" I hadn't heard him speak for some time, but he had a voice I'd recognize forever. We turned and looked behind us. Oliver and his wife were checking in. "Get me a drink!"

"I don't contribute to the delinquency of minors," I quipped.

"Grab me a beer. I'm growing up," Oliver responded. His wife, Amber, grinned but slowly shook her head in disagreement. I knew that was the truth. I had shared a barracks room with him and we'd done all the things standard of a young boot.

"Hurry and meet us at the bar," I said, waving my hand in the direction we were headed.

"Will do, buddy." It was already shaping up to be a good reunion, but it then ventured towards greatness. The group continued their march, rounding a corner with another added to the roster.

"Aww yeah, bro!" Sorbello roared with a drink in hand. Standing next to the welcoming bear, Doc Winsor raised a glass, also cheering our arrival. Sorbello and Winsor may have been on the opposing ends of the spectrum in the civilian world—the former was an extroverted West Coast bro, the latter a good ole cowboy from Arizona—but their mutual experience went beyond such naïve stereotypes. They were two more people who hadn't seen each other in a decade joining our crew of veterans eager to find out what each was doing these days.

"What the hell is going on here?" Jeff asked, not expecting an answer.

"Heck if I know!" Doc Winsor responded.

"Ain't that the truth, bro," Sorbello tacked on. The night was fresh, and an energy buzzed among us. It was a sensation we hadn't felt in a long while, but we knew the feeling well.

December 23, 2005 –

Our first mission. We were sent out on patrol with the guys we are replacing to pull surveillance along a dirt road. We got to ride in the Bradley's armored belly. While driving the main route through our area of operations, the supervising crew rattled the Bradley's tow-bar off into the middle of the road. The job fell to us to retrieve the massive rod resting in the center of the busy two-lane road called Route Pluto. Ramp dropped. Hello, Baghdad.

We recovered the heavy thing and continued mission to the spot we planned to disembark. Our team was inches from compromise on insertion. We jumped into a canal to avoid being seen but could have smacked the passenger side door of an Iraqi station wagon as it crept by.

That night introduced us to the dogs of Iraq. They bark and bark and bark. We found a suitable hiding spot, watched a building along a canal path, and waited for anyone to use the canal to access Route Pluto. They would remain unseen amongst the reed grass unless we got them first.

Soon, three young men left a compound not far from us and hopped in a car parked on the street. It was past curfew. We couldn't see much, so we elected to call our new Bradley buddies to investigate and they found no car there. The young men must have driven away with the lights off. There was not much for the rest of the night. It came time to make the call for exfiltration, and we heard the Bradley advance towards our position.

Minutes later, we climbed into the rumbling beast. We moved onto a road announced to have a high volume of bombs. Sure enough, an explosion added to the deafening noise inside the Bradley Fighting Vehicle, but it only jolted us in our seats no more than some of the other bumps we had hit. Stop. "Everyone ok?" We had hit an IED. In that same flash, the coaxial machine gun started going off. The smell of spent brass filled the vehicle.

The crew had identified three insurgents with AK-47s in the field. No doubt, they were the guys from the car. Do we get out? We were told to stay seated. They had called in Apaches to assist. The insurgents slipped into a series of homes. The large Bradleys were limited in their maneuverability through the narrow streets. As dismounts, we remained buttoned up and spent the next hour negotiating Route Pluto to the FOB. The vehicle's armor was damaged but not seriously. We got blown up on our first mission—looks like we are starting this thing with a bang.

It was like awakening from a sleep I didn't know I was taking. Now, that memory is like a daydream I know will be there for many years to come. Looking back, I can hear the whine of the Bradley's turret, smell the gunpowder, and feel the ramp crack open. Some journal entries snap me back into a moment filled with familiar details like these as if the episode had only happened yesterday. This entry—my first patrol outside the wire on the outskirts of Baghdad—was one of them.

As the sun settled, our team walked over to the Bradley Fighting Vehicle before the mission. The crew escorting us didn't ask our names or make much small talk. I wanted to ask what to expect, but they weren't interested. We climbed aboard, the ramp came up, and the lights dimmed. We clanked out of the FOB, over the bridge right out the front gate, and headed southbound on Route Pluto.

We cruised for several minutes when our vehicle lurched to a stop. Its loud engine purred, and a high whiny sound indicated the turret was rotating. A voice from inside the metal beast yelled that we had to get out and retrieve the tow bar. The bar designed to retrieve the vehicle from accidents or damage had fallen off on our maiden voyage on the two-lane highway.

The ramp dropped. The setting sun's light gleamed off the windows of the fifty cars or so that were following us, blinding me for an instant. As my vision returned, I looked out at scores of locals impatient with the holdup. It was my first look at Iraq, and it was angry. I gripped my weapon, cursed with a sudden fury, and ran towards the tow bar laying in the middle of the highway.

After loading the massive bar onto the Bradley, we cruised for another hour before the behemoth stopped a second time. After lumbering around in the dim crew compartment, I was

31

disoriented. It wouldn't have mattered. I had no clue where I was. The engines churned again, and the hydraulics whined. The ramp dropped a second time. The sun had disappeared, and the darkness of the Iraq night blanketed the sky. Not taking any time to gain our bearings, we rushed out of the vehicle and hopped into a canal. The feral dogs that were so common in this country barked and howled, alerted to our presence.

I scanned through my night vision to gain a sense of our location as fast as possible—a road here, a canal there, a house over there, some cover over here, bright lights right there. The team, after ducking from the civilian traffic following a safe distance from the Bradley, made its way to a position where we could conduct surveillance. After what seemed like the entire night—but was only a few slow hours—we spotted three men walking out of a compound a short jog from us, roughly 500 meters away. We called on the Bradley crew, who had moved elsewhere to conduct observation, to investigate the men on a late-night stroll. The crew lost track of them, and soon, without any other activity, it was time for exfiltration to the safety inside the armored belly of our new friend.

We climbed aboard and roared off in a direction known only to the crew. Sticking my radio handset in my ear, straining to gather as much situational awareness as I could, I heard somebody on the net remarking that we should not have taken this road as it had a recent history of IED activity. Not heeding this soldier's concern, we barreled down the road.

Our commanding officer, Captain Stanley, who was there to drive around with the Bradley crew and ask questions about the area, was sitting in the seat across from me. Hearing a whomp sound and noticing the vehicle jostling in the rear, we made eye contact. It was deafening in the troop compartment so any audible talk while we were moving, was futile at best. We came to a stop, and the turret whirled around, humming its rotation.

The voice from the turret asked if we were okay, and we answered in the affirmative.

The smell of the explosion was thick. After we cleared the kill zone and collectively confirmed our status, the voice in the turret yelled that three men with weapons were adjacent to our position. It was time for the music. The M240 coaxial machine gun sang its song to me. It was a welcome melody. The three men we had seen leave the compound after the curfew had emplaced the IED. Their attack unsuccessful, they had to deal with a colossal war machine and stood no chance of victory. Welcome to Iraq. Welcome to the insurgency and roadside bombs.

The IED—a broad term covering any ad hoc construction of an explosive—was the go-to weapon of choice for the enemy. The components were easy to procure since Iraq had many ammunition depots ransacked during the invasion, and the device themselves were primitive. They evolved at a rabbit's pace throughout the war, but for the most part, they were either ground wired or remote controlled. An artillery shell could be rigged to discharge with a garage door opener and blow a vehicle into a mess of steel and flesh in a matter of seconds. Remote detonation allowed for a decent standoff distance and mitigation of risk necessary to achieve the enemy's desired results. For the insurgency, roadside bombs proved an economical use of their resources and for the coalition, a sufficient obstacle to freedom of movement and security.

That night's fight ended after any surviving enemy slipped into a densely populated portion of a neighborhood. Dismount was discussed but disregarded. Air cover soared overhead, scouring the area for more insurgents. The Bradley rolled to the main drag of Route Pluto, where we waited while the fight was brought to a close. Eventually, we made our way back to the FOB.

The ramp dropped a third time, and I clambered out to inspect the damage. It was minimal, but the voice from the turret stood over me and lit a cigarette remarking that he was too close to going home to be dealing with these things. It was my first patrol, and we'd been bombed, so I questioned my future as the voice from the turret had. I walked to the company area, convincing myself that the enemy wanted me to feel this way and letting them do so would give them a victory. I was determined to not give it to them.

We replaced 3rd Squadron, 7th Cavalry, 2nd Brigade, 3rd Infantry Division. The unit was nicknamed "Garry Owen" after its marching tune carried most notably for General George Armstrong Custer. Most of the soldiers were indifferent or downright distant during the entirety of our transition and for a good reason. They were veterans, changed men, hardened from events like that IED attack. It may have been another survived bombing for them, but for me, it was different.

That blast did not simply rip away small chunks of steel and mangle the metal armor of the Bradley. Amongst the thunderous detonation and the rippling blast wave disrupting the calm Iraqi night air, were two other, less visible damages. Unbeknownst to me, the attack maimed my innocence and wounded my youth. Throughout the ordeal, I grinned a maddening half-smile—I didn't know how to respond. My bravado was misplaced. Years later, with incredible coherence, I can recall this jolt into the truth of my condition. This was real. This was happening. I was in a war zone.

December 24, 2005 –

The FOB initiated a communication blackout due to a Civil Affairs dude getting killed. Not sure what was going on and there was plenty hearsay about casualties. No phone calls for Christmas and no email either. Somewhere around this day, the Brigade Command Sergeant Major's truck hit an

EFP, explosively formed penetrator. The result, besides some more casualties, was a leadership swap among the squadron and brigade. We've been in Baghdad a week and we lost our top enlisted soldier. IEDs are indiscriminate.

Communications blackout was a term for severing phone calls and internet connections with home. It was a policy rooted in reaction. Thanks to the information age, updates from the battlefield were passed stateside instantaneously. Soldiers could call their loved ones or send emails discussing the details of a death or severe injury moments after an attack was over. Initiating the appropriate processes and gathering a notification team, to include a chaplain to ease the bereavement of the survivor's spouse or family, took the military a considerable amount of time, much more than an email or phone call.

Knocking on doors took a while. With the internet, the military struggled to keep a lid on the specifics of the conflict as it happened near real-time. It was much more efficient to simply sever communications home until the next-of-kin notification could be completed. Meanwhile, troops were isolated from an established expectation of contact with their loved ones. Families grew exceptionally close to email and instant messengers instead of their mailbox.

Unquestionably, this was an anxiety-producing policy for many families. The media would broadcast information on violence in Baghdad, but soldiers sometimes would not be able to contact their loved ones for days. Families worried—I hope it wasn't Johnny, I hope it wasn't Jane.

This compounded. Once, after being out on an operation for two weeks, we came back to the FOB expecting to reach home to send word to our families that we were okay but were unable to make contact for over a month and a half after a steady rolling blackout from the deaths and injuries of American personnel. Just as it looked like we might use the phones or email, there would be another successful attack, forcing the blackout to continue.

It was hard not to feel selfish or complain, but the reason for blocking communication was valid. It sucked, but we understood. It was a small price to pay for letting a family have proper notification of their loved one's death in service to the nation.

December 25, 2005 –

Today was Christmas, just another day. Around noon, another EFP strike less than 50 meters from the main gate killed a dude from Bonecrusher Troop. My friend was on radio guard with the dude the night before. I heard he was 19 and had a kid he hadn't met yet. So close to making it home. It doesn't matter if it's day 1 or day 361. The big holiday feast at the chow hall was solemn and carried an air of guilt. Merry Christmas.

The soldier killed on Christmas was nearing the end of his time in Iraq. On this particular day, his patrol did not even make it 100 meters from the gate. The blast was deafening, and a thick trail of black smoke stemmed from the traffic circle right outside the entrance to our base. I was standing outside my quarters when it happened, and I could feel it in my chest as the shock wave from the explosively formed penetrator detonated.

The base loudspeaker went off, announcing the attack, and soldiers scurried their way to the hospital or cover. I didn't move. I simply looked into the sky at the black smoke pouring from the vehicle as it caught fire. I stood, hoping the crew was able to get out before the flames took hold, but word spread as fast as the billowing smoke that it wasn't the case.

It was midday, and the cooks were busy preparing a Christmas Day feast to celebrate the holiday season away from home. The timing of this attack was purposeful. Several patrols had left the gate during the morning hours, and there had been no explosions. The morning commute provided a good deal of concealment, thanks to the mass of Baghdadi traffic.

You didn't need to be a forensic blast expert to understand that this was a big bomb that took a concerted, laborious effort to emplace. The enemy had taken considerable risk to get the bomb so close to the gate. It was a well-crafted message meant to ruin the holiday—and it did.

December 26, 2005 –

The morning started with a mortar attack. One round landed 20 meters from our door. It blew the hell out of a few trucks, and shrapnel peppered our door. Not an ideal alarm clock. Another incoming round impacted by the command post and sent debris everywhere. A guy took some shrapnel to the face. I went back to sleep, or at least tried.

A mere two feet from my head, shrapnel from the mortar impact riddled the cheap particle board door, damaged the HMMWV parked a spitting distance from our room, and punctured some boxes of Meals Ready-to-Eat stacked along the wall. Such events would become much more commonplace. Still, at the time, this was my first close indirect fire attack, and it garnered little fanfare.

I rolled over to go to sleep but was awakened by somebody doing a headcount. The concerned well-checker had looked at the damaged door and wanted to make sure we were alright. Instead of getting off the cot and investigating, I kept my head under my poncho liner, or woobie, as it is affectionately called, hoping to rely on the nylon blanket's legendary self-protective capabilities. I was not going to let the insurgents have the satisfaction of ruining my sleep before I had to climb off my cot for my radio guard shift.

Even though this was not routine yet, and even if I had not survived dozens more indirect fire attacks, I would be able to recall the sounds of incoming rockets and mortars with astonishing clarity. The short whine and boom created as one of these projectiles flies close by and impacts a short distance away is a secret each of us will carry forever. This recognition is unsettling at first but soon becomes a twisted mark of pride. Soon, you can gauge with remarkable accuracy how far incoming fire is from you—that is, until it is right on top of you, at which point, it doesn't matter anyway. I never knew how to react. I soon treated it like a game and sometimes laughed when I was caught out in the open. We reveled in the excitement. It was the misplaced sense of adventure inside us.

That would change. After we came home, anything that resembled that sound of incoming fire perked my ears most. My friends and I would hear the downward cry of a police siren or similar whine, and it would trigger a highly conditioned response. Return fire, find cover, assault the objective. In truth, a whole catalog of sounds—normal pops, zings, and bangs—drew reactions honed in a combat zone. Even to this day, over a decade later, hearing certain sounds prompts my mind to analyze an unseen level of threat.

Now, I have contained this to a mental process that those I am with won't notice. Nevertheless, it's there, harmlessly withdrawing me for a swift examination of my current surroundings before my brain releases me to reality. It's a natural process for survival. Life in a combat zone has made me vigilant, and time has made me a practitioner of calm observance.

December 29, 2005 –

DeLay's team headed out to set up an observation post by a radio tower on Route Pluto. We got stuck with gate overwatch to make sure no bombs were set in. Lightning doesn't strike the same place twice. Nothing happened.

While the other team went out on patrol, our section was relegated to nighttime surveillance of the area outside the gate. This was a reaction from the EFP attack days earlier, but as we sat upon a roof looking through the night optics, hoping to catch somebody in the act, we knew a similar bombing was unlikely to happen again, at least not here.

The IED cell that had built the Christmas Day bomb took a substantial risk of losing their emplacement team—a risk that might cause them to also lose their production team—to put that bomb so close. They could, with minimal effort, put one on the road in a more secluded spot that we frequented, not risk their own teams, and have a successful detonation.

While I didn't think we'd spot somebody emplacing an IED that night, I did begin to think how it would occur. I started to do this more and more. I developed plans for how our response would go if a particular event happened. I war-gamed constantly while in an observation post, driving on the cratered roads, or walking through a fire-burned neighborhood. Where is the next piece of cover? How far away is that doorway? What would I say on the radio? Do we have another weapon system close by?

Pulling overwatch throughout the night and fighting off boredom, I formed a ritualistic habit of contemplating contingency actions to stay engaged when fatigue started to get the better of me. Mostly, I wanted to be prepared for anything and everything—an enormously unrealistic goal. Chaos can be managed, but it cannot be predicted. Thinking on your feet is paramount, and relegating yourself to a preconceived course of action without examining details as they present themselves is ruinous. Take it as it comes, but have a plan.

May 28, 2016 –

"Pluto wasn't good, man." Jeff sipped his beer as we stood in a circle off to the side in the lounge. There were plenty of chairs, but for some reason, standing felt more appropriate. "It was the main route. We had to, we had to travel down it every day, man, and the enemy knew we had to travel down it every day."

Thus far, the conversation had consisted of updates from each attendee about what they were doing in their lives. Burns was working in an auto shop, turning wrenches and living the good life in Southern Indiana. Sorbello had gone to school in Southern California and found work before starting a family. Jeff had been a police officer outside Dallas, but his wife had taken a promotion and he had since moved to North Carolina. Doc Winsor had completed his education and put it to work raising his happy family in Arizona. Notaro had retired from the Army and bought a small subsistence farm in Louisiana, where he could live out his days hunting and growing his own food.

Each success story made us more comfortable, and as other names of other former Comanches came up—Keck, the medic from 2nd platoon pursuing higher education, Langford living his days surfing, Higgins the mountain man retreating into the wilderness, and a slew of others—we hoped they too were telling stories like these. We were getting acquainted with each other when the conversation moved from the long drive into Nashville to the long drive on one of the more notorious routes in Baghdad.

"Pluto looked like the surface of the moon when we got there," Burns piped in. Burns had joined the party with his brother, the lone family member he was comfortable enough with to share in the reunion. A well-respected squad leader from

First Platoon, Burns had fought through the invasion with another regiment but considered this unit his home. He was a quieter leader but one who worked behind the scenes as a constant advocate to ensure his guys and First Platoon at large were ready to go. Like a warrior sage, he knew what the war was like and what was required to survive it. "More IEDs went off in that sector than the country combined before we got there, but we shut the shit down fast. They weren't expecting our boots on the ground. The enemy was used to loud and predictable armor."

"Hell yeah," Notaro said, tipping back a mug to drain the rest of the beer. "The place was a shit hole, man." He wiped some foam from his beard.

Jeff took his turn speaking to the circle. "That road though." He shook his head. "Trash covered the place. Every 25 or 30 feet was something, something you imagined as an IED. We had to be on high alert the whole damn time."

"Well, you know you're gonna get hit," Burns said.

"Doesn't mean you can't try to not get hit," Jeff rebutted.

"By the time we left, though, dudes, that road was getting pretty terrible again," Sorbello said.

I agreed. The group tended to their drinks and looked away from each other. Everyone knew that the road and, in general, the entire area had become more dangerous as the deployment neared the end. It was a tough topic, and one we weren't prepared to dive in to yet.

Jeff steered the conversation to another subject. "Paul, remember that building you used to sit in, for like hours? You'd sit there watching Pluto."

"The paint factory?" Sorbello asked.

"That's it. That building was such a dump. We watched from there for hours. Felt like forever," I reminisced.

"Several days in the beginning," Eric said.

"Yeah," I continued. "We really had to take it one day at a time."

"We gave you at least a dozen rides, I know that much," Jeff recalled. "Driving those roads could drive you crazy."

"Yup," I confirmed. I was hesitant to engage. I had thought about these things and recorded my views as I compiled the journal. I just hadn't talked about them in detail, partially because I had been removed from the Comanches and my life had continued in a different direction, and partially because I just didn't know how.

"Hell, we sat in observation posts all the damn time in the beginning," Sorbello added. "Bro, just sitting could drive you crazy."

I puffed out a little grin. "Maybe it did."

January 1, 2006 –

Tonight, we set out for surveillance and route security with 1st Platoon on Route Pluto. We established an observation post from a 70' high building under perpetual construction. They call it the 'Paint Factory.' Sure, it made paint, but it looked more like it manufactured half-smashed bricks. Rambo'd into the building and snuck to the top. In place, we watched until 1100.

A large air assault by 2nd platoon planned for today was canceled. A high amount of car bombs struck in Baghdad, killing a lot of Iraqi Police and civilians. The concern is that more American presence on the streets would provoke outrage. We pulled off and rendezvoused with the CO's truck.

A young kid rode his bike there and was pestering the guys sitting security. His name was Hafar. I gave him some candy,

42

and he asked for money. He made fun of me for being short compared to Wright. Beat it, you little shit.

This is how we would do business during our initial operations. Rather than penetrate into the more austere outer villages, we pulled back to focus on protecting vital internal areas, and let the Iraqis take more responsibility for overall security. Echoes from the top told us that the host nation forces were ready and our unit may even redeploy earlier than expected. Until we got that news, our teams infiltrated observation posts or 'OPs' along busy thoroughfares while the other guys conducted route security in HMMWVs. We'd hang out looking for any belligerent activity related to IEDs and radio the teams in trucks to investigate or eliminate any targets as necessary.

Route Pluto was the primary path for anyone patrolling the region and was geographically well-suited for targeting American convoys. It was a two-lane highway, with considerable traffic, that carved its way into Baghdad through deteriorating neighborhoods dotting one stretch at a time. It also crossed the Diyala River using a bridge that was a significant bottleneck into the city. Securing it was an urgent first priority.

As the squadron's sniper team, this was our gravy. We waited for hours looking through small brick holes we chipped out of the shoddy masonry that allowed us to see for a few miles both north and south along the route. Anything we suspected that was not quite right, we would radio up for the guys a few miles away to investigate. Sometimes, in the middle of the night, there were zero friendlies to call who could reach us in short notice, and we would lay in silence watching and waiting for a shot, hoping not to get discovered.

Other times, and more often than not, deterrence was based not on being concealed but rather on being conspicuous. Long rifles with scopes, and those trained in their use, can be an off-putting sight. We once spent a night on the roof of a business, which also turned out to be the living quarters for a family. The kids awoke in the morning and played together in front of their store while the father made tea. Above them sat our team, who had spent a long, cold night making sure the enemy didn't put a bomb where their children played.

Hoping to avoid detection but needing to return to the FOB, we had no choice but to catch our ride. The family was flabbergasted when a sniper team climbed off their roof. No doubt, word spread and made any nearby insurgents at least think twice before putting in an IED, knowing we were out there hunting them.

It was satisfying to think that we were protecting the children of Iraq, but there were exceptions. Hafar, the cigarette-smoking twelve-year-old who rode his bicycle to our commanding officer's truck, was an ambitious dealmaker who, unfortunately, worked both sides for whatever reward possible. He sold coalition forces tips on the enemy, and vice versa.

They killed Hafar for assisting our efforts. It was quite probable that he was only doing it to provide for his family, but a degree of caution may have saved him, regardless of any noble rationale. Hafar should have done what the other kids did: take our candy and run. Instead, maybe he thought he could help. Who knows? He's dead.

January 9, 2006 –

We conducted a large force operation looking for a suspected stronghold. No bunker, no cache, no stronghold. We drove and walked through the knee-high mud to search a farm but departed empty-handed. The only thing to show for it was that the Screaming Eagles were in town and that we were looking for them, which I think was the intent from the get-go.

The farm had 15 men, 30 children, and some women. Trash was scattered like the morning after a carnival, but this was far less fun. Horrible conditions. The amount of litter in this country is overwhelming. I don't understand how you live like this.

Three years after the invasion, the Iraqi economy had crumbled and the black market was booming. Gangsters and local politicians controlled access to the markets, particularly for fuel. Lines several miles long ran along Route Pluto, snaking around the four-lane road, and taxi drivers pushed their empty-tanked cars alongside the road, hoping to get some black-market gas to make some cab fare. Moreover, if you weren't aligned with a certain militia group or sect, you wouldn't receive propane services to run your stove or gain access to electricity.

Neighborhoods divided economically. The Mahdi allowed Shia in their protected enclaves buy or sell their wares and controlled who could enter the market, but the overall inability to control and regulate also extended to government services. Utility work had ceased as the violence mounted and the government fractured. Lacking modern sanitation and waste removal, the farm we searched served as a refuge for refuse. The hovel of a house was a planet cut off by an asteroid belt of trash.

Lacking any sense of compassion at the time, I didn't have a solid understanding of the plight of the Iraqi rural citizen and was unable, or unwilling, to comprehend the factors that had forced fifteen able-bodied males to work a farm that one citizen from a developed world could manage with relative ease.

It was plausible they were gathered at the farm to plan attacks, but without evidence, we couldn't arrest them. Regardless of the circumstances leading to their predicament, I was incapable of expressing empathy towards them during this time. I had been conditioned to remove emotion and this separation of humanity aided in forming a boundary between *them* and *us*.

Without this barrier, operating in this environment becomes problematic, as the enemy walks among the populace, making it tough to know who was friend or foe. It was also problematic because it was difficult to engage the Iraqi citizens in a friendly manner without skepticism. Each interaction was crucial to foster a trusting and mutually beneficial relationship. My small worldliness, inability to relate, and cultural buffering didn't aid in our development of that relationship. We are the same stardust, but I hadn't yet been pulled from my ethnocentric gravity to understand their supernova of a situation.

Our leaders, however, did recognize the need for contacts and were quick to make deals and foster relationships where possible. Many of these associations dictated how our order of battle would develop, and it soon became apparent that after we had eliminated or denied Al-Qaeda sanctuary and stifled the Sunni insurgents' freedom of maneuver, targeting the Jaish al-Mahdi—the nation's Shia militia that was a local powerhouse—would become our next concern.

January 10, 2006 –

At 1700, I'm informed of a patrol set for 2000 start time. The teams needed to be out by the trucks in two hours. The patrol was to last until sunrise. I'd already been at it since 0500, so it was going to be a long day and night. Anyways, enough complaining. Hopped in with Higgins' crew from 2nd platoon to ride to the southern leg of Pluto right by a large traffic circle west of Jisr Diyala. Once established, and the trucks positioned, we sat for a few hours with no activity, so we rode to another spot hoping for enemy activity to happen.

We continued to sit for a while, and I fought to stay awake. The day-to-night swings made my eyes burn. It was boring, and I wondered if the top brass is right—maybe we can get out of here by the end of the year. A radio call came across the net that has been silent for hours. It's a team from 1st platoon calling for extraction from their OP. God bless them, let's go eat breakfast. Came in at 0445. Damn, I was tired.

There are two fundamental aspects of life as an infantryman—complaining and fatigue. In most cases, they go hand-in-hand. The fact is, I was not conditioned to go without sleep for as long as I was asked while deployed. Sleep was anything but routine. During training, sometimes an active twenty hours or more were required, but I'd get a solid four hours of rest, if not more. Here, we would go a day and a half without any sleep, punctuated only with statuesque periods of sitting and watching in an observation post or crammed in the threadbare seats of a gun truck fighting off the siren songs of slumber.

Compounding the issue of long hours, you would not be sleeping at the same time during the day. We'd lie awake all night and depart for another patrol that same day. The pendulum of our day-to-day operations ticked back and forth like a clock with broken gears. The regular to-and-fro was absent, but the danger was persistent. You needed to be alert. You were reliant upon your own personal discipline to remain attentive because you knew your brothers-in-arms were counting on you—even if you were grumbling about it in a journal entry afterward.

Complaining is a core competency of the grunt, maybe even servicemember writ large. A cautious grumbling or silent wish for somebody to go to hell while executing an unpopular order is normal. We understood it as necessary, for the most part. However, when they border vindictiveness, which they sometimes do, the gripes turn into genuine insubordination, which is unacceptable.

Fatigue, of course, exacerbates complaining. If it remains undirected, as in "I'm tired," that is acceptable, even warranted, in my opinion. Recognizing your condition is the best way to overcome it. That doesn't spare you from some choice words of encouragement, though. When father fatigue sets in, soldiers without wholesome discipline within themselves direct their gripes towards tasks or people. "I'm tired of this shit" is a different and dangerous phrase. Voicing that dark notion means your head is not in the game, implying that you cannot be counted on to do your duty when the time comes. You have also pushed your condition onto others, instead of chowing on some jalapeño cheese spread to keep yourself moving.

Being tired is part of it, but whether or not one gives in to dark, deconstructive imaginings is what sets people apart and demonstrates a person's character. Those who can divorce the two are the ones you will look to in the fray. Every veteran can spot the ones they know they can count on. They may gripe, but not in front of their troops. They may curse the situation but will direct their hate with well-aimed suppressing fire. They understand that complaining improves nothing and that deliberate action solves most everything. They understand that being the calm in the chaos is critical to bringing your fellow soldiers home. I appreciate that these elusive soldiers are the ones who win their nation's wars. I have learned much from them.

Regardless of the personal lessons of fortitude learned, this tiresome to-and-fro was in part by design. Our leadership desired unrelenting pressure on the enemy to loosen its grip on the artery to our AO. The insurgency had choked the area with IEDs, disallowing development and government services to engage the potential robust and diverse industries of southeast Baghdad. If the enemy saw continued presence on Pluto, they would direct their actions elsewhere to more lucrative targets, shifting the burden to other locations and buying the Iraqis time to develop more permanent security apparatuses. Ideally, they would be forced out of Baghdad completely, but that was doubtful. The capital was the crown jewel and destabilizing it was prime to the insurgency's goals of delegitimizing our efforts. But we remained hopeful.

May 28, 2016 –

As the night wore on, couples 30 or 40 years the wiser filed into the bar, forcing us to grab real estate in the corner, which we didn't mind. We broached a few more topics, ordered a few more drinks, and rekindled a bond that had been long untended. I glanced over to Kat, who had found a nest on a stool next to Jeff's wife. She looked content, and I felt at ease.

"Dude, um." Sorbello leaned over to me. "Do you think that it's senior night around these parts?" I looked behind us at the people who had come into the bar. They were busy talking with one another, like us, and were older, but Nashville attracts people of all ages.

"No, I don't think so," I replied.

"No, dude, look!" He thumped me in the chest. I turned and watched another group of five join the retirement crowd. We were out of place, and it was only a matter of time before our outlandish behavior would ruin their evening.

"We're gonna need to get you guys outta here," I said.

Sorbello chuckled. "This could get weird!"

"You mean weirder?" I pointed over to Doc Winsor, who was off reenacting another story involving his penchant for pushing clothing requirements to their limit and, judging by his rodeo charade, he was back in his element. We had called him 'Doctor Feelgood' for a reason. "We need another rallying spot."

I tapped Sorbello on the back and pulled out of the circle to see how my wife was doing and to get a refill.

"Hey," I said, speaking over the music, which had been turned up as the night progressed. "You two doing okay?"

"Yeah, we're good," Kat replied.

"I'm tired. It's been a long day already," I stated.

Kara nodded her head in agreement.

"You look like you're having fun," Kat said.

"Same to you," I said, motioning towards the tall glass of water sitting on a wet cocktail napkin. "But yeah, it's good to see these dudes."

Kat rolled her eyes. "We can tell. You guys have come alive. It's like this whole new energy I haven't seen in a while," she said, tilting her head at her new friend. "Jeff looks like he's having fun, too."

"I am sure he is." Kara signaled towards Jeff.

"This was a good idea." I nodded my head to acknowledge Kara's comment, but also to the beat of the music. I locked eyes with the bartender and pulled some cash from my pocket. "Can I get another?"

"No way!" Sorbello roared. "Get in here, sir!" The group roared, alarming the other bar patrons, and welcomed the newest addition to our reunion. In had walked the esteemed leader of Second Platoon, who was known for his no-gap leadership style—Eric. He cast his eyes toward the ground and did a sweeping wave before depositing his hand into his pocket. He was the lone officer attending, and we welcomed him and the perspective he provided as he bridged the gap between the former officer and enlisted.

"What's going on, fellas?" he asked. The circle grew.

I beckoned to the bartender, "Better make that two, please."

January 15, 2006 –

I spotted a new soldier and new officer around our company compound. New lieutenant is taking 2nd platoon. The dude seemed squared away. The new soldier, though, reports to the company commander. I watched him react to the CO's

*greeting. I didn't know if he was going to salute or shit his
pants. Joining a unit already in Iraq has to be tough.*

As fresh and inexperienced as we were, our training at Fort
Campbell had forged a tight bond over the year and a half we
spent in the sweltering southern heat and wet winters. Misery is
a fantastic enabler of bonding. For those joining the company
later in the deployment, an amicable reception was not automatic.
There'd be some trials, as Eric found upon his arrival to
Comanche a couple of months into the deployment.

Motivated and well versed in the emerging
counterinsurgency dogma trickling into the philosophy of the
military, he had a different attitude about how he wanted Second
Platoon to operate. He wanted to insulate, not isolate his soldiers,
notably his NCOs, when it came to his no-gap approach to
leadership. He wanted a close relationship that might spur clear
communication and feedback. Balanced with his platoon
sergeant, Sergeant First Class Schrader, a shrewd and devoted but
not overly welcoming soldier—the two developed the type of
strong team necessary for the challenges ahead.

Aside from building a great team, Eric also understood the
requirements of the emerging counterinsurgency fight at a time
when the squadron remained oriented towards the conventional
approach of large-scale capture or kill operations. Many of the
leaders also thought and were promoting the idea espoused by
the highest levels of our civilian and military leadership that we
were in the drawdown phase of the war and we were in the
process of handing things over to the Iraqis.

The priority was doing what we had to do, but also bringing
the squadron home with the least number of casualties. The
rumors flying around that we could head home early if things
progressed as planned troubled Eric who knew the situation was
abysmal. In addition to his initial assessment, he noted our spirits
were high, and we desired nothing more than to get after the

enemy. He also saw we wanted to see this American effort ended successfully. Morale was high.

At the time of the arrival of the squadron's newest lieutenant, the employment of our mission changed. Second Platoon became responsible for the Jisr Diyala neighborhood after the squadron reallocated forces and one of the cavalry troops was sent to protect journalists at a hotel outside the international Green Zone.

Without delay, Eric built rapport with prominent members of the community and gleaned information where opportunities presented themselves. His creativity and guile began to change how we did business. He paired well with our S2 intelligence brethren and together with our talented leadership, developed a robust mapping of insurgent networks. Using our innovative spirit, like tossing a cell phone in a sock over a wall to a woman connected to rising persons of interest, our leadership charted out the local Mahdi Army leadership—Abu Ayatt, Abu Sayf, and even the mayor of Jisr Diyala, a man named Fadil.

All of these men were complicit in the deaths of both Iraqis and Americans in some way, shape, or form. The militia was engaging in aggressive vigilante killing that was slipping more towards outright criminal murder. Despite this, they were valuable as cooperative passive security partners who would help to maintain a sense of order and preclude a leadership void far more nefarious individuals could exploit. In the end, Abu Ayatt—the leader of the equivalent of a brigade's worth of militiamen or a few thousand followers—and his pledged Mahdi Army served most parties better by cooperating, rather than stoking the fires of conflict.

The Mahdi Army, or Jaish al-Mahdi, was a Shiite paramilitary force that rose to notoriety in 2003 under the control of a fiery, ambitious cleric named Muqtada al-Sadr. The group was responsible for the first prominent Shia confrontation with the US, which led to a series of peace deals that had disintegrated by late summer 2004. They cultivated considerable popularity among the majority Shia population. Even more, the militia influenced government at all levels and pressured police forces to assist their ruthless agenda.

Located south of their headquarters in Sadr City, our area of operations maintained a substantial Mahdi presence which was a growing concern. Eric understood we weren't going to change the ingrained prejudices of generations of people by killing or capturing a few of them in a year, so why die when we could cut a deal to keep clean and give precious time to the Iraqis to organize a capable police force?

Like a mafia don, Eric leveraged mutual interests to keep the peace but, with a hard jaw, issued clear guidance that noncompliance would be met with swift aggression. It was a utilitarian relationship, but one we accepted knowing the end justified the means. Our S2 and leadership's targeting efforts ensured that we could—while our penchant for violence ensured that we would—accept a little bad for a greater good.

January 16, 2006 –

1730. I was hanging out when Wright busted in the door. "Get it on and be at the trucks in 30 minutes." Scrambled. Got it on. Radio needed some work. We met in the company parking area. I looked for a ride and hopped in with First Sergeant Lillie. We had received a report from an informant about a planned IED emplacement on a route adjacent to Pluto. We were going to pull surveillance and shoot them when they came to do their deed. We rode to a blown-out building with a tall cinder block wall around it. We discussed our plan while huddled in the darkness, "Alright, the target building the insurgents were using is to the right. 1st platoon is watching that compound. You guys will watch the route to watch for emplacement from this compound."

Roger. Moved out. Scrolled the road. Hopped in the shadows along the wall. Moving like a possessed demon, the first sergeant spotted a rusty metal door and cracked it open with one hand while the other gripped his rifle. He scoped out the inside and beckoned for us to come forward to the compound. Save some for us, first sergeant! We ran 150 meters across open muddy fields and entered through the door while Wright inspected the outbuildings to find the best position. Found it. Moved into place using some bent aluminum bracket that was 6 inches wide. It was a metal brace for some stairs that had since been destroyed. Good balance.

Got there, set up. Watching...temperature dropping. My watch on the gun. 1st platoon radioed that two individuals were lingering by the road. 2315 hours. Watched them. One wrong move and they are dead. Please make a move. Lose visual. Called in a drone and Apache helicopters on standby. Shit. Hoping to keep them from slipping away, Captain Stanley dismounted with his route security element to sweep the area. Walked them into the target area. Nothing but two insurgent cows. Joked over the radio for the next hour but we have another 5 to go. Temperature dropped to 35 degrees. I'm not dressed for it.

No activity. The decision was made since we have already been compromised with a dismounted team patrolling the area to move to a blown-out building and start a fire. I didn't object. Time passed as we took turns like bums around a barrel warming our hands and feet. Like vagrants under an overpass, we chilled, but the time came and we moved to the gate of the compound to step out. I stayed with First Sergeant Lillie since I had the radio.

Exiting the compound, two cars were stopped 100 meters north of us. They are full of military-aged males. The drivers saw us and split up. One ran north. The other one blasted off heading south nearing our position. We needed to stop these guys and search them. We signaled them with our flashlights. Nothing. 50 meters away, warning shots. My heart pounded. No reaction. Yelling. The sport utility vehicle was feet from Lillie, who was standing in the middle of Route Pluto as we ran to his position with weapons aimed at the speeding vehicle.

As the vehicle neared him, my eyes were wide open. Lillie took a few calm paces to the shoulder of the road, aimed his rifle, and shot the tires out. A strong gust of wind from overturning, the escaping vehicle skidded sideways across the road. "Get out, get the hell out!" We encircled the vehicle with guns pointed at the occupants' heads. Seven men cry out in terror. It's 0615. They got out and explain that they didn't see us. Funny how the other car did and headed north to avoid us.

Snooping around an area where known IEDs were emplaced was suspect. We could have killed those men. It was a couple of seconds to react at best, and First Sergeant Lillie did the right thing. I hopped on the radio and made the necessary calls after I botched the first one in excitement. We separated them, searched them, and searched the car. Nothing. I didn't trust them. We loaded into our vehicles and cruised to the FOB. It's 0720. It's a 13-hour mission. 24 hours with no sleep. Make that 25 after a nice long warm shower and some joke telling with some buddies and some journaling. I'm getting better at this staying awake thing.

The overall probability that these were the individuals we were looking for when we found the two cows ranked up there with bears shitting in the woods—it was a sure thing. Regardless, their statistical risk analysis led them to believe there was a pretty remote chance American forces were in the area. That's the thing about probability in combat—flip a coin fifty times and it will land heads up twenty-three times and tails twenty-eight. The math doesn't add up.

With the first sergeant, math had no place in dealing with the enemy. He had no time to pull out the abacus and realize it was fifty-one. He was a man of action and one who could rouse the fighting spirit of the most timid soldier in the company. He was the 'break glass in case of war' soldier archetype, but as we grappled with a counterinsurgency fight, his Field Manual 7-8 traditional force-on-force philosophy sometimes conflicted with the requirements of this irregular war.

Mission aside, if there was a man the soldiers looked to as a model for their own behavior, it was First Sergeant Lillie. Extraordinary is not a word that does justice to this man's ability to lead soldiers. He'd guide them with a colorful vocabulary of obscure curse words and a natural ability for taking care of the troops when they needed a boost. He wasn't soft, but his actions spoke to what the man had in his heart. That sort of relationship drove soldiers to march faster when it was time to move, to do more than what was asked, and to give nothing less than their all. He was the proverbial soldier's soldier. The men loved him for it.

On this day, as the mathematical insurgents attempted to make a break for it, the first sergeant was going to introduce another variable into the equation—his infinite courage. As the SUV carrying a group of them sped off towards an enraged NCO with his heels dug into their escape route, I remember watching in slow motion, thinking I was to witness the soldier's soldier being plowed over by a speeding sport utility vehicle.

Instead, I saw the poise of a man sizing up a chaotic situation with a skill foreign to me. With a nonchalance that almost seemed choreographed, the first sergeant took a few steps to the side and fired a half dozen rounds into the tires as the vehicle passed a couple of feet from him. Looking back on it, and putting myself in his stead, I wondered, would I have just shot the driver? Seven men don't pile in a car bomb and not one had appeared armed. They would've been the unfortunate victims of panic if we'd mowed them down. With the ROEs we faced, stopping the vehicle was the right call, and it was done in the most thrilling fashion.

The startled driver jacked the steering wheel in each direction, struggling to maintain control. Running on two flat tires, the vehicle skidded one way and another before coming to a stop a short distance away. With M4 rifles doing the talking, the escapees complied with our directions despite the language barrier.

My brain-to-mouth connection was not quite operable. I tried to sound composed on the radio but, bewildered and not sure of what was happening, muffed the call by forgetting to add any callsigns to the transmission. Nobody knew who the hell had asked for assistance. That's the difference between a man who has seen a great deal of combat in both the Afghanistan and Iraq invasions and a young buck eager to prove his worth to the herd. I couldn't even radio somebody without error.

The first sergeant acted as if he had scanned the threat and already planned to shoot out the tires. The composure with which he operated was a quality I have drawn inspiration from since. Say a few curse words before driving on with fists clenched. When the noise and anarchy of life threaten to deter you from your goals, remember, it is you and a speeding truck. Step calmly.

The fact is the scene between the first sergeant and that escaping truck was more than a singular instance. It was a snapshot of the struggle of a conventional military in an unconventional fight. The grace period after the invasion was over. The ROEs and the escalation of force meant that we had accepted more risk to ensure the right people were killed for the right reasons. The lines were grayer because the enemy didn't wear uniforms. The Iraqis, who were breaking curfew, attempted to flee when told to stop. They didn't just try to escape, they accelerated to run over the man standing in the road who was shooting over their heads yelling in broken Arabic for them to stop.

The first sergeant had spent years training for conventional war and was now engaged in a very different kind of fight—one where these types of calls are reserved for the police. The infantry was for killing, or so the drill sergeants will tell you from day one at Fort Benning. It was clear we needed to change to match the reality. And instances such as this demonstrated our need for adjustment. Nonetheless, it was a messy adaptation. It took as much courage to hold your fire as it did to pull the trigger.

January 17, 2006 –

Somebody told me to get the hell up and get to formation. Damn, man. I was sleeping. I was dragging ass but hoofed it over to headquarters to receive my combat patch. Old Abe is forever with me.

Even though this was not a patrol or a mission, it was significant enough for me to document in my journal. The combat patch was a rite of passage. Carrying the 101st Airborne Division patch on my right arm signifying I had gone to war with the unit meant a lot to me. Upholding the division's history was demanding, and we carried its charge on our shoulders. We had to maintain their blood-earned reputation, and the patch compounded that responsibility.

With 'Old Abe'—the name of the illustrious Screaming Eagle—forever displayed on my uniform, I knew I had to perform to the legendary standards of those who had gone before me. I was proud, but I was also humbled to think of the long line of other great Americans who had carried that patch into the halls of history.

Truth be told, we weren't seeing much in the way of combat, and what we saw was nowhere near the reality faced by those in places we had learned during our tenure in the 101st— Normandy, Bastogne, the A Shau Valley. Here, in our area of operations, we were looking for a fight, spending these first few passing weeks of January probing further away from Route Pluto. In fact, we hopped in Zodiac rubber boats and conducted a daylight search operation along the Tigris. As the sniper team sitting across the river, we wished that we would spot a would-be attacker before they even had a chance. It was dangerous and exposing but didn't draw a single shot.

Just like that first boat-crossing, we chased phantom sounds of rifle fire and whispers of armed men in the night. On the other side of the river, though, reports of significant engagements with a growing enemy force circulated through the squadron. We continued to keep the enemy off guard by conducting small dismounted patrols and raids, which was a departure from the actions of our predecessors.

Yet, we rarely encountered more than a few sporadic bursts from the enemy that, when pursued, faded away amongst the local mud shanties and shacks. As January progressed, we considered the thought that our leadership was right—the fight was on the downward trend. Yet, as we worked more with the Iraqi security forces, namely the National Police, our ideas changed.

During this time, the Iraqi military and police were functional, at least on paper. Our area of operations was patrolled by units called the Public Order Brigade, or POB, which had been chartered to restore and maintain security in areas where the local police force either had not yet been established or required reconstruction due to insurgent activity. They were more military than police and were intended to extend the reach of government rule. Wearing piecemeal uniforms and lacking the ability to project any sort of power without considerable American support, they were, by definition, a rag-tag fighting force.

These were the guys the future of their nation depended upon, and it was incumbent upon us to ensure they could secure the country. As opposed to cohesion as oil and water, we found it challenging to work with them due to cultural barriers that permeated our interactions. Our warrior ethos did not transcend to their battlefield prowess. Our organizational capacity to tackle the complex rigors of a changing battlefield far exceeded their ability to function on a basic tactical level. Notwithstanding their current capabilities, the most important thing we could do for the Iraqis was buy them time to organize, train, and equip a force capable of withstanding the pressures of a fractured government and splintering factional society.

Not unlike my inexperienced assessment of the farm we had visited earlier, I also lacked empathy for the Iraqi Police during my deployment as a young soldier in the most professional army in the history of the world. We all could do basic math. We could read. Heck, some of us could even write, albeit poorly. We had the coolest toys and capabilities edging on modern wizardry. We were ahead of the typical Iraqi regular whose only qualification for service was that he was a walking body capable of producing fog on a mirror.

I measured effectiveness in terms I understood—American terms—but this yardstick was ineffective for gauging this foreign policing force. It may have even been counterproductive. It blinded me to the merit of their commitment—signing up to protect their families, serve their country, and risk their lives to better their station. In the context of our mission, it pays to recognize this, exercise caution as necessary, and capitalize on such noble intentions. All this considered, and despite lacking technology and time, the Iraqis compensated with their own brand of courage. They were fighting for their country, which was a cause I could relate.

January 30, 2006 –

We headed out to pull an observation post by the Route Pluto bridge. Around 2 or 3 IEDs have exploded there in the last month. We can stop it. Hopped in the dreaded APC and cruised for 5 minutes. The radio called for the team to dismount. Climbed out and threw down my night vision. Complete and total ghostlike. Silent. We climbed into the trees lining the road and got back-to-back in a tight 360.

Satisfied we were safe, we moved out. We crept 20 meters before hitting the dirt for a string of vehicles that took 5 minutes to pass. Traffic was blocked while we inserted. After it passed, we lumbered onward soon coming to an abandoned building. I checked the inside. Nothing. "Endris, take point." Like the boogeyman, I snuck to the front to take us to the next building. I inched through the shadows. Cleared doorways and windows.

Got to the next suitable building. I went around the corner to check it out. About 15 meters away was a woman taking her laundry off the clothes line using a lantern. She didn't know we were there. It's an odd sensation to know that she went about her evening routine and around the corner of her house were 3 American soldiers. With this family so close to the building, this position wouldn't work. We moved 150 meters to another structure, our last option as far as buildings went. Nope, it wouldn't work either.

I called the CO and explained to him the last place we could see the river had too many avenues of approach. Do what you can was the response. Welp, went to the river bank in the reed grass and built a nice little hide site. It was uncomfortable with reeds poking us in parts of the body you shouldn't be poked.

About an hour into it, I spotted two men in a canoe gliding along the river. The boat meandered south, close to the bank, turned around, and paddled straight for us. What are they doing this late? Ferrying bombs into the city? Fishing? Those dudes came within 10 meters of our position. I grabbed a rock and threw it in the water. Bloop. Spook them. It's hard not to laugh, but we held it together. Their boat was empty, and these guys were doing some illegal night fishing, which I applauded.

The evening drug on until 0345 as we watched a convoy of 10 gun trucks careen around a bend in the road across the river from us. It's other 101st dudes from another regiment—the 502nd. About 10 minutes later, we heard a volley of RPG fire, and a hell of a firefight from where they had driven. We looked for targets through the trees with frantic energy but I saw only green-tinted foliage dotted with a zip of tracers through my night-vision.

Out from the houses came 5 HMMWVs. It must have been their medevac or their maneuver element. In either case, we have no radio contact with them. We wanted to help, but there was little we could do. It was frustrating but soon the fight was over and we were sitting in the reeds getting poked in private places. The temperature dropped and time marched on until 0445.

Our executive officer, out on patrol with the rest of the headquarters, had the Apaches clear the area around us to make sure it was safe to move out. It was free of enemy signatures so we headed for Route Corn. The route is a branch off Pluto that has become more and more dangerous, and we huddled along its ditches waiting for our ride.

We soon climbed in with Comanche 5, the XO, and pulled route security for an hour before returning to the FOB. One more day is gone. Somebody woke me at 0830. Time to pick up cigarette butts and rake the rocks—area beautification. Are you kidding me?

The Tigris and Diyala Rivers formed not just a physical barrier between us and a sister brigade of the 101st but also an operational barrier. Our sectors were poles apart and not due to the obvious geographical divide. Part of the insurgent infested "Triangle of Death," the enemy—both internal and foreign fighters—traveled through this region funneling money, weapons, and munitions into the capital city where it became virtually untraceable amongst the densely populated urban environment of Baghdad.

The 502nd, with their black hearts on their helmets, steadily chipped away at safe havens, forcing the enemy to seek alternative routes for moving into the city. Invariably, it would make its way east—to the land of the Comanches.

This night, we had no communication with them across this barrier, and as we looked for targets in the foggy dark, we could offer no assistance as the tracers lit the sky. It was frustrating to watch them do the work we were there to do too.

At the end of the night and in the years since it has become apparent to me that I should not measure my contributions against those of others. As a young soldier, I measured my value the same way others measured theirs, and this disillusioned me to the fact that I had a role to play not just in the military, but in life itself. Every person is better than you in some regard. Every encounter is a chance to learn. Comparison without improvement is vanity and it will blind you to that fact that heroism surrounds us daily. You can see it if you simply watch across the river. And sometimes, it's best left on the other side.

May 28, 2016 –

"Sir, welcome to the party." I walked towards him with an ice-cold brew extended as an arrival gift. He stood with his thumb in his pocket, baseball cap on, surveying the group, acknowledging guys with a quick nod, as if to say hello with his chin. He accepted the beverage, expressing gratitude with another tilt of his head.

"Thanks, Paul." As the sole officer in attendance, the enlisted veterans who had since left the service had to move beyond the old military pecking order of officer and enlisted.

"Eric!" Sorbello overcame this boundary with haste, "Good to see you, my dude." He walked across the circle with his arm outstretched, seeking a vigorous handshake. Eric obliged. Others followed suit, extending similar greetings.

"How are things?" I asked.

"Good."

"Sorry, I didn't hear that. The music."

"Good," Eric said louder, realizing how loud the music was or remembering that we had difficulty hearing from a history of machine guns and explosions. The evening had picked up and it was us that wanted the conversational volume, not the older crowd. "I'm glad you guys are doing this."

"Hell yeah," Notaro agreed. "But do we need another venue?" He motioned towards the growing crowd as a few more mature party-goers from a different generation strode into the hotel bar.

"Yeah," Jeff said. "I think we should jump up the street, grab some beverages, and find a place we can hear each other." We agreed, and soon the volunteers, Eric and I, were on a beer run.

"Thanks for coming," I said. We walked along the edge of the street. It had no sidewalk.

"No, man. Thank you." Eric had volunteered to leave the party he had joined just moments ago because he wanted to pay. The others remained, taking care of their tabs and joking with each other in ways not meant for crowds.

"It's nothing. Jeff and I thought it worthwhile. It's been a decade. Thought the guys might want to catch up."

"Well, honestly, it's more than that," Eric reasoned.

"What do you mean?"

"I doubt many of these guys have given a lot of thought about what happened that year. In the bigger picture sense."

"I see what you're getting at."

"Yeah." Eric looked at me. "After all my deployments, and I have many, this one was the most significant, y'know."

I knew how many deployments he'd been on and how consequential that statement was. I thought he was blowing hot air like leaders sometimes do. "Really?"

"Well, man, for starters, think of what happened there at the end, after we left."

"The surge?" I was well versed in the speech President Bush had given in December, and again in January after our return, stating how bad the situation in Iraq had gotten. The President was faced with a difficult decision that we knew needed to be made.

"Exactly. The place was unraveling."

"The President did say things weren't going well," I remarked. "I've thought about what that meant for a long time."

"Hey, man." Eric stopped and thumped me in the chest. "You can't change the outcome, you can only change your outlook. Remember what's in your control." I smiled. He was making sure I wasn't taking it too hard to the heart. Regardless of the results of our efforts there, we were alive and needed to live. We continued walking toward the glow of a nearby convenience store. Crossing the street, we scanned like two soldiers crossing Route Pluto.

"I guess you're right. I'm not sure that's what the guys care about anyway."

"You're right. Most of the tribe don't care to turn on the television, let alone read on the politics of that time. Doesn't interest the guys," Eric said.

"Right."

"What does interest them is that they understand what happened in our AO so they can process what it means to them on an individual basis." The door slid open. The cool air conditioning and the attendant welcomed us. "These guys are tough, tough as I've ever known." Eric paused in the entrance. He looked around the small shop loaded with the usual convenience store goods. "We came back and everyone scattered, so we didn't get time to talk, y'know, like a company after-action review or debrief."

"Well, there's no better time to do that than a ten-year reunion," I said. "Mind broaching the subject? Some of the milestones as it were. I figure a guy like you with a broader grasp on the deployment can speak to some of the larger pieces. It's easy to miss out on things when your lane is as narrow as the soldiers'. I knew what happened in one particular street corner, you knew what happened on the block or even the neighborhood. That's important."

"I could do that." Eric narrowed his eyes and scanned for the beer section before identifying his objective and marching past the chips, beef jerky, and candy.

"We'll have time tomorrow to talk it over," I said, racing through another aisle and opening the door to the cooler.

"Cold and domestic?" I grinned.

"Sounds good." Eric reached into another cooler grabbing some water.

"Gonna be a long night, early morning."

"We've had worse."

February 4, 2006 —

0330. Woke up and got my gear on. We waited 45 minutes for a briefing. The radios are screwy and it took a little while to iron them out. Tonight, we rolled in the M113 Armored Personnel Carrier. Everyone climbed in, and we are headed for the Paint Factory. The building has several stories allowing us to see a reasonable distance. Despite the blown-to-hell construction, it's a great position.

We rolled for 15 minutes. The tracks came to a stop. We climbed out of the top and ran to the entrance. The compound was locked. We took an instinctive knee. Wright handed me his rifle and reached in through the door window to unlock it. Ran into the building.

I got 3 stories up and saw a footprint through my night vision. Took off my glove, and the footprints were dry. It had rained the day before and it was muddy so I was looking for indications of more recent visitors but found none. Continued up the stairs and shooed away the pigeons. Set. Called in our status.

The dawn breaks at 0730ish. I was watching north through a 4-inch hole in the wall. Whomp—the low rumble of an IED detonation—it came from the market, south of the Route Pluto bridge, only a few hundred meters away. I lost my footing on the bricks I was standing on to look through the hole in the worn mortar wall. The blast had struck some engineer troops as they made their way out of the city. The debris hit some guy in the eye and disabled a HMMWV.

I watched as they responded and worked the recovery of the vehicle. Nothing else until 1000 hours. Davis was relieving himself in the corner on his knees. I watched as unarmed Iraqis climbed the stairs. They spotted Davis. I shined a laser on them from the M9 Beretta, gave a little whistle, and offered a whimsical kind of wave. "Hello, friends." We busted up laughing. The local nationals were pretty cool, and they wanted to squeegee the roof. We handed them what goodies we had in our assault bags and kept things casual.

Soon after, we spotted a van meeting the description of an insurgent's vehicle pulling into the compound north of us. We radioed it in and soon 1st platoon was on the scene questioning the driver. Night fell. Time for extraction.

We made it to the gate of the Paint Factory and the M113. Rode to the FOB, unloaded and conducted an after-action review at the clearing barrels discussing things we may have done better. I know I could have improved. I missed another opportunity. Davis and I are nabbed to pull a 6-hour radio guard shift, but Fogle takes one for the team.

This was the first, but not last, time I would track—through some sort of optic—friendly troops and watch them get blown up. Just like they had been trained, the soldiers continued to drive the HMMWV as far it would take them to avoid an ambush. Clear the kill zone, as they say. This time, the truck rolled a few hundred meters before the fluids leaked out and it came to a stop. It was trailed by a plume of dust and smoke from the explosion.

I watched one soldier exit and open the passenger side front door to check out the truck commander, who, I later heard over the radio, had suffered a catastrophic wound to the eye. I listened and watched through the scope as the team searched for a counterattack, tended to their wounded, and recovered the HMMWV. They responded well, and I responded poorly.

I relayed their progress as it unfolded. My communication skills were improving, but my overall assessment of the required tasks needed refined. I was so focused on their immediate action that I did not provide the single most critical thing I could do for them—overwatch. We were scanning the road but not looking among the shops, homes, and rubbish to spot those responsible for initiating the blast. We were watching the commotion and not the periphery, where the triggermen resided.

After the blast, survivors grabbed chains and prepared their disabled vehicle for a tow. I took a deep breath and came to a troubling realization. I had failed. I needed to learn from this and understand that when you are so focused on home plate, you will miss the other team stealing third. I felt ashamed but vowed to never let it happen again.

February 12, 2006 –

Another 0330 wake-up with not a lot of sleep, but I think I'm getting used to it. We climbed into the trucks and rolled to the sewage treatment plant south of the FOB. Nice little field trip, if you like sewage. Skirted around the outer fences in the shadows to find a way in before talking to the Iraqis guarding the place.

Once inside, we climbed atop a guard tower, but it was too exposed to our liking. I radioed our concerns and leadership made us leave since we are on the edge of our area and they are worried about fratricide. During the chatter, an Abrams tank whined into position right in front of us, and we agreed—time to go.

We edged down the ladder of the tower and walked to the trucks. We had time, so we planned a dismounted patrol through the Route Pluto bridge market. After pulling route security for a few hours, we greeted the sunrise. We dismounted to walk through the market as the morning business is conducted. Little kids skipped through trash as they played. Old bullet casings littered the ground. Trash was smoldering.

We spoke with a few people before loading into the HMMWVs. Comanche 6, Captain Stanley, who was to be our relief, was approached by the Iraqi Police saying that they had spotted an IED north of the Route Pluto bridge. Traffic was bumper-to-bumper, and they had a hard time establishing a cordon around the area surrounding the bomb.

We went to help them out but stopping the traffic was hopeless. Any of those cars could have had a bomb or a weapon, not to mention the pedestrians who could have explosives strapped to them. It was nerve-wracking. I battled to contain the crowd as best as I could, but I soon found myself alone. I was doing a lot of yelling and pointing, many times with my rifle. I was worried an unsuspecting gun shot from the crowd might end me.

After several tense, long moments EOD arrived and blew the bomb. All clear. Traffic exploded. We waved the frustrated drivers into traffic lanes so they could flow through orderly but that was in vain. In Iraq, people drive wherever they want: sidewalks, medians, wherever. The team regrouped at the trucks and we made our way through the mess to the FOB. What a day. I was beat.

Stalking through the crowd, I snarled like a wolf and brandished my rifle fangs for compliance. This was a precarious situation. For a moment, I was in a position where I could not see any other team member. Local nationals surrounded me.

Some were yelling about the traffic. Others were yelling about things I couldn't understand. The scene was ripe for kidnapping or worse.

As uneasy as I was, the locals were more so. I kept them at bay after a few escalations helped them understand I needed space. As I moved into a better position and peered into vehicles looking for anything suspicious, some were shaking and nervous.

The women in their black hijabs would keep their heads down. One man stormed to me, motioning for me to look in his back seat. He had two fresh skinned goat carcasses he had purchased that needed refrigeration. I couldn't do much except motion with primitive hand signals and make explosion noises to indicate a bomb was ahead.

I could not imagine the interruptions to their daily lives this conflict had caused. The central issue of war-fighting in the streets was one thing, but the constant nuisance it created would test anyone's sanity. The lack of electrical power, functioning sewers, transportation, fuel, health care, et cetera disillusioned the citizens' faith in the American plan.

On this day, we were the face of that plan, and the Iraqi people were aggravated. It is a bizarre perspective to think that through the disarray, success—and moreover, peace—comes in the form of a routine, frustrating traffic jam because of a vehicle accident, not a roadside bomb, spoiling your feast of goat meat. Peace is a damn hard thing to quantify.

February 16, 2006 –

Got up at 0100 with Davis standing over me, telling me I have radio guard. "What the hell? Are you sure I ain't going on a mission? Umm, yeah dude I am sure. Have you talked to any of the NCOs? Yeah man. Ok, be there in 5 minutes." I met Davis to tap him out and he was like "Man, you were talking in your sleep about a mission and shit. I was like, dude I AM going on a mission." It wasn't his fault. Fogle's home for midtour leave and I was covering down for him. Nobody updated the guard schedule. My day started at 0100. I got my kit ready and I was already fatigued. It's 0230.

Went through a mission brief and met at the trucks with our gear. We drove to the vicinity of the Route Pluto bridge, hopped out, and crept to our OP. We had to climb and make human steps to get a great view of the market and the bridge. We saw the entrance to Route Corn too. This place had seen a lot of bombs going off lately and I hoped we could get lucky but wasn't sure we'd ever find these ghosts.

We watched until noon. I couldn't hold open my eyes. I asked DeLay for a reprieve, and he let me shut my eyes for a bit. Thanks, boss. Intel says 13 people were abducted from this area last night. The insurgents cut out eyes, tore out fingernails, and threw the bodies into the river. Such evil. Even worse, it was reported they were dressed as Public Order Brigade members.

We made some radio calls to investigate some stuff, but those responsible were long gone. I was tired and frustrated. Where are these assholes? It was time to go, so we climbed off the roof, moving through the daylight. The Iraqis steered clear more than usual. I can't help but think it's because of our scoped weapons. We climbed into the trucks and made it to base after dinner. I skipped food and went to sleep.

After the first few months of patrols, I had accomplished little but had been witness to much—except the thing that we'd been hoping to eliminate, the enemy. The violence of the war orbited around me, leaving me unscathed. As the team I was a part of observed for hours, engagements from the enemy were sporadic and over fast. The phantoms would shoot at us, or detonate a bomb, and slip away into the periphery away from the main routes before we could catch them. This bothered us.

When deployed to a war zone, particularly as a member of an all-volunteer combat arms, you seek validation. You have trained your body and tested your spirit, shedding blood and tears, in preparation. You have hardened your heart and challenged your soul to face absolute danger, knowing the cost and risks associated, at least on the skin-deep level. We were ready to charge into hell's inferno armed with squirt guns. It is a foolhardy endeavor that sings a siren song to boys wishing to test their mettle.

The result, of course, is exposure to real and visceral consequences. It's a poignant song that can't be unheard. Still, I desired a listen to the fateful music I had so long demanded. It whispers to those aged warriors a powerful melody. Be careful what you wish for, as they say—such is the ignorance of youthful blood. You so often complain about being tired until you meet somebody who will soon never wake from their slumber.

May 29, 2016 –

The coffee was good. I woke after sleeping for a few hours and made a cup using the complimentary dirt the hotel provided. The signs were obvious. We had had a good time. Eric and I had brought the beverages back, and Jeff had shepherded the crowd into room 523 to round out the evening.

As the old soul of the group, I had maintained a degree of sobriety for damage control and knew we had a busy day planned. I thought it might have been a bit difficult to get the tribe moving, but the guys were sensible in their consumption, at least in a former infantrymen's sense, and were anxious to continue the reunion agenda. With a few text messages, the troops rallied.

I blew on the Styrofoam cup. Kat lay on the bed, wrapped like a mummy in the blankets—her usual sleeping condition. I pulled open the curtains, letting in the morning sunlight. She did not welcome it and rolled over with a groan. She had endured the mess of reuniting veterans with the greatest of fortitudes, especially considering she was growing another human in her belly. I peered out at the morning traffic zipping below, free of concern on their commute.

"Babe," I started, "we've gotta get a move on. Busy day today."

"Ugh." Her predictable response.

"Should be fun, though."

"Not enough fun last night?" she croaked.

I laughed. She was right. Last night had been a lot of fun. Eric and I had returned as conquering heroes, but times had changed. It wasn't wearing your helmet and body armor in contests of barracks boasting skill or running the obstacle course with flip-flops to prove your fitness as we had years ago. It wasn't executing well-rehearsed precision raids of other barracks to secure party supplies and pizza like we reminisced about throughout the night, but we felt youthful, like young soldiers again—if only for a while.

"How do you feel?" I asked her.

Kat de-mummified herself and stood, stretching towards the ceiling. She growled. "I'm pregnant, remember? I feel pregnant."

I needed to dodge the pregnant mother comment. "Yeah, I'm okay. I took it easy. Thanks for asking." Kat laughed, acknowledging my riposte. I stared out the thick double-paned window at the rush of silent traffic below, thinking about what Eric had said on our walk. We hadn't talked much about the deployment outside of a few remarks of Route Pluto, and I wasn't sure if talking about the more difficult topics was going to happen, or if the guys were ready to engage.

"You guys haven't talked much about Iraq," Kat remarked.

"That's fine," I convinced myself. "Let's have a good time."

"Kara and I think you guys need to get comfortable first," Kat said. She flipped open our suitcase and rummaged for the clothes she had packed with a mountaineer's talent.

"Maybe."

"No, it'll happen."

"Eric thinks that the guys want to understand."

"Don't you?" Kat asked. She threw a t-shirt and jean shorts onto the bed.

"I'm not sure what there is to even understand."

She walked behind me and rested her arms on my shoulders to look out the window too.

"Y'know, when you came back and we first started dating," she said.

"Yeah." I took a sip of coffee. Kat's entry had been a tremendous landmark in my young life.

"I knew you were doing some serious thinking about your time there. You read any book you could get your hands on, took classes, watched documentaries, hours and hours of self-studying. It bordered on obsession. All so you could get the bigger picture."

"Yeah, I wanted to understand the context."

"Yes, exactly." She spun me around while I balanced the coffee cup, keeping the black gold from spilling.

"You know what, when you went and threw together your journal, none of that mattered. You wanted to know what it meant to you."

"What it meant to me isn't what it means to them."

"Are you sure?"

I turned towards the window. Kat placed her arms back on me.

"When I read the journal..."

"You read it?" I interjected.

"I didn't let you see me reading it, but I read it."

I wasn't sure how to unravel that. I had wanted Kat and my family to read it. That's part of the reason I wrote it—so they would know what happened. But for some reason, I was nervous to share the story. It wasn't the thrilling Hollywood portrayal of war. I didn't want to dash anyone's expectations that it wasn't the battles of Fallujah or Ramadi. It was authentic. It was what happened.

"What struck me most wasn't the patrols or the fighting, but how you viewed it."

"I'm not following."

"You look at these things, and instead of looking for the bad side, you look to what could help you grow as a person. It's like you were using it to build a framework to look at the war on a more personal level."

"I wanted it to have meaning," I started. "We used to do after-action reviews following a patrol, which was a simple chat to learn how to improve as soldiers. We never did that when the deployment was over. We didn't sit down to understand what took place in the bigger picture. How we can learn from it? How did the Comanches fit in with the bigger picture? That's what I wanted to do by writing it down."

"You don't think your friends want that, too?"

"They are stronger than me. Don't need to waste time," I said.

"That's true." Kat laughed. "They are stronger than you. But who says it has anything to do with strength? It's about courage. You're one of the bravest guys I've ever known. Be the leader. Go first."

I didn't know what to say. Compliments from Kat weren't common. When she gave them, their rarity added value. I gave her a kiss. She walked over to the bed and sorted out her clothing for the day.

"I'll throw the journal out there and see if anyone looks at it this evening."

"Isn't that why you brought it?"

"I hadn't made up my mind."

"You wrote it for a reason. Why are you so anxious about sharing it?" Kat asked.

"I'm not sure. I can tell myself the story but sharing with others bothers me. It's not like the deployment was horrible; it wasn't. It was more about evaluating the whole thing," I said.

"You know as well as I do that sharing the journal, especially with the ones who were there, is not judgment," Kat said. She examined her clothing before turning to face me. "You're not evaluating anything but yourself. That's in the past, and there is nowhere else to go but the future."

"Well, I wasn't going to let our time there amount to nothing," I said.

Kat opened the mini-fridge and pulled out one of the waters before heading for a shower. "So, don't let it."

Ding. Jeff. "Breakfast?"

3.

STRIKE THE SPARK

The process of securing the central route into eastern Baghdad began to gain traction. Despite the continued presence of roadside bombs, a decrease of IEDs along Route Pluto tipped freedom of movement in favor of coalition forces. We spent most of those first few months probing, patrolling, and protecting the two-lane highway to secure the artery to the heart of southeastern Baghdad. As we developed a steady-state battle rhythm, it became time to push further into territory beyond the main thoroughfares and into more remote, isolated locations which were challenging to reach with our up-armored gun trucks.

Our operations transitioned from route security to a patrol-to-contact emphasis to deny the enemy's ability to coalesce freely and have safe havens accessible to the city. In actuality, Shia efforts likely forced Sunni insurgents to relocate elsewhere in the country, and the Shia militiaman remained in areas like Jisr Diyala and other enclaves more isolated. We were ready for the change in tactics because it meant reconnecting with our roots as light infantrymen, and it also meant tackling other dimensions of combat operations in which we were more well-versed rather than patrolling in HMMWVs for route security.

Helicopter insertion was a mission we were fond of, as our training before the deployment had consisted of several fast-roping, sling-loading, and other helicopter-related training events. It was outright fun to fly around with the doors open looking upon farmers working their fields across Kentucky and

Tennessee. Now we were going to do it for a mission in a dangerous part of the world, and the risk was genuine.

The energy was palpable. We were just salty enough to be comfortable operating in Iraq and also confident that our initial success on Route Pluto would translate elsewhere. Continued pressure on the enemy was precisely what young, bravado-filled soldiers anticipated, myself included. It might have been that we had something to prove, or it might have been that we felt that we had a job to do—it might have been that we were too tired to give a damn.

Nevertheless, I noticed a shift, not only in the employment of our combat capabilities, but also in our attitude towards combat. We felt a new level of fatigue, apparent in the contrasts of character that immersion in a wartime environment uncovers. We also carried a general sense that, as winter gave way to spring, a reinvigoration of violence and renewed aggression from the insurgency was blooming.

As we moved away from the main route in our area of operations and pushed into more remote areas, contact with the enemy increased. This was, at least in part, a result of more foot patrols and us entering areas that had seen less American presence in the last three years. This was also in part to a planned reaction by the Sunni insurgents to divide the country and bring the Shia militias further into the fray to destabilize the government.

It was common knowledge that if the enemy could convince the public we were unable to protect the populace, the largely Shia administration, boycotted by the Sunnis, would stalemate or worse, and the infant government could collapse. In our sector, the enemy targeting shifted to include not only US soldiers but also scared and vulnerable populations of civilians from other tribes and sects. As a matter of course, as spring grew closer, the conflict was heating up in more ways than one.

February 22, 2006 –

It was time, 0230. We milled around in anxious boredom before moving to the landing zone on the Iraqi Army side of the Rustamiyah. We did some rehearsals, and each soldier had their last smoke or joke before we split. Our stick boarded the birds. I was lucky and landed a seat next to the window. The Blackhawks took off and did one false insertion—a deceptive landing to draw the enemy's attention—before hovering into a gentle landing on LZ 'Viper.' We ran off the bird and continued movement through the orange orchards and woods in the area vicinity Salman Pak, a decent trek south of Baghdad.

The patrol was slow due to many obstacles. I think, in total, we had to cut, cross, or climb 7 chain-link fences, some over 10 feet high, and push through thick hedges marking property boundaries and making the movement laborious.

After a couple of hours, we found a suitable position to occupy that overlooked one of the roads leading to Route Wild, an extension off Route Pluto to the north. It was our job to stop vehicles from entering or leaving. The family's house we used was a one-story shed and there were two kids and a woman living there. We had to stop a few vehicles but had no issues. Lots of shooting was heard from the area where the outer cordon was at. We stayed there until around noon.

Soon, we got a call to rendezvous with the other team and move into a surveillance position adjacent Route Wild. There was some miscommunication with the checkpoints, and it resulted in us moving around a kilometer and a half to their position which was a precarious movement for three dudes in the middle of the day. We were lucky—we rallied with no issue.

The other team was hunkered down in some people's backyard and were talking with the natives pointing at drawings to gain some knowledge about local threats. We hung out for a few before moving 4 kilometers north to the observation post overlooking Route Wild. This movement was not fun. It was the warmest day yet, and the area was teeming with activity. Local nationals spotted us from a safe distance and were keeping tabs on our location and likely updating any interested party.

We pulled it in tight along a dry, reed-filled irrigation canal and stuffed MRE trimmings in our pockets to eat on the move. Making it to the OP, we weren't there long. We pulled off after seeing a flight of pigeons released off a rooftop. We had been briefed by intel that the birds were routinely used as a signal to notify the enemy of coalition forces. The jig was up. We hoofed it into a thick undergrowth of another, more defensible orchard less than a kilometer from our objective to lie low until nightfall.

As the sun set, plans changed. We got a call to move into the patrol base for the night. I was washed in a gracious relief because that meant we were going to be able to sleep for a few hours. We moved the two kilometers to the patrol base and bedded down for the night. The whole area had an ominous feel to it.

During this mission, I received the first of what would become my 're-occurring epiphanies.' Here we were in a foreign country, surrounded by a populace who cared little if we lived or died as we trampled through their backyards with scoped rifles. Moving in a three-man element like this was fraught with danger. One automatic weapon could pin us down, and our firepower would not be able to cover a break in contact efficiently. A single man wounded would result in another rendering buddy-aid, while the other was responsible for directing support and returning fire. That is a dicey proposition and a risk that required a certain strength of character to appreciate or a genuine ignorance to dismiss.

Some of our movements were in moderate to dense neighborhoods and villages. Sure, an M24 sniper rifle could reach out and touch the enemy, but whoever could put the most accurate fire on their foe won. It was about holding and maintaining the initiative. We had the most fire discipline. We had trained to shoot, move, and communicate far more effectively than the insurgents. Our teamwork and coordination were what made us most deadly, not our rifles.

As the small, cohesive element we were, we knew how to feed off each other. The surreal feeling of danger, however, never left me. I was aware that we each needed to be at the top of our game and that our fates were in each other's hands. It is a relationship unique to this environment and what is being asked of you at the moment. It is a bond that is not without its rough patches—after all, we could complain about each other with the best of them—but we also knew when it was time to ruck up and shut up. My 're-occurring epiphanies' captured these insights from those times.

Though I was cognizant of the hazards I faced, I was unaware that the conflict was fundamentally shifting instigated from a sectarian-rooted attack on the Al-Askari Mosque—the Golden Dome of Samarra—some 80 miles north of Baghdad proper. On this day, men wearing uniforms entered the mosque—one of the holiest in Shia Islam—captured the guards, and later detonated explosives, destroying the religious shrine. The attack sparked retribution on rival Sunni holy sites, inciting sectarian violence throughout the country despite national leaders' pleas to cease the bloodshed.

US forces appeared powerless to stop the attacks. Thus, we soon became targets of the hatred the sectarian violence planted in the fertile crescent. Yet, I remained oblivious to those larger geopolitical consequences and remained concerned with my little area of the war zone. I was unaware of how problematic and interconnected the events unfolding across the nation were. The first drop of water had made its way through the levee. It'd soon be joined by an angry river splitting apart every sun-dried neighborhood and farm.

February 23, 2006 –

We woke at 0300 in the middle of the orchard serving as the company patrol base. It was a cold, near frosting morning and climbing out of the fart sack was a chore. The skin on my face was stiff. I tightened my boots, threw on my gear, and moved out to get briefed on the day's events.

Today's mission was to once again overwatch Route Wild on our eastern flank to make sure the enemy didn't emplace IEDs to deter coalition traffic into the operations area. We were to move five kilometers northeast to our new position. Under the cover of darkness, we walked alongside Route Wild, skirting the road, using the houses as cover.

Ahead, was a checkpoint, manned by either the Iraqi Police or the Public Order Brigade. We moved, holding our breath hoping they didn't open fire. We kept walking until we saw a warehouse where we could establish observation. Oddly enough, there was a guard and he wouldn't let us in. It was best to move on. We got a grid to his spot for future reference and headed north until we came to an unfinished building with a massive field of view of the route.

Our teams cleared both sides of the building and set up shop in each corner. The building was perfect, but it was a little tight to watch each avenue of approach. We couldn't cover the multitude of entrances. To counter this, the teams combined to share the wealth.

We had some difficulty getting communications going, but I went to the top floor and unfolded the long-whip antenna. I sat listening to the radio communications from the other maneuvering elements to gain a picture of what was happening and relayed it to the teams scanning for targets.

We hung out watching the route until the POB made a hasty checkpoint right in front of our observation post. Perfect. Now, chances were slim any enemy activity would happen. Although, the POB are pretty large targets, so we kept our eyes peeled.

After a while, a young local national stumbled upon our location, setting off our trip flares. We grabbed him for questioning. He was some young kid, 13 years old if I were to bet. Scared shitless. We couldn't keep him with us so we gave him a job to see if he'd help us. We asked him to bring us food from a vendor across the street and he left to do so under the watchful eye of a sniper scope while we prepared to move out.

The kid delivered. He walked to the vendor, loaded a couple of bags with goodies, and carried to us flatbread, dates, oranges, little snack cakes, and a liter of Syrian-made cola. We gave him all the money we had. Nice kid. We sat there stuffing our faces and getting fat on Iraqi food when we heard a substantial amount of gunfire coming from the river banks of the Tigris to our rear. The radio went nuts. It was 2nd platoon. Time to move.

May 29, 2016 –

"Two eggs, fried hard, bacon, and toast."

"White or wheat?" the waitress asked.

"Wheat, please."

The waitress collected the menus and bustled off to pass our orders to the kitchen staff. Twenty people sat on either side of the long table of the hotel's restaurant. In various forms of morning composure, we recharged for a visit to the museum and the evening's reunion with more coffee and a hearty breakfast.

"Jeff," I said, unrolling my napkin. "Good turnout, man."

"It's great to see everyone," Jeff said. If the reunion-goers had a bond, Jeff was the glue. Even during some of the more unpleasant periods over a decade ago, Jeff had held us together when we wished nothing more than to be ripped apart. Much of the reunion was realized because of that glue.

"Agreed. After we visit the museum and the old company area, we'll get back here and rest."

"That's the plan," Jeff said. He chugged some ice water and continued to nod in the affirmative.

"I kinda want to get over to the VFW early to set some stuff up," I explained. I had coordinated the day's activities, and nowhere in the plan had I included an afternoon siesta.

"Yeah, man, of course," Jeff said, concurring with the potential for a busy afternoon.

"They said they have a spare room for us, and I figured we could move around a few tables."

"You bring the stuff we talked about?" he asked.

"I did, and a bit more."

"More? What do you mean?"

"Well, I got the letters some of the leadership wrote for us." I counted my fingers. "Four total."

"That's cool."

"All the newsletters from the trip, a few reports, and the pictures we had printed."

"It'll be good to thumb through all that," Jeff said. The guys and their significant others were continuing conversations from the night prior. The energy zapped back through the group. Coffee helped.

"I'm thinking about throwing my journal on the table."

"Oh, no kidding, you wrote a journal?" Jeff focused and looked me in the eye. I could tell that Kat was listening even though she spoke with Kara about needing a nap.

"Every patrol I ever went on, I scribbled a little note."

"Dude, I want to read it!" Jeff exclaimed. "It'd be great to remember those things."

"Well, I'm not sure it's worthwhile. I hoped to gather some meaning behind the whole thing. How the year unfolded but, y'know, more like how we draw lessons from those experiences," I said.

For some reason, I was still hesitant about sharing the journal. It wasn't that I was ashamed of my service, it was the contrary. It may have been a fool's errand, but I had believed in the mission given to me. We were there to kill the enemy and help those they sought to disadvantage.

As selfless as that may seem, I was also there to find what I was made of. The greatest mystery of a young person's life is whether they will measure up when faced with adversity, and I had scoured the pages I drafted hoping to find the answer. This sort of introspection was not a condition many veterans discussed, but I respected and appreciated most viewpoints— none more so than those of the men I served alongside.

"Well, hell, man. You don't think we want to learn from it in some way?" Jeff asked. His hands shaped the words as they came out of his mouth. "I've wondered how becoming an adult in a war zone has shaped this last decade, with respect to character. There are lessons in everything if you look hard enough."

"Paul," Eric chimed in. Sitting a few seats down, he must have overheard the conversation Jeff and I were having. "That's it, man. If you think you got a monopoly on learning lessons from war, you're sorely mistaken."

"There's no monopoly. I'm torn about sharing my thoughts about the whole thing."

"I get it. We all do," Eric continued. "I wrote my own piece. After some of the more memorable missions, I jotted notes to myself. I wanted to record my involvement in some of the significant actions that happened."

"See?" Jeff leaned his head in Eric's direction.

"That makes sense," I replied.

"I wanted to record the history." Eric motioned with his cup of joe. "So that others may know."

"Well, I guess I wrote some stuff so that others may learn."

Eric nodded his head in agreement.

"What do you mean?" Jeff asked.

The conversation continued along parts of the table.

"You ever ask yourself what it meant?" I asked. "What did we get from our time over there?"

"Yeah, what the hell does it mean? How do I move forward with it? How do I grow as a person after being IED'd, mortared, shot at?" Jeff lowered his brow and shook his head side to side. "It doesn't mean a damn thing. We can't change how it went down."

I looked at Eric. He smiled.

"Here's the thing, Jeff. Do you consider yourself better having experienced that?"

"Yeah, man. I'm more mentally strong, resilient, and…" Jeff trailed off struggling to think of his next words.

"You *have* thought about it?" I cut into his pause.

"I guess so," he answered.

"I'm not one to tell you how to draw conclusions about our time there," I said. "It's your own decision to learn from it. I tried. I tried to learn from it and apply it to my life."

"Aren't you a saint."

"Not at all, man. I wanted to get it out. It was my way of deciding I'm going to make the war work for me, not let the results be decided for me. What happens in Iraq will never impact me more than what I decide to take away from it. That's why I put the journal together. I wanted to look at those patrols and learn from them. Like an after-action review. A debrief. I wanted to use those events to make myself better. I'm just not sure I have."

Although leaders authored trip reports or wrote some dictation debriefing our deployment, the collective discussion concerning our year in Iraq had been held in a large circle surrounding a commander pontificating praise for our efforts. It may have been heartfelt, but thoughts of our performance and what we had learned over the last year about ourselves and others needed held in small, more intimate settings like a reunion ten years in the making.

"We should be doing that," Jeff said.

"We should," Eric chimed in. "Are you?" he asked Jeff.

"Actually, I've got some thoughts about the late part of the deployment," Jeff answered.

"Exactly," Eric said. "We got thoughts about those events and experiences because we wanted to record them. Paul, by sharing our story, you're sharing how things unfolded for those who were there. It ain't much, but it is history."

"It is history," Jeff echoed.

"Because I took those notes, I can remember that gunfight along the Tigris like it was yesterday." Eric looked around the table. "It makes me damn proud...to remember how damn brave the guys were."

We toyed with our coffee cups as Eric told his story, recalling the afternoon of February 23rd when I was huddled in a building along Route Wild listening to the radio, not realizing our conflict had changed course and with it, our lives. The table quieted one person at a time as they listened to him speak. Eric transported us to 2006, along the ancient river, back into the war, while we waited for our eggs and bacon.

February 23, 2006 –

We were inside an orchard, ten meters in from the east side of the Tigris, as the others made their way northward not far from the river's bank. We snapped a few pictures of each other not five minutes before the first shot. The orchard was a relaxing spot—it had terrific shade, the trees were blooming and smelled flowery, the grass was tall and soft, and the bank provided enough dirt berm for cover while not obstructing our view. We had a good position and could see up and down the river for several hundred meters in either direction.

There were five of us. Johnny rocked the M203 40mm grenade launcher and our automatic rifleman rested with the M249 Squad Automatic Weapon. Kelley, the radiotelephone operator, sported a long-whip antenna and an M4 rifle, and Bob, the interpreter, armed himself with a folding lawn chair he'd found earlier in the operation. The chair was bent and fraying, but Bob would open it to take breaks when the time was right. Johnny pulled rear, and Kelley pulled flank security, while the remainder of us overwatched over the far side of the river.

The other team was transiting a few hundred meters so we would be in place for ten minutes or so before it was our time to move again. Staff Sergeant Higgins, one of the warrior squad leaders we were blessed to have, called over the radio that he was in position, giving us a description of the terrain and his situation. We paused for a few more moments to let them get well set to cover us for our next movement across the danger area.

We moved out of the orchard and across a broad canal that was wide enough to slow our movement, steadying ourselves on the shaky earth. It took us a few minutes to get across, but we had plenty of time to make these movements, so we proceeded slowly, remaining cautious and maintaining security. I moved in front, Bob right behind me, Kelley a few meters off our left flank, the SAW gunner seven meters back, and Johnny maintaining rear security in a classic stop-and-go maneuver.

The field we needed to cross, past the orchard and canal, was 150 meters wide. As we made it a little past the halfway point, the height of the reeds on the bank became shorter for a dozen meters, exposing us to the opposite bank of the Tigris. We did have a foot or two of cover from the plowed field. The movement felt secure because we had plenty of support. Bob and Kelley were even bantering back and forth, teasing each other like soldiers often do.

About three-quarters of the way across the open area, two sets of two shots each came from across the river. This fire was disproportionately loud, and I knew it was not the harassment fire we'd been used to receiving. We hit the ground and sought cover. Training kicked in.

Everything happened at once. Those first shots were followed by another burst, which I thought was outgoing at first, but saw otherwise as bullets popped into the dirt around us. Barnett, the M249 SAW gunner, was a veteran of the invasion and, without needing to be told, unleashed hell at a rapid rate of around 200 rounds per minute, but it wasn't enough to stem the initial legato of fire. In fact, the enemy's fire gained momentum and escalated into a sheet of bullets—we were being ambushed from a wadi, or ravine, just behind us and 200 meters across the river.

Within those first few seconds, each of our guys identified the enemy and returned fire at a rate so high the sound formed one continual blast. Kelley, Bob, and I were in the open area, covered by shallow plowed trenches. I rolled onto my back to gain situational awareness. Bob was lying as flat as he could and not moving, wishing his broken lawn chair would transform into a howitzer. Kelley, too, had hit the dirt but with a combination of a groan and a scream.

As Kelley shrieked, I got on a knee and yelled at him, "Quit being weak; we're getting shot at! Get up and shoot back!"

He replied, "Sir, I'm hit!"

I smiled and laughed a little to myself at the dark humor of it all before yelling for a medic. Having done so, I realized Keck, the future archaeologist now medic savior, was 400 meters away with Higgins, so I hit my push-to-talk radio and revealed my excitement, "Kelley's hit, we need the medic here, and we need some support by fire!"

The same time I sent that message, I could hear Higgins returning fire from his position, and I got a speedy reply from him, "We're on the way!" I knew the wild man would not miss out on the opportunity to fight.

On my knee next to Kelley, I looked at his blood-soaked pants and could see the thigh wound. I put my hand on the other side, where I could feel the exit channel—he screamed, confirming the location. As I did so, I had to chuckle again, as the humor of my initial words to him lingered while I assessed him. I could see the wound was sizable, but it had traveled through his flesh and exited. Based on the proximity, color, and flow of the blood, it hadn't shattered bones or severed a major artery. He was going to be okay, but not if we didn't end this fight.

It was an eternity. Fifty seconds had passed, and the gunfight was raging. Counting to fifty in your head turns out to be an uncomfortable amount of time while under fire. The exchange had become a total two-way fusillade of bullets that was as loud outgoing as incoming, shredding the reeds on the banks and kicking up dirt around us. Our easternmost guys had spotted the enemy position and were pouring fire into them, and, with the least amount of prompting, were yelling reports to me.

As I worked on getting the radio off Kelley, I could hear Higgins' fire getting closer. Johnny fired M203 grenade rounds, which were welcomed and sounded magnificent as they impacted. I smiled with each small explosion. Combined with Barnett's SAW's high rate and Higgins' rapid fire as he moved towards our position, the growing firepower gave us the decisive advantage in the fight. My heart rate was through the roof. The heat and adrenaline amplified its thumping. It was to the point where I could feel my heart beating through my neck and into my temples. The fight continued.

By minute two, I had gotten the radio off Kelley's back, told him to stay low, and scrambled a few feet to cover. On a knee, I was a huge target and was drawing a lot of unfriendly fire. I sent the first situation report, and I could see both Higgins and Keck sprinting full speed toward us. There was an eight-foot-high berm between us, but Higgins—like a scene right out of the movies—ran to the top, waved and yelled at Keck, "Go! I got you covered!" Higgins stood on the summit of the berm, and while standing, took aim and emptied a magazine into the enemy position. I watched in awe for a moment as Keck stumbled toward me and bullets skimmed off the earth surrounding Higgins. The man was a warrior.

Keck reached my position and together, we scrambled over to Kelley. Taking a knee once we got there, we both looked at Kelley as the incoming fire increased and the dirt shattered around us. Higgins was shooting again from atop the berm after reloading, and again drawing an enormous amount of fire. I bounded towards the radio, noticing Keck had begun working on Kelley in the open. I yelled to move him to cover, and we grabbed Kelley and dragged him to where they were at least partially obscured from the fire. Just that small amount of movement kept us removed from the fight as long as we stayed low. Ten feet is like ten miles under fire.

Keck did what medics do and Kelley was in good hands. I scurried to the radio, which had been secured by Sorbello, arriving at the fight alongside Higgins and Keck. Together, we sent a second report to stir up some attack aviation or fire support, which I assumed were well out of range, but remained hopeful that a 60mm team was close enough to respond.

Johnny was firing his fifth or sixth carefully aimed 40-millimeter grenade, and I yelled to him for a report. Higgins had moved to the berm, run across our position, and was in the process of establishing another firing position closer to our grenadier and SAW gunner. He was creating sectors of fire and he had the immediate tactical situation under control, so I focused on getting us some assistance and getting Kelley evacuated.

I took a few deep breaths to get my heart rate under control before keying the radio on the command frequency to send an update: "This is Comanche two-six, in sustained contact with six to eight enemy. My forward observer has a gunshot wound to the right thigh, stable and being treated by the medic at this time; requesting air support pushed to this frequency; request quick reaction force and medevac for wounded. I say again…" I sent the report twice and received several responses from other command elements with squads conducting dismounted clearance operations on routes parallel to ours.

Every response came back in a short-breathed manner.

"We're on the way!"

"About one click out."

"Be there in five mikes!"

Everyone who responded was running at full stride toward the sound of the fight.

I heard First Sergeant Lillie shout over the radio, "Is it Kelley? Is he okay?" It was apparent that as tough as the man was—and he was incredibly so—he viewed his soldiers as his own children. The first sergeant mustered the supporting troops and marched them off towards the sounds of rifle fire, knowing that his soldiers were well prepared. Like a father, it pained him to not be in the fight that, across the radio and across the river, sounded like a downpour of steel rain with the occasional clap of grenade lightning.

Despite the storm, the frequency was saturated with each leader wanting communication, but, after Sorbello's forceful interjection into the net, he raised the company commander who asked me to re-send the report a few more times until he had a clear picture of what was going on. It could not have been any more crystal to anyone listening to the radio on the other end. There's no question they could hear the automatic gunfire and impact of the M203 rounds.

Bullets were still zipping and cracking within a few feet of my face after seven or eight minutes. The tribe was identifying enemy personnel and pouring steady fire into them. The incoming fire was just as steady but less accurate than it had been earlier. We had gained fire superiority.

My heart said I should put down the radio and kill some people. Sorbello wanted to get further into the fight as well. One look told me that the boys had it under control, and they loved every second of it. They were blood red, with veins sticking out of their necks, eyes narrow and locked on the enemy, as focused as I'd ever seen a man. It was a sickeningly beautiful thing to watch—broken only by the cracking bullets reminding me to get my face out of the way.

I threw the radio handset to Sorbello and grabbed hold of Kelley's magazines—we'd been shooting for a while, and I knew they had to be low on ammo. Between bursts, I ran over and gave a few mags to the soldiers. When I got to Higgins, I slid prone next to him. He believed they'd killed most of the threats, save a few guys who were staying low in the grass, still firing, and could not be observed. The enemy had the advantage of being able to move along the wadi without being spotted. After ten or so minutes, the incoming fire slowed to sporadic bursts, and the outgoing fire was directed towards suspected enemy positions for suppression.

Sorbello soon reported friendlies were south of us, requesting us to mark our position. As soon as I saw the first friendly, I waved an orange VS-17 panel until he caught sight and signaled to the others that they'd made contact with us. They navigated across the canal we'd crossed moments earlier and closed on us to reinforce our perimeter.

It was First Sergeant Lillie leading a squad from the headquarters platoon. I linked up with him and laid out some priorities. We established security and moved Kelley to a better spot for evacuation. By that time, the entire squadron had shown up. Everyone wanted to fight. That's the thing about warriors—it's the peace that can bother them.

May 29, 2016 –

Eric finished his story. We looked around at nothing in particular. Some looked at their food, some looked across the hotel restaurant, but not a soul made eye contact. We had for our first moment been transported—we were halfway around the world again. Remembering the first blood of the company, the first time the enemy stood to lock horns with us—our pulses quickened, our senses sharpened, our warrior spirit that most had long since tucked away, crept to the surface, manifesting in a sort of maddening smile.

It had been a decisive victory. Our team won, and that was an affirmation of our ability to overwhelm the enemy. But many late arrivals to the fight, including the sniper teams left on the fringes of the battlefield, sought further confirmation of their warrior spirit. As the arriving Apaches reported a few bodies floating in the Tigris, many of us wished, in the backs of our minds, that it was we who had sent the corpses into the river. As gruesome as that may seem, we wanted to make sure that when the enemy confronted us, we too might best them.

That meant killing more of them than us. It was an overzealous bloodlust if there ever was one, but it also meant we were validated as warriors. The question remaining a decade later as we sat around eating our breakfast—to whom were we to prove ourselves? We did a job. We did it humbly. We did it because it needed to be done. We do it so the person sitting next to us eating breakfast can savor that bacon, sip that coffee, and enjoy another morning alive. That's it. That's your validation. That's your approval. That morning, with Eric's story transporting us to the silence of memories, our eggs tasted better than usual. They tasted like appreciation.

February 24, 2006 –

Woke up at 0300. It was cold, but I took the Band-Aid approach and ripped out of the sleeping bag, puncturing the night with an expletive. Got my gear, went to the truck, grabbed an apple from a crate procured from the support company, and zombied off with the team to our final objective: a group of possible insurgent safe houses. We were to isolate the targets until the platoons could reach them and clear the objective.

We humped through a few orchards until we made contact with a group of people that scurried off. No shots were fired. We did a kind of horseshoe movement to come around to catch them. Never found the individuals, but locals typically aren't out for a stroll at 4 in the morning. Somebody was out there.

We climbed one fence, then another. We hopped into a ditch, and an individual carrying an AK-47 was walking toward our position. He was 100 meters away when we spotted him. He kept coming. He hadn't done anything wrong yet so we couldn't shoot him. He kept coming. We called out to him when he approached 25 meters. He dropped his AK and babbled before bending down to retrieve it. We yelled, and he discontinued his reach. From the shadows, we circled around, crossed the ditch and surprised the man.

We searched him, cleared the AK, and radioed it in before discovering other dudes at the end of the road listening to the commotion. We told the detainee to call his friends to come. They didn't comply, so we told him that if they didn't come we were going to shoot them. They came running.

Soon, the shimmering light of the morning sun broke through the trees and we spotted 2nd platoon crossing the road a few hundred meters away. I called for their interpreter to help us out. We recorded the information and passed them off to the cavalry scouts so we could continue mission.

Our team walked through some difficult terrain as we made our way out of the orchards into another series of irrigated fields—mud to my knees and, at one point, water to my neck chilling me to the bone. We arrived late to our hide site and I was chilled to the bone after getting covered in that sludge water from our hike. We overwatched 2nd platoon's movement until they got too far for us to shoot with confidence and we moved again. This time we climbed to the top of an abandoned building. We watched the fun, wondering if another fight would break out.

Alas, the enemy didn't show themselves but sent a few rounds of harassing fire from across the river, just to let us know they were there. Without fanfare, the call came for us to move to the pickup zone in the salt flats for our ride home. The dried salty soil quaked under our muddy boots. We moved out like slugs, leaving white, dusty residue in our wake. By this time, even after all the sock changes, my feet felt raw.

It took us an hour to get to the PZ. We sat and the birds came in three at a time. We got in and took off throwing enormous clouds of white powder into the air. We landed at Rustamiyah and the word spread about how much indirect fire the base received while we were gone. I wasn't much interested in the scuttlebutt. Time to clean my gear so I could sleep and maybe relax a bit. Indirect fire is coming in as I write this. They're pissed.

The price the forward operating base paid for our offensive operation was significant. Seeking to deter our aggressive foot patrolling by mortaring the base was counterproductive—it galvanized our spirit and told us that our dismounted operations were pressuring the enemy and served as a surprising source of motivation.

The attacks were also indicative of the growing capabilities of insurgency and deteriorating sectarian conflict, but we just sat and took the barrage, hoping we all could make it to the chow hall without the hassle. With a twisted sense of selfishness, I would much rather be on my feet, where I could defend myself, rather than on the FOB, where soldiers were fish in a barrel for insurgents to launch ordnance.

Like so many things at this time, I hadn't given much thought into the experiences of other soldiers, the ones who, for at least a year, endured being surrounded by tall, concrete barriers enveloping our base. They had to deal with indirect fire without a way to deter it but came to realize they depended on us, as we depended upon them. It's warzone homeostasis and a frustrating balance we needed to strike. There was one way to end the mortar and rocket attacks, and that was to get after those responsible. But first, we took a knee.

Our company would bring the full-court press in less than a week. We reconstituted by wrapping our feet in moleskin, drinking copious amounts of water, and eating several thousand calories a day. We were ready to put the pressure on the enemy, but, in preparation, took the time for warm showers and Kellogg, Brown, and Root-supplied hot meals. We were spoiled. There is no doubt. And we felt a sort of guilt with the level of comfort we enjoyed. We'd not complain, but we knew. These small things bring a degree of gratitude that you cannot begin to appreciate until you do without, and the knowledge, in the back of your mind, that there was a chance you'd not enjoy such little luxuries again.

Warm food not from a bag, being able to relieve yourself without fear of getting shot at mid-stream, or merely having a discussion with friends without whispering are some of those elements that become sacred when deployed. They sound trivial, but trivial becomes meaningful among the fields of shared strife. I was less concerned with not being killed than I was with being able to shower. It wasn't hubris. It was knowing you're alive, so live.

March 1, 2006 –

It was a 0400 wake up after pulling guard until midnight. Grabbed my gear. Radios need some work. Fixed that. Our communications dude is top-notch, always willing to hook it up. Headed out. 1st platoon dropped us off at the Paint Factory. A sharpshooter had been firing from across Pluto at passing POB trucks the night before. We hung out, drew a sketch, and filed a log. Nothing. It got to be 1400 and we met the trucks for a trip north.

We get near the Route Pluto bridge and turned around. Comanche 6 wanted us back in position to support a raid of that compound later in the evening. We handed off the sketch and log to Schrader. Captain Stanley got a hold of it and wanted to have a look himself. He climbed into the compound and came into our position. He gave us an intel dump on what to look for and expected activity. They wanted to take a few people for questioning.

So now, it was a waiting game. Soon enough, we spotted some people moving around in the compound and a couple of vans entering through the access road. The place is much more active than we've seen in the past. One particular dude hung out at the entrance and got on his cell phone. He matched the description. He walked across the street to a roadside shanty store with his buddy that also matched the description. Bingo. They had a seat and people talked with them. He looked kind of nervous and got on his cell phone and pointed towards the compound opposite our position.

Darkness was creeping in and 10 other guys came to the shop. I radioed the CO to inform him of the meeting. The HMMWVs roared in and flicked on their headlights. Nobody ran. It turned out the two guys failed an explosive residue test, so they are zip-cuffed and taken for questioning. Explosives are in the compound. It feels like we are policemen, not infantrymen, but this is what the fight requires.

We rolled into the FOB and were greeted with guard shifts through the night. Wonderful. Used the time to write this journal entry. The bonus about hanging in the CP all night is that you get the word early—we are heading south for an extended operation. I get to sleep at 5 a.m. I'm tired, but alive for another day.

Coming back, we were notified that the snipers and mortar section were going on a special mission to assist the Public Order Brigade near Salman Pak, a city fifteen or twenty miles south of Baghdad. The POB had established a headquarters along the Tigris at an old Baathist resort for Saddam and his cronies. We were returning to our primary duties—our roots—what we had trained to do, and the operation afforded us the opportunity to act like snipers again. Our task was to eliminate the indirect fire threat harassing the resort which had limited the POB freedom of movement both within the compound and out.

Our teams combined with the mortar section to increase the level of firepower, enabling us to reach across the river with both bombs and bullets. Operating from a central location, the mortar teams would monitor the radio and stand by to launch counterfire missions using distances and bearings we provided from our vantage point—a hide site we had built on the fourth floor of the hotel. This hodge-podge collection of soldiers, at its core, was economy of force in action.

To that point, we also wheeled and dealed to have a medic attached to us: my good friend, Dombroski. A first-rate medic in the company, the infantry dudes felt safer when he was around. Dombroski was one of the first friends I had made when I first came to the 506th.

Stocky and athletic, the Polish descendant from New Jersey was a favorite in the company for many reasons. He stood out in his dedication to craft and his relentless pursuit of perfection. He was also good-natured, and I was proud to have him as a friend because he made me better. He was not unique. The brotherhood of arms is filled with guys like him.

On the roof of the hotel, we harnessed our technological edge to enhance our low-light capabilities by bringing along a cavalry trooper and his night optics to help us knuckle-dragging cavemen. Despite our wizardry, we were several miles from the nearest friendly American forces. Although this was an ally's compound, the distance contributed to a sense of uneasiness.

Though the term 'ally' was appropriate, the Iraqi troops who manned this compound were also divided across sectarian lines. We were sure that some POB soldiers were sympathetic to the opposition, and to a larger extent, the Mahdi Army, who was shadowing the Sunni insurgency in our sector. They would give us up if the situation arose.

As we watched our six and simultaneously scanned for the enemy, we weren't sure who the enemy was, or if that POB soldier climbing the stairs was well-intentioned. It didn't matter. We were here to do a mission—to aid the Iraqis exposed to an endless routine of murderous fire from across the Tigris—and we had the team to do it.

March 4, 2006 –

The mission planned for next week got bumped to this day. We gathered what intel we could and staged the trucks for departure. I pulled routine maintenance on one of the gun trucks. For hours, I melted in the motor pool preparing one of the vehicles for the mission. The beast has seen better days.

We wrapped that up and are given tan desert uniforms to mirror the Special Police Transition Team soldiers that train the Iraqis at a Public Order Brigade Headquarters at an old Baathist resort hotel complex. We convoyed south of the traffic circle and rumbled into Salman Pak before turning west for the river. We made it into the POB compound and pulled into the SPTT's ad hoc command post in a villa overlooking the Tigris.

Soon, the POB soldiers were crowding us asking questions as to who we were and what we were doing. We got communications established and unloaded the trucks as fast as possible. Our observation posts were planned for the fourth and fifth floors of the main hotel building, but we waited until most of the POB soldiers were asleep to move into our positions some 200 meters from the CP. We spent the time preparing our gear, discussing our plan, and eating chow.

Dusk settled in and we got our second welcome. Boom! Wam! Boom! Mortar fire blasted throughout the compound, peppering the Hesco barriers outside the villa. Knowing the POB didn't have any night optics to see where it came from, I grabbed a few parachute flares, grenades, and the platoon leader and ran into the fight.

Together, we dove into some cover, and I loaded a flare into my M203, hoping to see across the Tigris and brighten the night. A steady stream of bullets was sailing over us. Scanning behind me, along the elevated bank, I could see the machine gun positions manned and spouting flame across the river in a blanket of suppressing fire hoping to stop the mortar barrage.

I laid low and peeked around a barrier toward where I wanted the first one to go. I saw a little patch of grass to my 12 o'clock. That would do. I let one go with the 203, but there was not enough hang time, and the flare goes 30 feet in the air. It lit and deployed its little parachute in enough time to show me that the grass was an island in the middle of the river. What a dumbass. I could see the opposite side of the bank and it's 50 meters farther. The platoon leader busted my chops for being *a bonehead. We laughed and remembered machine guns were shooting over our heads.*

Back to business. Thump. I launched another, and the flare illuminated the entire area like a shimmering, miniature star. The teams scanned for enemy movements but found none. I doubted anyone would be moving with that much suppressive fire. After the star's light faded, we clambered along the bank to the CP before the POB shot at us by accident thinking we were the bad guys.

Not long after we got into the command post, the fire slowed. The mortars had stopped so Davis and I got our stuff and rushed to the hotel positions, hoping to get a better vantage point with the help of some optics. Joining the team, we dropped our gear and began to build a hide sight, but the fight was over.

We worked through the night, and I got a half-hour of sleep due to the humongous rats in the building desperate to steal our food. To keep us going, we have a little coffee pot and a small Coleman propane burner. DeLay always thought of everything. We're going to need that.

The rats in this old resort hotel were scurrying in and out of a variety of holes, defiant of their new neighbors, and the temptation of open MREs was irresistible to them. The first floor housed several Iraqi soldiers, who would sleep together in one room, with a large four-foot diameter plate filled with rice to share.

Without a doubt, the rats were the only ones calling this place a resort. The hotel had been ransacked when Saddam was overthrown—wires had been ripped from the walls, the furniture looted, and the maintenance neglected. The elevator sat on the first floor as a permanent fixture of the building in a couple of different pieces. Rumor had it that underneath the metal heap were the remnants of some unfortunate Iraqi looter, which was untrue, but the blood stains on the walls near the elevator lent the story credence.

Bullet holes riddled the glass and plaster, and scorch marks, where individuals had started fires indoors, pockmarked the rooms where squatters had spent the night huddled together for warmth. It was a war-torn building at its utmost. Despite not having modern amenities like toilets, this building had everything we needed, and—when the shooting ebbed—radiated a sense of calm and tranquility as steady as the flow of the ancient river in front of it.

The Special Police Transition Team (SPTT), pronounced 'spit,' had set up shop in a smaller villa located a few hundred meters away from the hotel. We had borrowed it as our command post. Their villa was in better shape—it had mattresses and a sink, a relative five-star upgrade to our observation posts. Hesco barriers provided protection, but the building also showed the scars of war. Bullet holes and fragmented infrastructure told a story of some fun vacation evenings at the resort, with an Mk-19 grenade launcher on the roof headlining the entertainment.

The SPTT welcomed us into their swanky lodgings on the premise that we'd take care of their pesky neighbors—they even offered some of their orange soda acquired from contractors' stockpiles. As they left us alone to take care of business, it was fair to say we got along just fine.

March 5, 2006 –

Woke up. Stand to. Looked to make our position better. Made it better. Pulled observation and got down the routine of the day—saw what went on, who went where, what time, grids to key buildings, ranges to targets, range cards. The usual junk fills the majority of the day. Darkness came and the team leaders headed for the CP to help with the High Frequency radio.

Davis and I were chilling at "Hotel California"—the name we chose for our position on the fifth floor. Tyler and our cavalry troop buddy that had joined us to run the thermal vision were relaxing at their hide site on the fourth floor—"Motel Six."

I was eating an MRE when I realized we didn't have comms. I crept to the fourth floor to ask who had the handheld radio. Nobody was there. I remembered the guys asking me if I had an infrared strobe, so I climbed the stairs to the roof to see if they were there taking care of it. The roof was empty. There was no strobe. Where the hell are they? I talked to Davis and decided to head to CP to track them down.

On my way, I met the dudes on the stairs from a trip to get batteries for the radio. Communications reestablished and finding the strobe, we made our way to the roof to get it done. Thump! As we were emplacing the small blinking box on the roof, staying low, a mortar was launched in the distance. I ran for cover in the stairwell. Boom! Explosion, not far. I yelled at Davis through the stairwell. "What do ya got?" "Mortar. Off to the right." I radioed a situation report to the CP as Davis scrambled to the roof to meet us.

The report completed, Davis scurried into the building, waving me inside. Incoming! We dive. Wham! A mortar lands 10 meters away. Loose debris fell around the rooftop and walls. "Time to dance." Pissed, Davis and I ran onto the roof, spotted the enemy in thermals, and called for the mortar team to start raining hate. Fireworks.

Soon, we are joined with the rest of the gang who tapped out Davis and me, who pull off to get lucky with the guns. Rock *and roll. Our mortar team was dropping rounds of 60mm mortar fire while we made the necessary adjustments to the target. It's quite the show with a series of mortars back and forth until we walked rounds right on top of them. We blew them to hell. The fight is over and we are victorious.*

When your adrenaline is high, confusion will make your head spin if you are not careful. You must be deliberate and venture on about your work. Regardless, with so many soldiers moving and partaking in the action, you can only speak to your role and how you interpret the uncertainty. Reexamining this journal entry brings these details to the front of my memory. It may have been chaos, and it may have been over quick, but it remains vivid enough to recall my actions amidst the battle— these dueling mortars.

That's the unique thing about the perplexity of battle, you can remember so much, but also so little. The wildest details stick out while the most significant events go unnoticed or even fall silent in your memory. I recall this evening, or more correctly, these disordered few hours, with astonishing distinction despite the frenzied commotion.

In this instance, I recall sitting in a rare moment of bliss eating my #9 Beef Stew Meal Ready-to-Eat. The sense of dread washed over me as the food warmed in its pouch. I hadn't heard any comms for a few minutes. I searched for a radio. Things escalated in intensity when I realized the dude carrying it had walked off to find more batteries. We would take turns eating, but without a radio, I felt just as uncomfortable as if I didn't have a weapon. That discomfort helped etch the smallest of details— like what type of MRE I was eating—into my memory banks, where they remain embedded to this day.

I had used the MRE heater and was excited to have a hot pouch of food, but the enemy made sure I would eat it cold. I remember that after establishing contact with the mother ship, I was on a knee, doing my best to stay concealed, positioning the small strobe on the rooftop, when I heard the familiar, distinct sound of a mortar firing. I galloped for cover, ducking into the stairwell that led to the roof, and listened to shrapnel from the impact pepper the walls of the building, scarring it even further.

After making a radio call, I met my teammate, Davis, and we charged into the open, but a blast soon sent us reeling into the building. We repeated this dance a second time before a round impacting fifty meters away granted us a brief reprieve, so we took advantage of the poorly aimed fire and scanned for the enemy as best we could.

Looking through the thermal scope, I could just make out a pixelated, block-looking figure that represented the heat signature of a man with a mortar tube. A one-second exposure of that image is stamped into the tissue of my mind, and an equally clear image exists of that same Atari-like figure launching another round. We hung tight, jaws clenched, taking a risk to stay engaged with the target.

I had initially called for counterfire due to the type of concealment the belligerent mystery mortarman and his compatriots were behind, but Murphy's Law was in full effect. Our own mortar crew had just shifted their position, and we had not completed calculating our pre-sighted points, introducing another complexity and delay into our communication and fire coordination. Fortunately for us, but unfortunately for the enemy, our guys were good, so it was time to meet fire with fire.

By the time the first enemy round impacted, our mortar crew had already reacted. They ran out of the villa and oriented their tubes. The mortar section sergeant would hand fire our request as relayed through Dombroski—the medic manning the radios—using a vernacular with which he was not well versed. Dombroski knew tourniquets and hypovolemic shock, not echoing commands to coordinate indirect fire, but he caught on, recognizing the importance of the lingo.

The mortar tube bellowed its distinct thump, launching a 60mm gift for the enemy that landed with a yellow blossom of embers across the river. The shower of sparks from the impacting rounds and the delayed sound from the reports were hypnotic—it was like our own small Independence Day fireworks show. I smiled and called for adjustments to guide the pounding footfalls of the mortar impacts as they walked around the Atari mortar team.

When our section leaders, DeLay and Wright, made their way to the rooftop, I handed over the radio and got behind the Barrett .50 cal sniper rifle, which was sitting nearby, ready to engage the enemy if they maneuvered. DeLay continued to pour on the heat, walking repeated mortar rounds along the river banks. As fast as it began, it ended, and a deafening silence consumed us. We gathered around, thinking another attack was imminent or that we'd run across another insurgent attempting to retrieve bodies. We were anxious to discuss it, but we knew one thing: we had been initiated. Despite this, I remained unsatisfied.

My baptism of fire had told me I was not prepared. We should have been more proactive when the mortar team repositioned the guns. We should not have allowed the radio to walk away from us, and we should have placed the night optics in better positions. Each of these fouls was overcome, but we were lucky that we did not have to pay for any of these mistakes. The payment for errors in combat is blood, and many can only afford one bill. Still, it was a valuable learning experience of fallibility.

Yet, you cannot be too hard on yourself because it will eat you up inside or create a sense of reluctance to jump into the action. There is no perfect plan—there is no perfect circumstance—and you will never be perfectly ready. In life, as in combat, you won't be perfectly prepared for what the world may throw at you, and sometimes, you need to act. Imperfect conditions breed perfect performances. The reward from any experience is achieving your goal—not because the cards were in your favor, but rather, despite the challenges, your response overcame doubt and reflected your best. Only then does personal growth happen.

When we were attacked, we responded like a hungry pack of wolves. We rained angry mortar rounds of justice accurately and stopped the threat swiftly. Could we have done it better? Without question. There was much to learn. These experiences taught me that if you are exceedingly hard on yourself, doubt can take root, and that uncertainty inhibits action. Seek improvement, learn from mistakes, but tackle things regardless of the conditions being less than ideal. As that night along the Tigris taught me, frustration with yourself is best resolved by learning from failures, no matter the severity. Life goes on—that is, unless you attack the police with mortars.

March 6, 2006 –

The same crap during the day, nothing out of the ordinary. As darkness falls, we were primed after the night's prayers, which were when these attacks happen. Some mortar fire came as soon as the sun slips away, but it's due north and impacted in Salman Pak. We had no visual through the thick foliage of the surrounding orchards, so we unleashed the Apaches to helicopter in and check it out. The insurgents launched 9 total rounds but the casualties will remain unknown. We had no eyes in that direction.

March 7, 2006 –

No enemy activity until the Squadron Commander, Lieutenant Colonel Winski, came to resupply us to continue the mission and to keep hunting the bad guys. Riding with the boss, the Sergeant Major hit an IED right outside the gate while I watched their entrance through a spotting scope. The blast knocked me from my roost.

It was 50 meters from our position and right at the gate to the compound. C'mon, dudes. There is no doubt in my mind that that bomb was meant for us. Whew. Somebody around here is up to no good. Mahdi? Anyways, the bosses are okay. They gave us a pat on the back and some MREs. Our mission is extended to ensure we keep the heat on.

After getting knocked on my rear end by an IED that exploded a short distance from me, I radioed to the dudes to tidy their uniforms because the big-wigs were visiting—classic Army priorities. Everyone in the convoy was fine, and the truck was towed behind the walls of the resort compound. Any doubt that the enemy knew Americans had led the counterattack, though, was gone.

When that bomb detonated—it was a message. They knew who was capable of returning accurate mortar fire, and it wasn't the police. It was unnervingly thought-provoking that the IED was emplaced yards from the Iraqi-manned gate. We could not shake the idea that it was meant for us. Whoever had placed it was no doubt tipped off by a conspirator within the riverside POB headquarters who was sympathetic to the anti-Iraqi forces. Even though it may have been intended for us, it was detonated on our visiting leadership.

Our squadron-level leaders were a great team, and we were fortunate to have them. Warrior 6, Lieutenant Colonel Brian Winski, was a man born to command. He led from the front and carried himself in a way that garnered respect. Tall and well built, with salt and pepper hair, he resembled the classic infantry commander. Command Sergeant Major Fields was the perfect complement. He took charge not long after a series of unfortunate injuries early in the deployment had forced replacements to our enlisted leadership. Large, gruff, and booming, Fields had been doing pushups in the womb. He cast a large shadow that could either induce complete fear or provide welcoming shade. He could swap his leadership style to fit the situation, but most guys endeavored to stay out of the sun. Both men made an effort to know some anecdote about or happenings of each soldier in their unit, making them popular among the troops. Together, these two created a team environment that made you give your best. That combined with their zest for going after the bad guys, made them legends.

The reason behind their visit was to commend our actions from the days prior, and also to inform us that our mission had been extended. We were resupplied with MREs and told to get after the enemy. When asked about the IED attack, the topic was dismissed as a simple indicator of our pressure on the enemy. With this information in hand, we worked to improve our position. We drew sketches, marked ranges, and discussed courses of action, which after the IED attack, included insider threat.

Consolidating our positions on the top floor of the resort was determined to be our best bet. Our gear was deposited at the top of the stairwell, in a room that led to the roof and had line-of-sight through the steps to the ground floor. I placed some debris on the steps below, hoping to slow any would-be attacker or at least tip us off to unwelcome visitors. It may have been unwarranted, but we felt it was in our best interest to ensure we had enough ammunition to hold out like Texans at the Alamo if it came to it. Our work drew the watchful eye of the POB but we needed to make ourselves hard targets to deter aggression from both inside and out.

March 8, 2006 –

I am starting to smell pretty ripe. We caught a guy with a shovel sneaking through the orchards around 11am. What the heck was he doing? Farming or digging in caches? Disappeared. The thick vegetation surrounding the hotel makes it difficult to see in many directions, including to our rear and south.

A call came over the net that a local Mahdi leader was killed by coalition forces nearby. Crap. The POB's ranks are filled with Mahdi guys that may pursue revenge. We pulled off and regrouped at the CP and established a defense. Nothing happened, but we spent the night talking with the POB Commander. He pleaded for us to stay and not to worry about any insider threat. He was grateful for us getting rid of the constant barrage they had endured of late and insisted his compound was safer than the Green Zone.

To express his gratitude, he put on a dinner for us consisting of fish from the pool in the courtyard. That was an experience unlike anything I've ever participated and yielded awful consequences. I got to sleep on the floor in a crowded room of the CP. Better than in that rat-infested hotel.

The dinner with the Iraqi Public Order Brigade colonel shot me into the center mass of their culture. He was an overweight, round-faced Iraqi man of fifty or so years, and we gathered together around a long, flimsy table complete with a cheap tablecloth and fresh fruit in a plastic dish in the center. We sat along the sides of the table, while he and his deputy sat at the head on either end. Our interpreter sat with us, translating the discussion. I do not recollect the subtleties of our conversation, but I do remember the substance.

He sang praise for our actions on the riverbank. He said his soldiers felt comfortable enough to linger out in the open in his compound again. He asked us not to leave, which was a request we did not like to hear. We wanted him to take charge and inspire confidence in the abilities of his own troops—we would not be here forever. I remained off to the side thinking these things, immersed in a growing sense of desperation, knowing our departure would expose them to even more attacks.

Soon, another orderly-type Iraqi brought out the main course as the colonel boasted of the excellent fish from the "*land between the two rivers*." I was raised eating catfish caught out of a muddy river and was intrigued by the idea of eating the fruit of the Tigris, although the fish was just netted from the resort pool right outside. The main course, however, was a variety of carp, and when the orderly sat the platter on the table, the freshly baked fish stared right back at me. My curiosity vanished, leaving a nervous apprehension; but good manners and my cooperation were critical to fostering an amicable relationship with this man and with the Iraqis. It would be a condemning act of disrespect to refuse the food.

Mirroring the actions of the deputy at the head of the table, I took some flatbread, filled it with rice, and sprinkled on a bit of carp I had pulled off the bones with my fingers. The colonel, who was walking around overseeing the meal, saw what little meat I had taken and interpreted it as me not wanting to be selfish. He reached in and grabbed a large chunk of meat to add to my meal. As gooey fish meat slid off his fingers onto my bread, I forced a smile, and his nod indicated approval. Time for a bite, and one more for the cause.

The orderly gathered any rice that was dropped on the floor until a nod from the colonel allowed him to retire to the kitchen. I choked down my food and, with help, the servants cleared the table. We soon sat around in a semi-circle. Cigarettes were distributed, and even though most of us didn't smoke, we obliged the colonel in his simple acts of appreciation and respect.

The most bizarre thing happened afterward, though, when an orderly came into the room with a glass perfume bottle with a squeeze bulb. He walked around the room and each soldier, who hadn't showered in several days, soon smelled like flowers. We were treated like kings among men—the very best the colonel could do to reward us for helping eliminate his aggravation.

Not surprising, the reward I received from that dinner was a case of what was either severe diarrhea or mild dysentery. It hit me as I was walking up the several flights of stairs to relieve Davis from his position and start breaking down our equipment. My stomach grumbled, and by the time I reached the third or fourth floor, it was letting me know it was not a fan of the fruit of the Tigris. I also knew I could not make it to the lobby and out the door to the nearby bushes and brush.

Since there was no indoor plumbing in the building, I sprinted, with beads of sweat popping out on my forehead, to a room furthest from the stairwell in the hall. Booting in a closet door, I was not prepared for the calamity that was about to happen—I made a new camouflage pattern on my trousers. Later, more angry than ashamed, I asked for cover and crawled out to wash my pants in the muddy waters of the river. I spent the remaining days of the mission smelling a bit like shit and a bit like the river, which is one in the same. Needless to say, this mission could not end fast enough for my teammates' sake.

We'd leave soon, but not long after the operation concluded, and before our return to the hotel compound a few weeks later, the colonel and one of his kids were murdered for cooperating with us. Words spreading through the company indicated what we already knew—Mahdi militiamen, who had infiltrated his ranks, had fragged him from within the perceived safety of his own base. That was commonplace in Iraq circa 2006—the threat we celebrated eliminating with the carp feast was not across the river, but rather internal, and unfortunately, right underneath his cheerful, round nose. When he asked us to stay, his concern wasn't about the insurgents across the river, but rather those a grenade throw from his villa.

March 9, 2006 –

Morning came and we hung out for a few moments enjoying some coffee. Got the word to start packing it in. Once we left the compound and hit the streets, you could tell the nation was changing.

The police were out in force. Damn, what has been going on the last week? Disorder. Made it to the FOB in one piece. Unloaded. We have word we are going across the river in a few days to find more assholes. No rest.

We were to conduct another waterborne movement across the Tigris River. The sniper teams were tired, and, after some debate, we talked the company commander into allowing us a couple of days to refit. Scuttlebutt around the company was abundant, and my buddies wanted to know what it was like at the riverside resort. I told them in as subtle a way as possible that they would find out soon, and it was actually kind of fun.

To a larger point, the gossip circle became so big that the military reporters wrote a lackluster article that was published in our base newspaper. The role the snipers played was relegated to one sentence, but I was even more disgruntled when the story was released because the authors hadn't spoken with any of the guys there.

Had they asked, we would have expressed to them that the mortar section—and the radio-relaying Dombroski—were the heroes of that battle. Regardless, after cleaning and prepping our gear again, we were back on the banks of the Tigris, back in the cinder block skeleton of one of Saddam's former Baathist getaways, laying again amongst the rodent tenants and shrapnel decor.

May 29, 2016 –

In telling the first story of any significance during the reunion, Eric had taken the group to the banks of the Tigris—back a decade—back to when we stomped our way through the slums and villages of southeast Baghdad. We finished our breakfast and herded ourselves out front of the hotel, where we regrouped and stretched before embarking on another long day.

"I don't know if you guys remember, but we operated out of an old Baathist resort, not unlike this joint, for a few weeks," I said, not directing the statement to anyone in particular. Eric's story had me thinking about how we all operate differently under fire. "Of course, this place has far fewer rats and bullet holes."

"Yeah, I remember that," Jeff said. "That's when we went across the river in boats," he added, making his way through the group.

"Hell, the company got so worked up over what you guys were doing there, we had to come to take a look." Burns walked over to join in the conversation. Smoking a cigarette, he scoffed. "What a waste of time."

"It was a bust, but sometimes you'll have that," I said.

"The cool thing is, we got to cross the Tigris in zodiacs in the middle of the night," Burns said, redeeming the value of the operation.

"That was pretty cool," Jeff added. We stood on the curb waiting for stragglers before dividing the group for the drive to the museum.

"I think the important thing was we were showing the enemy we weren't afraid to reach out and get after them," I reasoned. "But I still wish we could've found something."

"Definitely," Burns added. "So much of their weapons and ammunition had funneled through that area into the city without much stopping them."

"Triangle of death," Schwartz said.

Burns repeated Jeff, pointing with his cigarette.

I interjected. "You guys ready to head to Fort Campbell? I got room for two." I stepped in front of the group. "We're headed to the museum on post. We'll meet outside before going in. If you don't have a ride, find one. We have plenty of vehicles with room. Questions?"

"Race y'all there?" Notaro dared the group.

"Hell, the only race you've won happened…what? Forty-something years ago?" Jeff countered.

"You can crack that joke, but I can crack that skull, Jeff," Notaro chided. The group laughed and headed toward the parking lot. Kat and I climbed into my truck and were soon cruising Interstate 24 towards Clarksville, Fort Campbell, and the Don F. Pratt Memorial Museum.

As the Assistant Division Commander during the 101st's drop into Normandy, Brigadier General Pratt was the highest-ranking Allied officer killed on D-Day. The museum named for him housed a plethora of military artifacts throughout the interior and exterior of the building that told the story of the illustrious division's history, up to and including Operation Iraqi Freedom.

"Haven't been to Campbell since I left the Army." I sought conversation, although I knew Kat was looking for a bit of shut-eye.

"Why would you?" Kat challenged my attempt.

"Well, it's a bit strange to return, if you ask me," I conceded.

"I can understand that," she acknowledged. "It's weird visiting anything from your past."

"I wonder what unit is garrisoned there." The 506th Infantry Regiment had been disbanded, with a couple of the battalions realigned under different brigades as part of the Army's attempt at preserving its heritage. Our history was diluted, but even though things had changed, the unit maintained a tremendous legacy that made us extremely proud.

"Who cares?" Kat dismissed the notion.

"Well, whoever it is, they can't be as cool as we were." I chuckled at my own desperate attempt at humor.

"I think the last time I was on Campbell," Kat fiddled with the radio, looking for a suitable channel, "there was some big thing where you guys were marching on the big field."

I smirked—Kat prided herself on not knowing the military lingo. "It was a division change of command, a full pass and review. The ultimate dog and pony show," I remarked.

"Gosh, things sure have changed," Kat said. "Kids, jobs, that normal life stuff."

"We've gotten a lot more boring," I said, half-heartedly. "But not as boring as standing in formation for hours for a general's speech."

"We've changed. It's life," Kat said.

"It's funny, though. Sometimes I feel like, yeah, we've moved on, but then again, we haven't."

"That's certain. It's hard to let go of such a powerful experience. I mean, it makes you who you are. All of you. Not a lot of people have been to war these days."

"Well, people still experience tough things."

"Of course. And the same skills to overcome them apply," Kat added.

"Absolutely. It's a framework, or a frame of mind." I thought about the conversation with Eric. "Like Eric said to me earlier, 'You can't change the outcome, but you can change your outlook.'"

Kat agreed.

"I think one of the things that made us different is the bond. We trained as a team for a year and a half before deploying. Not everybody gets that kind of time together before deploying. We were a—"

"Band of brothers," Kat finished my sentence, referencing the unit's fame in popular culture. If Kat knew the phrase band of brothers, it had made it to the mainstream.

At its inception and reorganizing in 2004, the regiment had been a handful of soldiers meeting in a parking lot. The newest brigade combat team, the 506th Infantry Regiment, had deployed to Iraq from Korea, but upon its return, was organized back at Fort Campbell under the original 101st Airborne Division umbrella. Parsed out from various regiments across the division and new accessions from across the Army—including many Ranger Instructors like Notaro—we were part of the new Currahee lineage.

With that reputation to uphold, we trained and trained hard. Our leaders made sure of it. We rucked, we hit rifle ranges, we set out into the field as often as it rained. This included visiting Fort Knox and setting a range on fire when a tracer round flew into the soft headliner of a Chrysler, duking it out in mock villages where one soldier's claustrophobia trapped him in an underground sewer and hitting shoot-houses with live rounds blasting inches from our faces. Once a soldier was electrocuted by an open power wire during a mock urban assault, and the only response was to treat him like a casualty. There were no time-outs. We trained on the zodiac boats and fast-roped from helicopters. One mistake meant drowning or falling, and we were okay with that. If there was training the NCOs wanted, our leadership made it happen. The result was fierce confidence and loyalty to the team that prepared us well for Iraq.

"Yup. Some things change." I leaned into my seat. "But just as many things stay the same."

"Example?"

I hadn't expected her to respond. "Uh," I delayed, "well, for instance, Iraq is in trouble, but another generation is working the issue."

"Did you think it'd be different?"

"Years ago, I wasn't sure. Now I'm watching the fighting and seeing Iraqi troops taking on a difficult enemy. Think about it. Today, you can visit many sites of American battles—Europe, South Korea, Vietnam—but I'm skeptical the State Department will ever say it's safe to travel to Baghdad in my lifetime. Will I ever tour the sites of our battles? It seems so unlikely. I want the country to do well. It deserves to do well, but will it forever be hostile to guys like me?"

Kat smiled. "Don't be so sure. Crazier things have happened," she said. She reached for my hand. "Who knew we'd be here?"

"I did."

Kat wrinkled her brow. "What?"

"I knew I wanted to start a life with you," I said. "I made a decision a long time ago to move with a purpose towards things. This family." I made a circle motion with a finger. "Once we were together, I wanted to build a life with you."

"Oh, so confident," Kat teased. She was less of a life planner and more of a party planner, taking it as it came.

"I knew there were going to be things I couldn't control, but the things I could affect, I was gonna try to," I said. I heard my own words. I needed to apply that principle universally. "I guess that should go for the Iraq thing, too."

We drove through the Tennessee countryside towards the Kentucky border and the Army base we had lived on for a few years. At Campbell, the Comanches had trained together, partied together, and grown into adults together. Kat was right. We may have changed, but some things remained frozen in time or in memory. It felt like we hadn't been away for a year, let alone over a decade.

"Tunes?" I asked Kat.

"Yeah." She landed on a frequency just in time for a news break. Some stock market summaries led to a world news update.

"The US said late on Friday it had killed the top ISIS commander in Fallujah in airstrikes that also struck 70 other fighters," the radio DJ announced. "The Iraqi military commander said the final assault to regain the ISIS-controlled city would come within 'days, not weeks.' The attack comes amid growing reports of civilians starving to death..."

We drove on. The rolling green hills of Tennessee were a stark contrast to the Iraqi landscape. Some things change, some things stay the same. I turned the station. The Eagles came across the radio.

"You good with this?"

March 12, 2006 –

Today, we returned to the Baathist river hotel. We may have stirred up a hornet's nest according to intelligence. We arrived after dark and marched to the hotel as we had done before, except there was no indirect fire to greet us. We built positions on the roof again.

This time we were joined by our Forward Observers with high-powered optics that turn the dark night a bright green. Together with the newest addition to the sniper section roster, Howser, we pulled surveillance until the morning's first rays poked above the trees to our rear. Nothing except a firefight somewhere in Salman Pak through the thick foliage. We tried to organize the POB to respond, but they were unwilling.

March 13, 2006 –

I woke up in the hotel and heated some food. The MREs they gave us were rotten. Great. I didn't even know those damn things went bad. We sat around telling stories of the dumbest of topics. 1st platoon arrived that evening to go across the river with us to reconnoiter some objectives.

The day became night. Despite the risk and the unknown on the other side of the river, the mood was kept light. Our team headed to the riverbank and hopped in the zodiac boats and zipped across the Tigris. Of course, I got wet as soon as I hit the ground on the opposing bank.

Walked around the entire night, cleared some houses that were abandoned and so forth. We wanted to get to the area the mortars impacted but ran out of time. I'm not sure why we wanted to inspect the area. Our team met the boats around 0400 and rode across the river in the early morning light. We debriefed intel, and I get to sleep in the CP tonight. Bonus.

One might think that gliding across the Tigris River in southern Baghdad as the moon dances over the rippling water was cut straight from a Navy SEAL action flick. We did it, though not as elegantly, as our boat motors were underpowered and not by a little. The phrase "zipped across the Tigris" is not straightforward, as the small engines on the boats and the ridiculous amount of gear we carried made it more of a chug than a zip.

To make matters worse, the Tigris is less than 150 meters wide south of the Diyala River intersection, which is not even enough room to open the motors up before you reach the opposing bank. It was comedic, at best, but we kept our laughs quiet and our grins wide because we were unsure of what we would find across the ancient river. Gossip was rampant, but our team was hoping to uncover more than enemy activity.

We wanted to see the fruit of our destructive labor. We wanted to verify our lethality. Were we warriors? All the teams had a set amount of time to execute searches on designated targets, which were far to the south and west. Even if our team wanted to comb over the area where we had engaged the mortar team earlier, doing so meant we would have to move fast and, more importantly, find little reportable at our tasked locations to slow us down—both were less than ideal.

The darkness and distances between objectives limited the speed with which we could search these places before the call would come to catch a ride home. Priority one—don't miss your boat. On the raft, you are exposed. Crossing any danger area is risky, but if we made contact with the enemy, there was little hope of making it unscathed. Worse, there was the possibility of drowning. Waiting on the banks for your ferry was not an option.

The crossing was uneventful, except that I got one boot entirely soaked. My foot made a squishing sound as we set off at a pace better suited to a forced march. We powerwalked towards our first objective—to look for weapon caches in a defilade that we were unable to see into from the other bank but had seen people visit before. There, we found only traces of normal human activity—empty soda cans and garbage. We continued mission.

Our second objective was a reportedly abandoned house. As we approached, we could see spray-painted writing on the exterior. We lay prone in some bushes and watched for a long few minutes to see if anyone was squatting there, maybe taking a stop on the underground railroad of foreign fighters sneaking into Baghdad.

Howser had joined us for the mission. He stayed in cover with a borrowed M249 Squad Automatic Weapon to give the sniper team some added bang-bang. He was a champ when it came to machine guns, so it was nice to have him watching our six. Wright and I galloped towards the door and did a two-man stack. We listened but heard only ambient noise before entering. We cleared the house without talking before huddling in the central room, nodding in acknowledgment of our teamwork.

The finds were rat-chewed bedrolls, propaganda painted on the walls, and recently discarded water bottles. This was an insurgent safe house. Howser, after covering our advance with the light machine gun, posted at the entrance, whispering his arrival. We flagged him in. In a blatant display of bravado, we complained about the lack of occupancy but soon stomped off to our next objective—another weapons cache.

In keeping with the theme of the evening, that cache was also a bust. With our assigned objectives complete, we were nearing our zodiac rendezvous time and the sunrise. We stalked towards the scene where we had killed the insurgents a few days prior. I am not sure what we were hoping to discover—a body part, a dropped mortar tube, craters or some blast marks would have been noteworthy finds.

These were possibilities, but I think we were looking for more than our gruesome handiwork—we were looking for affirmation. A picture from a drone isn't fulfilling, I suppose, and we wanted to visit the scene of the fireworks. Though we were making decent time, I glanced at my watch and whispered to get Wright's attention. We had a few hundred meters to go, and it was nearing our boat time. I asked if I needed to radio for an extension or if we needed to peel off towards the river, adding that cresting the elevated road in front of us would put us in view of our overwatch element, which was atop the hotel scanning for our return. They sat watching for heat signatures from any lurking enemy fighters and would notice if we detoured away from our boat pickup. We looked at each other and knew we were sunk.

We took a knee and glanced at the map, ensuring we were on the right track. Getting to the boat was the right choice, and the best option for our psyches as well. The zodiac was on time, and we made it across the river to the Public Order Brigade compound.

We walked into the buzz of the ad hoc command and control position and told our story to the intelligence troops. The first sergeant burst in, took one look at us, and told us to sleep in the command post, an order we gratefully obliged. I lay under my poncho liner, wondering if another team would come across the remnants of our battle. On and off, over the rest of the operation, I asked around—no one ever said they did. The answer to that question would remain unknown.

March 14, 2006 –

The raid was canceled for tonight due to the lack of aviation support. We chilled out and pulled observation from the hotel. Some mortars were launched southeast of our position on our side of the Tigris near another POB unit. Slept in the CP.

March 15, 2006 –

0700. With a tip from a local national that enemy forces were planning to launch attacks on the hotel today, we got hustling. I collected my gear at the CP and ran to the hotel. We waited, hoping they would start a fight.

Darkness fell and the rest of the company along with Bradleys and some of the squadron staff arrived at the party. We hit the river and went across around 2230, headed for a blocking position near an intersection to interdict any traffic that'd compromise the teams as they raided some objectives.

We found nothing significant that night. Some dudes failed the residue test or have a few extra magazines than they should for their AK-47s. Nothing big. The dudes had been using a fertilizer that day on their fields, leading to their failed test. Or not. We headed across the river at daybreak and packed to return north to Rustamiyah. Operation complete, but more on the way.

The obvious problem with raiding at night is that it is dark. You can miss a lot of things when you do not have a clear view of the area. Months later, another unit in that same area of operations made a concentrated push south towards the objectives we had searched earlier. Right across from the compound, they discovered massive caches of ammunition and weapons dug into the ground. With the Iraqi colonel dead, Mahdi militiamen embedded in the ranks, and plenty of weapons to go around, attacks on the compound reached new levels—such was the nature of our operations.

Some were complete successes, others less so, and some were even total flops. The most important thing was that we got after the enemy and showed them there were no safe havens from which they could move into the city. Infiltration into Baghdad would be stymied, but there were already enough fighters in the city to fuel the insurgency and sectarian violence. As we transitioned from spring into summer, that violence would swell across the city and move into our sector, challenging our fragile security.

That evening, while waiting for the show to start, we waited on the top floor of the hotel watching for any indications of the enemy. Joining us was a tall, thin Iraqi named Hamza. He was a young recruit of the Public Order Brigade, and I did my best to discuss with him the current predicament. He knew much more

English than I knew Arabic, but his reasons for volunteering were clear—he desired security for his country.

Safety and security remained elusive for him and millions of other Iraqis, but not only in the physical sense, in the psychological sense, too. Security is an emotional state that brings a feeling of comfort, of ease, that grows faith in the future. These days Iraqis made life plans, but these plans included little more than Maslow's hierarchy of needs of water, food, sleep, shelter—with a smattering of health and well-being. An army can protect you, but security, provided by said army, is far more than guns and grunts—it's a psychological belief that you can stroll through a resort without rockets ruining your day, as Hamza could attest.

All these things considered, the operations along the Tigris and our time in the Iraqi POB compound were satisfying because we felt like we were doing our job. We were providing not security, but its close cousin—protection. Like an umbrella, we could keep away the rain, but would also black out the sun. We needed the police to provide the faith that the clouds would clear and the skies would be blue again.

In providing that umbrella, we also felt like we had been tested and arose victorious. Although we missed our chance to travel to the point of origin of those mortar attacks, even under the watchful eyes of our covering elements, it was best we avoided the scene of the mortar duel. Perchance, we needed to not revisit the site—thereby allowing us to remain disconnected from the results of our labor. The overhead imagery provided told us all we would ever need to know about what had occurred.

It is essential to enjoy the little successes, in whatever form they take. We had destroyed the enemy, enabled the police to resume operations for the time being, and allowed leaders to verify what was happening across the river. Our plan was a success, and as we gathered around the chow hall table back at the FOB, we emitted a noxious odor you could chew. We grinned from ear to ear, joking and ridiculing each other.

More was to come, and in the back of our minds, we knew it—but we knew too that you must take time to enjoy your achievements, as trivial as they may be. In combat, as in life, big differences are made with small victories—just make sure the celebration is commensurate with the feat.

4.

THAT WILL ALWAYS MAKE MEN FREE

May 29, 2016 –

After stopping to grab the necessary lunch supplies, top off with gas, and have another coffee, we made the turn to the main gate towards the home of our band of brothers—the Screaming Eagles—the 101st Airborne Division. A long line of flags lined the divided road that approached the guard position. A young soldier on duty welcomed us to the post with a sharp "Air Assault" greeting to highlight the pride in the unit's unique capability.

We continued driving the aptly named Normandy Boulevard toward the museum and our rallying position. On our way, we passed the giant garrison flag waving in the tender May breeze and the old division headquarters where so many historic decisions had been discussed. We cruised by the Dreyer Fieldhouse, where deploying soldiers had stood in long lines, readying themselves for their trips overseas, before coming across a few aircraft and monuments, which signaled the approach to our destination—the museum.

The reunion group was already inspecting the various aircraft, vehicles and monuments dedicated to the many wars in which the 101st had been involved. I rolled a window down and announced my arrival, which Notaro welcomed with a traditional American greeting involving one very specific finger. I laughed and parked in the Don F. Pratt Museum parking lot, ready to peruse the pieces of history as well.

"Got the lunch," I told Sorbello, as I walked with Kat towards him and towards a C-47 Skytrain. The important airplane had played a crucial role in a critical war. It sat dignified and accomplished—a permanent fixture of the museum's collection.

"Can you imagine?" Sorbello raised his arms out towards the aircraft.

"No, I can't," I confessed. Kat broke off to inspect another aircraft, nodding her departure to me.

"Yeah, it's hard to fathom," Sorbello admitted.

"We thought we had it rough."

"Dude, we had it so good."

"Everything is relative, I suppose," I said.

"These guys were loading into this bird to change the course of history over territory that musta' seemed like hell itself, bro."

"We drove out on patrol and came back in time to hit midnight chow. How good is that?" I roused.

"So good," Sorbello answered with a smile.

"This generation had their own set of challenges—we had ours. I'll take ours any day of the week."

"Uniformed enemy, known fronts, and, like, the noblest of causes, bro." Sorbello edged closer to the aircraft.

"Yeah, D-Day, Bastogne, places like Okinawa and Iwo Jima, man. Brutal." I added.

"Yeah, you're right, man. Can't compare apples to avocados, man. Just different fruit," Sorbello remarked.

"I kind of feel guilty, though."

"No, I hear ya."

"I mean, we think we know what war is, but really it's these dudes who know war."

"It's a tough reputation to live up to." Sorbello raised his eyebrow, turning to face me. "I hope we didn't let them down."

"Tough act to follow."

"Big boots to fill."

I smiled. "Different boots."

"Much more comfortable." Sorbello smirked and continued to meander around the Skytrain, which was named the 'Brass Hat'. "You think there will ever be a HMMWV sitting out here? Getting rusty with people climbing on it, thinking of the good ole days?"

I couldn't answer.

"Hey, you dirtbags!" Notaro shouted. Sorbello and I turned towards his voice, noticing that the crowd had moved on to the 506th Infantry Regiment Memorial. Notaro waved for us to join them. "Bring it in!"

We closed the distance and met them on the north side of the circular pavilion. It was sacred ground. The circle was centered on a black spade, the symbol many veterans have come to know as synonymous with the Currahee name it represents. Surrounding the circle was a number of granite parachutes, with titles of 'WW2,' 'Afghanistan/Iraq,' 'Vietnam,' and 'Training Service,' each dedicated to the fallen. A small Currahee flag flapped in the wind at the southernmost point. We felt a tremendous sense of pride standing there, at the memorial, among the monuments. It was humbling to think of those who had come before us. Our chests puffed up a bit more, and we took the opportunity to snap a photograph before moving the herd towards the museum entrance.

"Hey, here we go." Jeff found the Iraq memorial and motioned for us to join him outside the circle. The marker was shaped like the country we had fought in and stood upon a black granite rectangle engraved with the unit insignia of the various battalions associated with the Currahees.

"No shit?" Notaro asked rhetorically, walking towards the monument.

"Wow, we got our own rock!" Sorbello said, sounding more nonchalant than intended. Before anyone could call him on his sarcasm, we saw them—chiseled out of the hard stone under the unit crest and the words 'Forging Destiny,'—two names with which we were familiar: SGT David Weir and CPL Edgardo Zayas.

"These guys deserve their own damn monuments," Jeff said, kneeling to get a closer look.

"They have 'em," I said. "I dug the holes to place the markers myself."

"That's right. They sit on each side of the walkway as you enter the headquarters building, man," Notaro said. "One for Zayas, one for Weir." Notaro knifed two spots in the air. The stones sat out front of our headquarters where Zayas had cracked that wide grin and shouted encouragement during a number of our demanding training sessions and Weir had popped a sharp salute, offering the perfect Army greeting on his way to train with his forward observer brethren.

"I hope they're there. The 506th being deactivated or broken up or whatever," I said with a shrug.

"That shit better be there. You don't just toss those things away, man." Notaro said, with a hint of fire in his voice.

"There's only one way to find out. We'll go over there after we're done here," I said.

"Yeah, but for now, we should cross the street and hit the museum." Jeff stood. "I'm glad to see their names are here, though."

"Yeah," we murmured in agreement. We crossed the street that we had so many times ran shouting cadences about the deeds of the soldier and strode off to inspect the history of the 101st.

All of the major, and most of the minor, roads in Iraq had been given names that the American military could understand. Instead of Omar Bin Al Khatab Street, for example, we would use the name Route Pluto. The inspiration for street names came from any number of things, some humorous like Route Cartman or favorite college teams like Route Irish or remembering hometowns like Main Supply Route Tampa.

One highway, which cut through the southern part of our area of operations was named, I can only guess, after its condition: Route Wild. It led to Salman Pak. The town was home to the ancient ruins of the imperial city of the Parthians which the Persians called Ctesiphon, but also to a biological and chemical weapons facility under Saddam Hussein's reign—an insidious and contentious geopolitical issue only a few years ago.

The town was named after Salman the Persian, a friend of the prophet Muhammad, who was buried there, and it also contained the world's largest span unreinforced of brickwork in a remarkable vault. Here, ancient beauty recalling the glorious expansion of civilization met the dark side of modern society's most destructive creations—it was Iraq's dichotomy, and it was right here in our area of operations.

After having some success on Route Pluto early in the deployment, the leadership wanted to extend our efforts to the southern portions of the outer communities surrounding Baghdad. Specifically, the goal was to make it safe to drive from Salman Pak into eastern Baghdad. To accomplish this, we needed to pull some assets off Route Pluto and transfer them for use around Route Wild. In doing so, we were expanding our reach away from Rustamiyah to more austere locations farther away from the nearest American base.

We were pioneers penetrating deeper into the Iraqi Wild West—it wasn't exactly hostile, but it wasn't safe either. We used the same tactics we had used before—gun trucks in conspicuous locations to deter enemy activity, as well as OPs, hid away from the road from which to pull surveillance. We set about our business, which was finding out why the route had earned its brutish title.

Name aside, though, the route was not the sole thing that was wild. Three months in with no significant opposition encountered, we were becoming almost cavalier in our approach to operations. We took more risks probing further into areas less and less infiltrated by American forces. Most of us were thirsty, and we wanted to make sure we did not leave Iraq without taking a drink of combat—such is the way of the volunteer infantryman.

Violence is life, and Comanche Company was seeking maturity. When you go looking for trouble, though, you will find it. The dilemma is that trouble seldom results in anything but more trouble, which for us at that time was acceptable. The insurgents, however, only wanted it when they chose it.

Therein lies the fundamental problem—rarely can you decide when conflict will find you. Sometimes it finds you laying along a canal under the glow of a high moon, or sometimes it finds you on top of a resort. No matter where you stumble upon it, you can't hide. This fact makes readiness imperative.

Thus far, we had toed the line, following the overarching strategy of maintaining a "light footprint," as proposed and instituted by the highest levels in the Department of Defense. Our leadership was creative, though, in their interpretation of limiting direct American action and presence in specific areas, leaving it to the local forces to stabilize the region. We knew they needed breathing room and we were going to give it to them.

As difficult as it was to employ the Iraqi forces, tracking the enemy was equally challenging. Securing the major thoroughfares was a prime example—these roads were used by the populace and by the insurgency as well. The difficulty lay in differentiating the two, but there was no better method of finding out who was who than getting away from the FOB and seeing what trouble we could stir up.

As a small reconnaissance company, we maintained a light footprint by design; but, as we uncovered more and more evidence of the enemy, we began to convert that light footprint into a hard boot print—right in the chest of the enemy.

March 19/20, 2006 –

Time for another operation. The whole company was put into observation posts along Route Wild and Route Pluto to extend our presence southward. We rode with the first lift somewhere around 2300 and were dropped off to go hide in foliage next to an orchard. We hurried across the road, one at a time, to an abandoned building and got to work on another night of observation.

Sporadic gunshots, firefight in the Pak to our south. Nothing else. The sun marched up the scarred walls and the day turned from orange to blue. About that time, a kid walked into our position. He was terrified. We radioed it up higher, and the CO pulled us out of the operation. I can't help but think the enemy sends kids in here to confirm our position.

In their vehicles, we cruised the route with the Quick Reaction Force for a couple of hours before heading into the FOB. Communication was spotty at best and taking us out of the picture put the whole chain in jeopardy. Our radios have a certain usable range, and we had to relay up and down a chain to pass information. It was a battlefield telephone game.

Our teams returned to the chain the next night to fill in the communications gap. It was pretty calm, but we spotted an unknown patrol coming north along the road. We were ready to smoke them but determined they were POB as they entered our kill zone. Their mismatched uniforms confused us. We called to verify because death squads have been reported moving into the area. Even more disturbing is that the murders have been committed by those in Iraqi uniforms. It's complex and we have to get the targets right. The night is quiet until

2nd platoon finds an EFP. That's one less powerful bomb off the road. Good work, dudes.

When one unit was pulled from the operation, the whole thing peeled apart. We were a chain—pull out a link and it cannot reach as far, but it may also unravel altogether. Our posts were dispersed, so the team furthest out relied on an intermediary, like us, for communication back to home plate.

It was risky. If you had to break contact, or maneuver on an enemy force, you were running a gamble of doing so without reliable communication with friendly forces. Our company was spread out but making the best out of the situation in light of the size of our sector. We needed to be judicious in our use of forces to maximize our security efforts, but we also needed to rely on our Iraqi partners for assistance.

The company was responsible for patrolling a swathe of land that required our full capacity but also that of the Iraqi POB troopers to conduct effective security efforts. They manned postings that dotted the roads in the form of exposed traffic control points, which were, by design, ripe targets. Their job was to search vehicles, protect government facilities, and build confidence that the Iraqis were beginning to take responsibility for their own protection. It was dangerous work, and the recent attacks along sectarian lines made it even more so.

It was clear, however, that the Iraqis needed more help. Route Wild was a beast—uncertain and unreasonable. With most of the company focused on river operations during the previous weeks, a resulting period of absence needed to be addressed to ensure the enemy knew we were out there hunting them. Thus, for now, we were scattered from one corner of our AO to the other, making the best out of the situation to secure one of the major thoroughfares leading into southeast Baghdad.

Despite our efforts, retribution violence of Sunnis against Shia and vice versa was increasing throughout the country. Talk around the company centered around groups crossing the river to incite violence, rob, and kill rivals. Rumor had it that the POB had taken part in some of the killings, or, at the least, had loaned weapons to sectarian murderers for pay, or to save their own hides. It was anyone's guess as to what was going on, but we dedicated ourselves to finding out. Like the road we were watching, the situation remained unpredictable—we needed to stay wild.

March 28, 2006 –

Patrol of Route Wild. Took off at 2200 hours. I was driving on patrol for the first time in the deployment. We cruised to Wild, cleared the route and hung out shooting the breeze. We came back and drove right to midnight chow. Bonus.

Driving the monster that is a HMMWV was an experience synonymous with combat in the Middle East. These unwieldy beasts were birthed in the 1980s and proliferated across the United States following Operation Desert Storm. In the Middle East, they would again play a central role during the next war against Iraq. This time, the nature of the conflict had changed, and roadside bombings did not mesh well with the soft exterior of the trucks. Rapid improvement to the armor was paramount to defend against the increase of elaborate and powerful improvised explosive devices.

Our small fleet reflected those adaptations—we had a green truck covered in weld marks from the artless addition of steel plates, and a few desert HMMWVs sporting gun turrets that functioned only if you sweet-talked them and air conditioners gasping on life support. Our maintenance teams were champions and force multipliers who enabled continuous squadron operations and fought extreme temperatures, both in the motor pool and inside the vehicles themselves. It turns out that if you cannot put the window down when it's 120 degrees outside, it can get scorching hot inside a rolling metal box.

Of course, the heat is not the only threat, but it is the easiest to mitigate—drink water. The HMMWVs themselves provided targets for the insurgents that were plentiful and low in cost to exploit. The roadside bomb, or IED, became the top killer of coalition forces in Iraq. More and more news clips of exploding HMMWVs and cargo trucks plastered the media, painting a grim picture of the conflict. Our training at Fort Campbell before our deployment reflected this increase, and we ran several counter-IED drills before our departure. This is what you look for, this is how you should drive, these are the actions you take upon contact, and this is how you exit a vehicle—these were topics covered in briefings and learned in practice.

The magic, however, was not parking by or driving by one. This was easier said than done, as the insurgents were experts at camouflaging the bombs and emplacing them without us noticing. Driving HMMWVs around Iraq required a high level of alertness, forcing a maddening scan of each potential stone or every pile of trash. Here, however, those were every ten feet. It did not take long in this environment before you developed more realistic expectations—you drove ahead looking for the big ones, but hoping that when you hit a little one, you wouldn't be hurt or killed. That is not to say we didn't do our due diligence, but instead, we balanced risk versus reward.

Our patrols needed to move across a large area, and we needed to sustain this initiative with increased freedom of movement. We did our best to eliminate the threat, but all we could do was mitigate it. We changed our technology and tactics often, but so did the enemy. It was a cat and mouse game. Sometimes you were the cat, sometimes the mouse. It took no time to appreciate the danger, brought home when driving a HMMWV across routes like Wild or Pluto. If you didn't understand this on day one, you did by day two. It was life. You left the wire knowing you were going to get hit—it was a matter of when and how bad.

March 30, 2006 –

Davis and I were rallied at 1915 out in the parking area with our gear ready for a briefing before a mission. Our team was to overwatch an objective we searched when we crossed the river last time. Davis and I sat there, wondering if we were going to find anything, throwing gravel into a helmet placed a fair distance away. Our game was interrupted by a faint explosion that rumbled over the churn of the generators.

We looked at each other. Zzzzzzzzmmmm Boom! Incoming. Close. I ran for the company command post. The rounds came in nearby. I could hear debris, rocks, and shrapnel impact the trucks. Ran faster. Got in the CP. I paused, I got to get my radio. Ran. Incoming. Wham! Nope. Turned around. Boom. I clobbered somebody to make it into the room.

It was over a dozen rocket rounds and was pretty exciting. Everybody in the CP laughed. Anyways, we went on the mission and rode to Salman Pak for a one nighter. No activity so we make it back to the FOB unharmed. Communication blackout was in effect because somebody died in the rocket attack.

My memory is as sharp now as my vision was then. The sparks from the impacting projectiles filled my peripheral vision as my eyes fixated upon the safety of the command post. Taking those first few steps, I looked at Davis, seeing his eyes widen, watching the spectacle of the fireworks show. I reached to put my hand on him and it brought him back to the situation. We sprinted for cover together. With each explosion, I could feel the heat on my face as rounds impacted near us.

They were landing close enough that I could hear the gravel smash into our gun trucks, making a sound like metal rain. Once we made it under cover, even after sprinting for the radio before abandoning the task and diving into the CP, we were grinning. We had made it. Once the barrage eased, I ran out and scooped up my gear, fearing not the rockets, but a reprimand for leaving my gear unattended. Once the all-clear came, I was told the fun was over and to get the hell out of the command post—I obliged.

Yet, looking back, there is no fun when you're dodging mortar rounds. However, people like me—a brash, bulletproof twenty-one-year-old—did find a bit of sport in avoiding indirect fire. It was fun until you knew somebody wounded or killed from one. At that time, I was unsure of the reasoning for my actions. We thought ourselves too fast, too nimble, and too lucky to take a piece of shrapnel, and that is not the case. It could also be that we were somewhat feral and that the adrenaline in those instances fueled our desire for a cheap thrill. It could also have been that we understood that the fire was so random if you got hit, it was destiny. In actuality, it was pure naïveté of youth.

The average age of the men in our company was around 21, maybe 22. Most enlisted right out of high school and had no understanding of the world outside the military. What we did understand, though, were indirect fire attacks. We were accustomed to rocket and mortar rounds striking with a slot machine's unreliability. They were a daily occurrence. They pissed you off when you were on your way to chow, pissed you off when you walked from the latrine, pissed you off when you should've taken them seriously.

April 13, 2006 –

Left the FOB at 2100 hours for the Tuwaitha Nuclear Research Facility. I was driving, which sucked. We took an hour to get there. We ran into 2nd platoon that had found an IED on Route Wall Street, off the traffic circle on South Pluto.

I thanked them and took a detour around the cordon to get to Tuwaitha.

Once there, we left the trucks with the mortar section and had to climb a mountain of a berm 50 meters or higher. The infantry God was smiling on me and I found a rope somebody had tied to something at the top to pull myself up. I was smoked and it took me a bit to ascend the hill with the 70 pounds of gear and ammo strapped to me.

At the top, we could see several kilometers in the night. We watched from there, scanning Jisr Diyala and the major roads nearby. I took a walk around the berm and found a fountain with a picture of Saddam and some 30mm casings from a battle forgotten. We called in some stuff but pulled off around 0300 and drove through Jisr Diyala. This place is a total shithole—sewage in the streets, dilapidated houses. I felt an uneasiness steering the truck around that neighborhood at night.

Tuwaitha was one of the central features of our area of operations. Located south of Jisr Diyala and a stone's throw from the Tigris, it once housed a nuclear research facility and a yellow cake factory. The facility had been bombed by the Israeli Air Force in 1981 and again by the US ten years later. The area had been used as storage for spent reactor fuel and medical wastes. With that in mind, it was an interesting place to patrol.

The complex was protected by massive dirt berms that rose like mountains from the dust below. We used these, as well the adjacent guard towers, to pull surveillance of the surrounding area, including the dirty slum neighborhood of Jisr Diyala. Tuwaitha was guarded by Iraqis who lived within its walls, and I often speculated what health effects they suffered in doing so. In fact, to this day, I am not sure what particulate matter we stirred up during our patrols. Every one of us discussed our concerns on this in typical Army fashion but continued mission without complaint.

Geographically, Tuwaitha was a significant point of interest for us in that it allowed for surveillance with a considerable degree of cover but also served as a staging ground from which we circled the wagons from time to time. We used it to facilitate a quick response when our company commander and other leadership would attend local council meetings.

Further buffering the nuclear complex, a small wall separated the outer cordon of the complex from the outside world, but that didn't stop the local children from trespassing. The kids would come and put on a show, hoping for a handout which we supplied. Their liveliness contrasted with the bleak backdrop of Tuwaitha and the repugnant dereliction of Jisr Diyala.

On top of the kids' antics and the desolation of the place, Tuwaitha was such a strange feature to have in our area of operations. The nuclear hub once belonged to an enemy of the United States. We did much to inhibit Iraq's pursuit of the bomb. Facts like this, however, were lost on us because, at the time, we were focused on the mission and keeping an eye out for the next attack. It was not until we rotated home that we realized that we had patrolled areas relevant to the history of Iraq and the world at large. And that maybe, we wrote some of that history.

April 25, 2006 –

Our section got the word at 1600 hours that we were to head to the hotel compound for another 3-day mission. Hustled to get the trucks loaded and steamed out the gate. We cruised to the POB headquarters and there is no welcome. The place is quiet. I helped establish communications and proceeded to the top of the hotel. Davis and I dropped our things on the top floor of the building and it was a moment or two until the rest of the gang arrived with their gear.

Like a leaky faucet, the night dripped with the occasional rifle shot. It was peaceful. We sat and watched the stars twinkle on the blackest of canvases. Without the lights from the streets, cars, and homes—the night sky filled with winking stars. I chomped on MRE pound cake and did my best to look for targets, but the sights of the cosmos were hard to beat, so was the camaraderie.

Five months in, we were back strewn across the roof of the ruined hotel gazing at the night sky. The heavens on those bright, crisp Iraqi nights reminded us of our insignificance. Without the city lights to drown out the twinkles of those far away stars, we felt a sense of calm.

We lay awake that night discussing home and other more trivial things. It is in these moments when you get to know the other guys. Most soldiers can spout off the whole life story of another soldier. Not only do you rely on these guys for your protection, but also for your humanity. You have one another to complain to, to seek advice, or to, more often, shoot the breeze with. And we did a lot of that.

Sometimes we talked about the most boring and random topic, but I remained interested because I knew it was important to listen to the other person's story. When you are unsure of your future, you discuss topics you usually avoid. Nobody would care about your fifth-grade monkey bar experience, but somehow, we managed to talk about it. I got to know more about the dudes I patrolled with than I did about some of my own kin.

As the stars faded and the sun painted the clouding horizon, we pulled stand-to with a renewed family-like sense of connection. This connection was a bond built from shared misery and strengthened with devotion to duty. It was a fraternity pledged with blood and sweat—a camaraderie most will never understand. It was a brotherhood.

In fact, this brotherhood is a source of motivation, of reliance, of pride, and it's the foundation the military is built on. Nothing happens through a single line of effort. Everything the military ever asks involves teamwork. No exceptions. Brotherhood is an accelerant to stoke the flames that burn in the team, forging extraordinary outcomes from ordinary individuals. In this way, the exceptional results demanded by the armed forces become routine, and anything less is deemed a defeat. Failure is, instead, channeled into the best teacher.

That ethos is based on the team, the individuals working the mission together. It creates a connection so strong it's replicated nowhere else in existence. You've trusted others with your security, with your role in the universe, and even more than that, you've trusted your brothers borne of battle to carry your spirit onward if anything should happen to you. Like an unobserved communal ritual, our tribe pledged to one another our most valuable possessions—not all of them physical.

April 26, 2006 –

We're chilling at the hotel. This was great—like R&R or a vacation. We kept our eyes open and made a few radio calls, but we got to listen to music and reported little in the way of enemy activity. Most dudes caught a tan or fell asleep when they could. The SPTT showed up, and they allowed us to eat their hot dogs which were a welcomed switch from MREs.

April 27, 2006 –

It was the same deal as yesterday. Except it was even more calm than last time. We sat around and thought of new and exciting ways of wasting time, like launching a soda can into the air with gunpowder. I played harmonica attempting the

Star-Spangled Banner on top of a Baath party retreat. Take that Saddam!

We ate hot dogs again that night. We saw an amazing shooting star, which was cool, and later that night, there's a loud, sustained gunfight in Salman Pak. We called some attack aviation and walked them into the area in question, but it was unsuccessful. We again couldn't see, but it was clear that somebody was having a hell of a time. We slept awful.

Identifying the moment you become a veteran is difficult. Is it when you qualify for DoD benefits? Return home from a deployment? Have your DD214 separation paperwork in hand? Many do not come to the realization when they are in the service, but as I looked around the rooftop riddled with bullets and crumbling concrete from old mortar and rocket impacts, I saw it. My best Star-Spangled Banner harmonica jam, although terrible, cast an extraordinary atmosphere on the rooftop. It amplified the setting sun bathing us in orange sunlight as the day retreated.

We slacked a bit on the grooming standards, using what water we carried up several flights of stairs for drinking or brushing teeth, and did not get the greatest sleep due to the constant guard we kept against the enemy and the rats. We were manning and cleaning various pieces of military hardware, grumbling our different grievances and tossing the occasional insult back and forth. Instead of being miserable and cantankerous, we were soaked in rare tranquil peace.

We were veterans by the definition of the word, but it became more than that. I understood I was experiencing something unique and something that I have since found difficulty in articulating to my friends and family. A world away, the sun melted across the horizon past the Tigris River, taking with it the shimmering, fading light of another deployed day.

Back home, people sipped coffee, greeting those same rising rays of sunshine, and went about their lives as free people.

While the serenity of another dusk clinging to life crept across an ancient river, a harmonica played our nation's anthem. It was in this instant we grew into veterans with a different type of understanding. We were more in tune with the complexities of our fight. We were continuing to adjust to a different skill set required for the mission and continued to defer to the local Iraqi forces for security as the decision makers had directed. Whether we were veterans or not, the fight required a mature warfighter, not simply in the sense of tradition but in the application of violence. We were still kids, but we'd move into the spring matured by this evolving reality.

April 28, 2006 –

I went to the CP to hang out until it was time to leave. We drank some coffee, and I disassembled the radios. Out of nowhere, First Sergeant Lillie and his 1st Platoon convoy barreled in, wasting no time doing first sergeant things. He told us to shave and had a look around to make sure our stuff was squared away. It was. He was satisfied and began asking about the activity. There was zero significant activity, so we got to shooting the breeze when the POB started engaging targets across the river with a heck of a lot of automatic fire. They saw some guys in ski masks rummaging through the trees along the banks and were now trying to shoot anything that moved.

Every POB machine gun unleashed hell and the 1st platoon dudes came running so I directed them to some cover so they could get eyes on the opposing bank. I returned to grab some more ammo, but they lost visual with the suspected enemy as they slipped away through the orchards.

Soon enough, the firing stopped except for the occasional Iraqi that wasn't content, claiming that somebody is hiding in the bushes across the Tigris. They blasted a few more rounds into the shrubbery to make sure. If they were there, they weren't happy. Walking back to the CP, I found my coffee cold.

May 29, 2016 –

We entered the museum to a warm greeting from the curator behind a reception desk. I had called earlier to inform her of our reunion, but she didn't need help to recognize we were veterans. She'd been around enough to tell. She welcomed us with a big smile she displayed for the usual visitors, not only those that had served in the division. "Please take your time," she insisted, and gave us a memorized run-down of the museum, emphasizing our heritage and the exhibits dedicated to contemporary conflicts.

"Our history is in a museum, man. Pretty wild." Notaro stroked his beard in approval.

"I'm sure it's not our stuff, but it is cool to think that an Iraq exhibit is in here," Jeff added.

"It's probably a lot of invasion stuff," Eric said. "Saddam stuff, Republic guard, Mosul, not our unit stuff per se."

"Yeah." Jeff shook his head. "We're small potatoes."

"It doesn't matter," Notaro said. "It's our stuff, our story and all. We're part of it."

"You're right, I guess. By extension," I offered.

"Yeah, man." Notaro agreed. "By extension."

We strolled through the halls, looking at relics from the infancy of the 101st. Although the division had existed in one shape or another since World War 1, the museum launched visitors first into its more famous history. From Camp Claiborne, where Major General William C. Lee famously noted in 1942, "The 101st has no history, but it has a rendezvous with destiny," until its mobilization as part of the country's rush to develop parachute infantry units at the beginning of World War 2.

We examined uniforms and memorabilia from Operation Overlord where 6,600 soldiers loaded into over 1,400 C-47 Skytrain transports, like the Brass Hat parked out front, to drop as part of the D-Day invasion of Normandy. Nearly 1,500 of those brave Screaming Eagles were killed or captured that day.

The division continued through Operation Market Garden and into the Battle of the Bulge where near Bastogne, Brigadier General Anthony C. MacAuliffe delivered his famous "Nuts!" reply to the German surrender demand. Towards the end of the war, the Screaming Eagles captured Hitler's mountain retreat of Berchtesgaden when the German surrender was received. The division was soon deactivated, but America would call again.

"Humbling," Burns said to Notaro as they combed through the exhibit of US military weapons and captured German gear from the period.

"These dudes were tough as hell," Notaro said.

"It's incredible what these guys went through. They saw indescribable things and went on to build a nation." Jeff stepped in behind us as we examined an M1 Garand and other accouterments of the period.

"Greatest generation, man," Notaro said. He gave a little subdued nod and stepped off into the next area of the museum.

We wandered into Vietnam exhibits displaying the division's role in the conflict. From 1965 to 1972, the 101st soldiers had fought across the country—in areas from Saigon to the hilltops outside Quang Tri while also battling in the notorious A Shau Valley and participating in the Tet Offensive. The history on the walls and scenes of another generation's war echoed to us more so than the war against Fascism.

"Fighting an enemy you can't see, in a land you don't know, for causes you don't understand," I mused.

"Easy, it doesn't take no Greek philosopher," Burns said. "It's much simpler. You know that."

"Is it?" I asked, looking at an M79 grenade launcher soldiers referred to as the blooper, or thumper, for its distinct sound upon firing. "Fighting for the guy next to you, I suppose."

"That's it. That's all it is." Burns said. Boiling it down to the tangible result of our fight was necessary. "Don't act like you gave much thought to the cause, or how this whole thing was going when you were outside the wire. We had a mission."

"Leave the debate to those that weren't there, man," Notaro proclaimed. "It's not our role."

"Yeah, but I can't stand the thought of having my morality tested by somebody whose morality remains untested," Jeff interjected.

"It's easy, guys," Eric joined in. "We were there to do the job asked of us. We did it. We tried to help them as much as we could. We did it. We tried to bring as many of the team home as we could. We did it." Eric put his thumb in his pocket. "We did exactly what these guys did." He pointed with his free hand towards mock paratroopers wearing olive drab set in a command post bunker deep in a forgotten jungle. We all murmured agreements.

The group moved towards Desert Shield and Desert Storm where the 101st fired the first shots of the Gulf War, not to mention where the division made one of the longest and largest air assaults in history. The attack cut off the Iraqi forces by taking Highway 8, securing the flanks for US armor. The Iraqis stood no chance.

Soon, we inspected the Screaming Eagles role in Panama, Haiti, Bosnia, and Kosovo before coming upon an exhibit dedicated to our response to the 9/11 terrorist attacks.

"Where were you?" Jeff asked me.

"Walking into class, junior year," I said. "You?"

"Changing classes junior year. Figured it was an accident."

"I thought so, too."

"Kids, man," Notaro commented. The light shined on his beard making it appear a bit grayer. He slapped me on the back. "Look at this shit." He pointed to where the Operation Iraqi Freedom exhibit rested. Burns and Eric were already hovering over a glass-enclosed scene of mannequins wearing uniforms and holding weapons set upon a backdrop painting of Saddam Hussein carrying a rifle.

"Look at these NCOs," Burns pointed. "Uniforms jacked up! Looking like Endris was back in the day!"

"Hey, follow the leader, right?" I asked. Burns was the leader of the second team in First Platoon. Responsible for an element smaller than a squad but larger than a fire team, he led his six or seven soldiers on tasks that could've been given to a platoon, but he'd get it done. He was a team leader many guys wanted to work for but never got the chance. Instead, we watched his actions to gauge how to be a competent sergeant. As a sharp NCO, he knew what it meant to lead troops in combat, and when Burns spoke, you listened.

"Jokes aside, leading soldiers will be one of the highlights of my life. Being an NCO made me a better person. I mean, look through this museum. It's a heritage of non-commissioned officers. You're always training your replacement." Burns took his hand out of his pocket. "This dude," he pointed across the museum towards a mannequin WW2 paratrooper, "trained his replacement, who trained his replacement." He motioned towards the Vietnam exhibit. "Who trained his replacement and so on."

His hand stopping at Desert Storm, Burns' eyes locked with those in the group with a flicker of seriousness. "That's how we got here. We are the legacy of these guys. They learned stuff and shared those lessons, sorta like us. We've grown on the coattails of their experience. It's the NCO who carries the Army and carries a country for that matter. We stand on the shoulders of these giants."

As Burns spoke, guys gather around him. Being the more reserved soldier and friend, I knew it was tough for him to be the center of attention unless he was giving orders or having a cold one. His insight as an NCO was golden. He was a man that could crack a perfectly-timed joke but also a man who saw the bigger picture. It doesn't matter how you got there, you do it for the man next to you he would say, a lesson passed down from generation to generation. Learn from their examples.

When he finished, Burns disregarded the circle of listeners and turned to read a placard on the wall elaborating on deeds the 101st had accomplished in its storied past. "The bars have been set high. I hope we've passed on a good example," he muttered.

May 11, 2006 –

Tonight, we were tasked with an observation post along Route Wild. We moved out around 2200. We crammed in the RG-31, the newest addition to the fleet that smells like vomit because somebody earlier today puked inside. The vehicle is from South Africa and has a V-shaped hull for deflecting blasts. It was safer, but I got some puke on my glove, so I got to sniff somebody's stomach for the next half-day.

Drove. The call came, and we hopped out and ran for the target house. Cleared it, sat tight and listened. Once quiet, we climbed to the top to begin observation. We got the radios working for us, or at least functioning for us. Howser, my river-crossing machine gun friend, was with the other team adding to our manpower but we weren't there for an hour before Wright decided to do a small dismounted patrol around the OP to investigate reports of caches.

Tyler and I volunteered so that others may chill. Howser wasn't going to let us have all the fun, so he handed off his radio as I threw mine on my back and grabbed his gear. It was time to hump. We headed due east into farm country and we didn't make it fifteen minutes without running into local nationals conducting backyard business. Salman Pak doesn't have a curfew enforced. We did some maneuvering and got around them, staying in the shadows but skirting close enough to another neighboring house.

As we neared the home, in the backyard area, the residents came out. We leaned against their wall a few feet away in the shadows. It made me smile, but I also wondered if we couldn't get some help spotting local nationals in our vicinity. I radioed the other team at the OP and told them to cover us with thermals. Davis peeled off from watching Wild to scan around us and locate targets before we could.

Behind the neighborhood, there was a series of ponds that we would have to navigate, and the banks left us exposed without much in the way of cover. We walked and walked and walked in a zig-zag fashion along the berms dividing the bodies of water before hitting open fields.

Soon, we were a few kilometers out and our only find was an empty hole in the ground. I signaled for a tight 360 and the team gathered around. I asked, "What the hell are we doing? We are too far out." I complained about medevac and air cover, mutual support, Davis losing visual on us, no communication...it was dangerous as it was with the four of us. What if they saw us before we saw them? We didn't need to get any farther out. I didn't think it was worth the risk.

Wright acknowledged my points. Time to head for the OP. He knew we were pushing it and took my input without issue. We got within 150 meters of the observation post. I called Davis to again peel off surveillance of Route Wild to scan our approach route.

"STOP!" Davis radioed us the bad news. I told the team, "Freeze, get down, shut up! Two, make that three guys tailing, armed with AK-47s. 100 meters out." They were stopped, taking a knee, pointing at us. Our sister team was covering us and I radioed back and forth as we searched for cover or concealment. "Do you have visual? Shit. No. Where? You got a bead on them? Roger. Distance and direction? Can't see through the reed grass. Shit. Get cover, I say again, get cover. I got visual. They are closing on your position, say again, closing on your position."

I waved for everybody to get comfortable with the dirt. We weren't close enough to whisper any further directions. Hand signals would have to do. I saw them. They had guns, but they weren't at the ready. They have demonstrated any hostile intent. But it was go time. Clenched my jaw. Waited for Wright's move.

Following him, we hopped out of the ditch, weapons pointed, tac light from our rifles blinding them. Everyone spouted their limited Arabic spiced with some American curse words. "Don't move! Awgaf! Le tet-Harak!" Communication barrier overcome. They dropped their weapons. We waded across the creek. Howser led the way. Disarmed and searched them.

The quick reaction force is too far out so I need to move to get reception. Risky. After a jog, I got reception with the platoon leader to get the trucks to our location with the interpreter. We separated and questioned the young men one at a time. They talked. Son of a bitch. Fish farmers.

I am not an old man, but at least I have the chance. Remembering this night, it became clear that nothing is guaranteed, but events played out to at least let seven men have a shot at telling a story to their grandchildren. The particulars of such a close call are etched into the deep recesses of my mind. But, the reason for this predicament is something I've thought about more since facing down those armed fish farmers. In these details, the truth is hidden.

As we wandered out in the countryside, we were exposed. It was a small group of soldiers, four to be exact, surrounded by hundreds of Iraqis, and one of us was carrying a bolt action rifle—a weapon better suited for precision firing from concealment, not suppressing automatic fire pouring all over you. The situation was risky with little reward.

The 'recurring epiphany' struck again, and this time I verbalized it. Wright took no issue with my list of concerns and complimented me on voicing them. He was a leader building another leader. The dubious nature of our objective lent itself to criticism and questioning.

After finding a dry hole of a cache, we trudged off in the direction of the fields and ponds. Again, several 100-meter-long bodies of water stood between us and our destination—the observation post. They limited our avenues of approach. The moon was high in the sky on a cloudless night, and it was otherwise peaceful, but we were forced to highlight ourselves in the strong lunar illumination. The four of us marched across the berms separating each pond, raising us a few meters above the water line or the canals linking each. We moved quickly to limit our exposure across the danger area.

The ditches were filled with reed grass jutting well above six feet from stagnant, foul water. We knew we were pressing our luck, hoping our figures in the dark would go without notice. My shadow was hard to miss as I had erected the long-whip antenna on the radio, which made me waddle back and forth a bit. Our team of volunteers were spread out twenty meters from one another, scanning through night vision that may have well been turned off in the abundant moonlight. It was the home stretch, but our luck ran out.

When I got the call, we had crossed a drainage ditch from the ponds one by one across a pipe, keeping us dry but testing our balance. Dropping and getting the others to follow suit, I saw the opposing bank through a small V-shaped slit in the tall reeds. The stalks provided a few feet of concealment if you laid low enough, and I pointed in the general direction of our pursuers. Being the one with the radio and more than three or four arm's lengths away from the nearest teammate, I was the sole person getting the radio relay of these dudes' paths as they crept towards us.

Davis watched the scene through the scope and gripped the trigger of the M24 sniper rifle. He whispered information to the medic, Dombroski, who had joined us for the evening and again found himself relaying communications. I did my best to pass updates to my teammates using arm signals until the Iraqis walked right into my view.

Through the V-shaped slit, I saw the moon glisten off the AK-47's stamped metal frames. I heard them speaking to each other, debating our location. My finger slipped into the trigger well, inching closer towards releasing a rapid succession of bullets into center mass. The scene is burned in my mind. I eyed Wright through my periphery, waiting for his decision.

We did not have time to debate whether to engage them, but I had asked Davis to take a shot if they brought their weapons past 90 degrees or broke the plane as we called it. We stuck to our rules of engagement. A shot from the M24 would be trailed by a volley of 7.62 and 5.56mm rounds to ensure the targets we eliminated, but only if threatened.

That was not deliberation, only the sentence. We were judge and jury. Unless I had clear intentions from the men across the canal, I determined I wouldn't shoot first as I was the lowest ranking, and the thought of military prison time at Fort Leavenworth wasn't appealing, but as soon as the opening bullet was fired, I was going to sling the most lead. It was time for aggression. It was time for violence. It was time for action.

With a nod from Wright, we launched. Jumping up to challenge them, four men made the sound of forty. We roared like beasts, spewing curse words like flame and blinding the men with beams of light from our weapons. We unleashed a fury so surprising, they dropped their weapons into the muddy canal banks and raised their hands high into the bright moonlight.

Before a rational thought could form in their minds, we had forgone the pipe, crossed the reed-filled water, and secured the scene. One of the individuals, in a half-ass, confused attempt to reach for his dropped AK-47 which was sliding towards the murky soup of the canal, met a size 14 boot to his chest. He decided it was best to let the thing get wet.

Radio coverage was spotty, but I was able to take an exposing, dangerous jog and report our situation. After patting them down, we grabbed their weapons, separated each of them, and forced them to wade the canal to meet the platoon leader arriving with the QRF. Accompanied by the interpreter, they each related their story while Tyler, Howser, and I played with their AK-47s like children with new toys on Christmas.

Their testimony, a trigger pull away from nonexistence, spoke to the situation of the nation at large. Due to the declining capacity of the Iraqi police to stop thievery and with food being at a premium, the three men had taken it upon themselves to patrol their livelihoods—the fish ponds. Their elder, who lived

r away, had requested they keep their remaining
 market.

police, this was their option, and it was a deadly
ied that theft from the fisheries was frequent
.... thought we were another group of hungry criminals. They
didn't think US soldiers moved in such small groups, and when
we jumped out of the reeds, they were stupefied. If they were not
more careful, the only thing they would have caught was a bullet.

In fact, we could have been a few rifle shots away from
ruining their whole economy and hindering others dependent
upon the fish. We'll never know. For their sake, and ours, I am
relieved that our discipline precluded us from taking the easy way
out and, more selfishly, that my integrity remains intact.

However, the rules of engagement we operated under on
nights such as this were not there to protect my integrity or
mental condition. They were there to further the mission by
directing the use of force congruent to the goal of a free,
independent Iraq. Never in the history of warfare have decisions
at the lowest level been so consequential. Our efforts to secure
Iraq depended on each interaction with citizens of the host
nation and enormous discretion foreign to young soldiers. When
the last ounces of your soul compel you to shoot, sometimes
courage means not taking that shot.

I hated it. I hated it because it was hard, and because it was
risky. It challenged what I thought it meant to be an infantryman.
I long thought compassion and courage were mutually exclusive.
They are not. They feed one another. It takes compassion to
stand up for those that can't defend themselves. It takes courage
to be empathetic. Many people who consider themselves
warriors despise the words empathy or compassion, thinking
they would have smoked those dudes with AKs without thinking
twice. I myself stewed along the muddy canal shivering wet in
foul water, trying to rationalize the situation and justify the risk
we'd taken.

Without exception, the conflict at this time demanded more scrutiny of targets. I wanted the clear fight with an enemy willing to go toe-to-toe with us, making it easy for us to kill them, and not to worry about murdering the wrong people. We don't get to choose the hand we're dealt, but we have to play it. Decisions like this were part of it. This dilemma required a discipline that challenged every one of us. We'd have to adjust.

What this meant in practicality was that risk was carefully leveraged against reward until the return on investment diminished. It was business. It was simple escalation of force. When it came time for force, particularly of the deadly variety, the response needed to be overwhelming, accurate, and swift. Channelized aggression is what brings soldiers home.

Empathy aside, when the moment arrives and the threat is existential, there can be no quarter. Existence is at stake, not only your own but your team's as well. The force applied should not be disproportionate, but should make the receiver unable to mount any response capable of threatening your life. This is demanding and calls into play the judgment of the warfighter. This was not an easy fight, and it asked us to go from infantryman to policeman and back again, but it was the mission. Make no mistake, when the wolves threaten the flock, when the moment arrives, when it's them or us, it will be us.

In the end, the chaotic scene made such a ruckus that we knew our surveillance wasn't going to be effective. We sat around pulling security and eating beef jerky from care packages sent from home. There was no way we were going to get a sleep rotation going, as we were soaked to the bone and too excited, too angry to throttle back.

The rest of the night was uneventful, but we took turns debriefing the situation, making certain we did not miss any hint or sign that the fish farmers were being dishonest. Being on good terms with the Iraqi people was a top priority. I hoped that our gamble had moved us closer towards that objective. I hoped our risk matched the reward. I hoped those fish farmers understood how close they had come to dying.

May 13, 2006 –

The day starts at 3am again. Why do I even care? We climbed aboard the RG-31. We are going to pull observation in the area where Kelley got shot. To help draw some fire, 1st Platoon was doing a baited ambush north of us. We are also to interdict any combatants that use the river bottom to flank the teams set in positions along the Tigris.

We drove towards Salman Pak, turn off Route Wild onto some dirt road. Once we stopped, we hopped out and moved west towards the river through thick trees and lush vegetation. We reached the road paralleling the river and stopped to listen. It was clear, so we continued across the road, named Route Gator, and got into the irrigated orchards running along the river.

The team combed the area looking for a suitable spot and found one in a dried-up irrigation canal that had been reclaimed by some broad-leafed plants. We set in and camouflaged as best we could. We even threw on some face paint and used a lot of natural vegetation as we were semi-exposed.

Around 8 in the morning, a blue bongo truck rumbled into the orchard and parked a short distance away. A family unloaded as I watched from behind a rifle. Great. They gathered a dozen fruit baskets and started picking dates from the trees. They had no idea we were watching them as they tossed baskets around the orchard to revisit as they filled others. The father of the family came within 10 meters of us and had no idea.

Soon, a young boy, not more than a few meters away picking dates, stopped his harvest. His eyes focused, and he caught a glimpse of us and, startled, bolted to tell the others. They were scared at first. I know I would have been. We waited to see their reaction. They didn't leave. The father asked as best he could if they could continue picking. We obliged but did our best to motion for them to keep their distance.

The harvest continued with them watching us and us watching them while scanning our objective. One was a teenage Iraqi girl. Her father was zealously protective of her even looking at us. She pulled her veil around her face the best she could as her father yelled at her each time the wind blew. I pulled some candy from my pocket and threw it to the children busy picking fruit. They didn't make a cell phone call or appear apprehensive to the point of escaping. They looked like honest farmers similar to those from where I called home.

The operation was over with little more than some harassing fire and some weapons seized. We packed it in to head towards Gator. The kids followed us out in a sort of backyard march. The girl said goodbye in English, making her father shout for obedience. We made it alongside the road and a convoy rumbled in at the perfect time. We loaded up, the family waved, and we headed for the FOB. Another adventure.

The difference between our purposes in the orchard was absolute. Our observation post was camouflaged well. The fruit harvesters moseyed into our position without a care before I whispered and gave a gentle wave. The young kid and his family continued picking dates while we maintained surveillance. If they were not worried, we were not either. The minute the farmers wanted to leave their harvest behind and flee, our concern would pique but, for the time being, the best reaction was no action.

In many coordinated attacks, the surest indication of looming contact is when the families and children slip away. As they picked their fruit, we felt safe, but with a camouflaged sniper team a short distance away, I doubted they felt the same. All of us went about our work in the light whispers of a breeze, enveloped by a green patch of date trees providing us all a degree of relief.

It was a stark contrast. The date farmers' implements of harvest—hands and a few baskets—were at work right next to our implements of death—the Barrett .50 caliber sniper rifle and the M24 sniper rifle, most notably. In the breadbasket of the Middle East, the cradle of civilization, the heart of Mesopotamia, conflict was no stranger. Unassuming fruit farmers, who wanted nothing more than to pick their dates and raise their families, witnessed perpetual fighting and came to know the Americans from interactions like this.

For a whole generation of America's history, we've been engaged in some form of conflict in the Middle East. Iraqis, for good or bad, have grown accustomed to Americans and, as representatives of our nation, their impressions were formed by our conduct in situations like these.

Whether it is promoted or not, today's American military is the most disciplined in the history of the nation with an infinitesimal fraction of host-nation interactions proceeding poorly, even fewer criminally. Illegal acts have happened and each time they did, they blemished and overshadowed our endeavors. We own those blemishes. For a single act of misconduct, there were thousands of other interactions that went untarnished and even polished the bonds we were forging for a brighter future.

Like those fruit farmers harvesting their crop and kids enjoying candy on a pleasant sunny day with a sniper team hidden among the shrubs, there was much to remain joyful about in this life. The smiling family continued their labor and didn't let the drudgery or near constant reminders of war overwhelm them. Even though there may be unpleasant circumstances behind you, do not fail to see the goodness in front of you, if you can spot it.

May 14, 2006 –

It's getting warm. The bitching about it flowed like the sweat from our brows. I swung by the CP to grab some ice water and get the scoop on the current situation. I overheard a radio call notifying the tactical operations center of an IED attack on Pluto. It turned out that the SPTT team dudes had hit an IED and it sounded serious.

Time to roll. Now! Hustled to get our gear ready. We raced out the gate and drove to the scene meeting 1st platoon already providing assistance. The explosion had flipped one of the SPTT's HMMWVs. It had caught fire and two of the four dudes made it out—both severely wounded.

Still, they were in better shape than their friends. Those inside fared much worse. They either caught a round as the ammo cooked off or burned to death. I prayed they were unconscious. The medics from 1st platoon rushed into the carnage, but Dombroski and Winsor did what they could before they too would have been casualties. This will haunt them, I'm sure of it.

I'm sorry, guys. There wasn't a thing more we could do. It's time to move out and clear the grisly scene for the work required of the recovery. We put it behind us and moved forward. We continued to the vicinity of Route Wild and Salman Pak. We unloaded and headed off to investigate some areas of interest. One team stayed to keep eyes on another farmhouse while we went off into the wilderness to check out an old Republican Guard facility.

We walked around 5 miles, inspecting the various abandoned buildings along our way. Some had spent brass littering the floors, others were full of crude anti-American graffiti. At 0230, we were done walking and made our way to Route Wild for extraction.

We rode north, passing the scene of the attack identified by a black scorch mark on the ground the size of a gun truck visible under our night vision. We, the lucky ones, returned to the FOB in one piece. Upon making it to the company area, I read the details. It was an EFP, and it was detonated right downstream from an Iraqi Police checkpoint on Pluto. Are they not doing their job or are they involved with the IEDs? Is the militia running the show? Why are these bombs going off right next to checkpoints?

The SPTT, special police transition team, were generous hosts when we had conducted operations out of the hotel, and when we heard about the attack, the platoon sprinted out of the FOB, pushing the HMMWVs hard. Crossing the Route Pluto bridge a few miles to the south, we saw the smoke.

Beaten to the incident by First Platoon, we drove onto the scene of the attack, slowing to position ourselves for security, but it was hard to turn your eyes away from the calamity. The truck lay in a heap with shards of twisted metal protruding from the mangled carcass only slightly resembling our own ride. Smoke billowed out from a dozen large breaks in the skin the vehicle. The flames betrayed the extent of the inferno, but the longer we were there, the larger the fire grew.

The EFP launched projectiles through the armor plates like they were made of butter. The fire danced off the armor plating as the flames grew in intensity. There was little anybody could do to help the soldiers trapped inside, but that didn't stop our medics from trying. Winsor, with a bit of rage in his voice, requested a truck swing around for protection of the wounded and so they could attempt a recovery of the two individuals inside the wreckage with a bit of cover. With the truck in position, Dombroski ran towards the flames, hoping to pull the remaining casualties from the HMMWV. Not to be outdone, Doc Winsor charged ahead, disregarding any sense of self-preservation. These guys embodied the medic spirit. They were saviors not simply by trade but by nature.

As they approached, ammunition cooked off, sending zips of lead through the air and striking the dirt in front of the responding soldiers' legs. The small caliber rounds were soon followed by Mk-19 grenades exploding inside the growing inferno, sending shrapnel whizzing through the air. It was over. The risk of creating additional casualties precluded further rescue attempts. After accepting the woeful foregone conclusion, a fire truck from Rustamiyah arrived to extinguish the blaze. Dombroski felt that the recovery of the remains was his duty and sought to remove his comrades from the dismal scene and spare them the graphic image. Winsor dismissed the idea and assisted. It was not a one-man job. They were brothers taking care of another brother.

With hands burned and uniforms charred, the medics set upon their work in an almost ceremonial fashion. Not wanting to hand the initiative to the enemy, we ensured security was sufficient and drove south to get out of the way of the recovery. We left a dreadful scene behind us and locked it away inside the back of our minds, knowing that dwelling on it is not good for the spirit—not then, not now.

It was war, and we went about its brutal business. Our mission complete, we drove right by the scene on our way to the FOB. They had cleared the debris as best they could. The smell of smoke lingered in the air. Back with the tribe, not a single Comanche spoke of the incident. We knew the unshakeable truth, if it wasn't them—it was us.

May 29, 2016 –

"Well, I guess that's it, man," Notaro said. We poked around the exhibit, examining the last of the equipment and artifacts from the conflict we had fought.

"Eh. It's pretty cool," Burns said approvingly. "Makes you feel a little older to see this stuff in a museum, though."

"Only old as you feel, ain't that right, graybeard?" I faced Notaro and stroked imaginary whiskers.

"Shut the hell up, man," Notaro retorted but followed with a gentle laugh. "This stuff is good, but we need to see if those pieces of granite are out there."

"We will, we will," I said. "But first, let's eat."

We strolled through the gift shop, browsing the souvenirs we never thought we'd purchase a decade ago. A coffee cup with the 506th PIR logo, a sticker for a vehicle, a t-shirt, the things to let the world know you were a Currahee were desired now. I bought a sticker for my garage refrigerator. It defends my adult beverages, but it can't keep me from liberating a few from time to time. It felt appropriate being a veteran to have these tokens.

Outside the building, we had assembled a tailgate buffet. During the luncheon, Jeff unveiled his hard work. The group had raised enough money to purchase two stones for an additional facility the Don F. Pratt Museum had planned. The bricks will forever read "Comanche Co 1/61 OIF 2005-06 Blood Does Not Define Brothers."

Everyone appreciated the gesture. We knew the names of our fallen existed in a monument across the street, but it was fulfilling for us to know that their names would grace the entrance to the museum dedicated in part to the conflict in which they were involved. From there, they would greet thousands of visitors that wanted to look at fabled airplanes like 'Brass Hat' and stare at 'Blooper' grenade launchers. The bricks would let those know that the history inside was written in blood—our friends' blood. It was humbling.

"Great job, guys." Eric congratulated Jeff on the surprise and his effort to memorialize our fallen. "This is good stuff." His compliments made us feel like the officer was talking to his troops again. We felt ten years younger and ten years closer to the war. The memories were being kept alive.

May 22, 2006 –

It was going to be an all-nighter...again. Indirect fire came in while we were preparing and one landed a hundred meters away, but the others hit somewhere on the other side of camp. We mounted up in the RG-31 in our usual fashion and rolled to squadron headquarters. There, we got news that mortar rounds had hit around the aid station with 1 KIA, 3 WIA. Damn. Drive on.

We tracked due south to our natural playing grounds. This time we were to walk a straight-line distance of around 4 kilometers, hitting phase lines through the night to disrupt enemy forces/mortar teams operating in the area. It was a sweep and clear operation.

Our start point was along a route south of Tuwaitha and from there, we were to work our way south to the intersection of Route Wild and a road that parallels the Tigris River, not far from Salman Pak. The geography pretty much worked us in a cone to the point where we would rally.

We were dropped off and the platoon leader walked with us. We made it 20 minutes when we had to cross a canal. It wasn't too wide but was filled with 2 feet of standing water. With a running start, one-by-one, we leapt over it. It was easier said than done with all the gear we had. The platoon leader ran and jumped but he didn't have the smoothest of landings. He dislocated his shoulder in the process. Tyler jumped across and helped him pop it into the socket. While adjusting his shoulder into place though, he disconnected his radio tie-down. The radio fell into the tall grass. It took us 30 minutes to find that thing.

During this, I got a call saying the RG-31 was stuck and they would need to call for a wrecker to tow it out. Beautiful. We got it together and humped for hours, scaling fences, crawling underneath vegetation. We were walking along a creek bed when a white light came from out of the bushes. I crouched. It was a few feet away from me. Easy does it. It didn't see me. Tension. Everyone fell into firing positions. Challenge. Response.

Turned out after we got the interpreter to talk, the individuals on the other side of the hedgerow were our friends, the white light owner—my buddy, Hughes. We cracked a few jokes and made a few jabs before moving on.

Our section got to the rallying spot first. We called for extraction but found out that when the wrecker crew was towing it out, the earth gave way and flipped the RG-31 on its side. It was floating in a canal—or at least laying on its side in the muck. The two dudes inside of it were banged around with some bruises to their extremities and pride.

Since that was our ride out, we established a security halt to wait for words on how we were going to get home. Nothing.

We sat there from 4am to 11am. It was rough, over 100 degrees, little remaining water, tired, concealed but with little cover, tempers flared before we got transportation to the accident site.

We had to hang out and work on the RG problem before hitching a ride. They pulled it out with the help of a colossal M88 wrecker, but a guy got his hand caught in the crane, which chewed it up something awful. I was running hard for a good 28 hours, but when it came time to sleep, I crashed hard.

Driving the RG-31—a South African vehicle built with sheets of bulletproof glass with portholes that would burst eardrums if you shot through them—was tricky business down narrow winding roads of dirt that gave way constantly. Before the days of the MRAP, or Mine-Resistant Ambushed Protected, or the answer to some of the HMMWV issues, we used this behemoth of a vehicle to insert squad-level elements into areas without manning additional vehicles.

It came with risk though. It was heavy, and as light infantry, most of us weren't used to driving HMMWVs, let alone the RG-31, which was twice the size. Accidents were going to happen. The earth along a canal gave way that night, and the truck slipped into the brown waters of the ditch. We were sunk.

Several kilometers south of their position, we waited. The night sky dissolved, and the sun greeted the day with spits of fire. The Baghdad morning commute came to life despite the heat. Our radio was at the limit of its range of reception, and we were bordering a busy two-lane road intersection. The location had been planned as our extraction point for pickup at 0400 when the route was dark and void of traffic. With the RG-31 overturned, we were stranded without a ride, little water, and exposed, concealed by a thin line of vegetation a few arm's lengths from a busy road.

169

We held there after receiving word that our ride was soon to come, but those estimates were impacted by a multitude of difficulties that included the wrong type of recovery vehicle initially being dispatched. The temperature rose as did our tempers, but all you can do is maintain the faith and monitor the situation.

The bonus to having a radio is that you have a higher degree of awareness. Even more so, you feed decision makers information so they can relay guidance. As I threw out my long-whip antenna, I heard the chatter from the convoys going to and from the accident site, giving me an idea of what they were facing. It was apparent this was not a short operation. Facing water supply issues and knowing it was a matter of time before somebody walked into or by our position, we had a choice, and the platoon leader knew it. We either sat and waited in the heat after a long night's march, moved into a better position, or proceeded towards the RG-31 recovery site. All options had risk. Surrounded by several NCOs, the debate began.

Tyler, one of my closest friends and confidants, had little problem speaking up and interrupting when he thought the time called for it. He was passionate and an adept soldier. Tall, athletic, and a crack shot, he got picked first if you lined up for teams. We had trained together at Fort Campbell, so I understood how he operated. When I scooted over to the platoon leader to give him an update, Tyler wanted to make sure the situation was clear. He artfully insisted we articulate that our risk was not being prioritized over the overturned vehicle, a situation that wasn't going to improve anytime soon. That was true, and the PL acknowledged as much but had orders to sit tight.

The only problem with that was we were in a terrible position. A single grenade from a passing car could ruin our day. He turned to me, sweating it out with the radio, for some informal counsel. As a young enlisted soldier, you did not amount to much outside of a warm, fleshy trigger puller, and I was there to follow orders, not influence them. It was time, though, to speak my truth calmly and clearly. I explained that with the intermittent radio reception and the potential injuries at the accident site, we needed to take the risk and at least move. He agreed.

We busted out the map and looked for better concealment or cover. The platoon leader pointed out a position as if he already knew what we were going to do before he had asked us. He nodded, first at me, then at a satisfied Tyler before crawling over to inform the accompanying NCOs.

We moved out, crossing a road one-by-one and diving into a defilade between a few houses before making our way into an orchard. Tired, hot, and parched, it was one of those times we were thankful for the rigorous conditioning and physical training our leaders demanded. Scurrying under the thick leafy cheese grater of sunlight and shade, I felt that I had the opportunity to voice my concerns, even though the platoon leader appeared to have already made a decision. He empowered others.

The stress was as palpable as our growing thirst. It had been a long night, and it promised to be a longer morning. That said, the PL had given us a chance for buy-in, to become part of the process, and express our points of view. It was a lesson I have carried with me since. Without conceding his authority, he vested in his junior leaders and diffused any tension. It was a sign of respect to allow us the chance to be part of the discourse and not dismissive of our inputs. I was thankful to be a part of that team, even if there were few worthwhile options.

May 27, 2006 –

I went out to gun for our Fire Support Officer, Lieutenant Slaughter*. I spent the whole night in the turret, sweating like I was in a sauna. We cruised through a neighborhood north of Salman Pak, called Wardiya. It looked rough. Burned out hulks of Iraqi Police trucks littered the streets, spent bullet casings freckled the earth, and other scars of battle pocked the masonry. What has been going on here?

As soon as we turned into the main road through the village, people began slipping away into their houses. One kid threw a brick at me, striking me in the helmet before running away. I shook it off, and I scanned like a laser for every little asshole peeking around the corners. I'm not sure what I would've done once I spotted one, but a brick? C'mon, man.

We circled the wagons outside of a mosque and engaged with some local leaders. The Mahdi Army has moved into the area and is targeting the Sunnis of this mixed neighborhood. Insurgents are also crossing the river to fight the police and target civilians. Locals are not happy with our level of protection, which, judging by the scenery, I can't blame them.

At this point, the deployment was getting a bit routine, going on patrol and coming back to do the same thing the next day or so. Although no mission was ever the same, they carried the same tone, waiting for the enemy to attack. That is a dangerous way to think as monotony breeds complacency, the silent killer. You

---

*Four years later, Captain Garrett Slaughter was evacuated from Afghanistan to Walter Reed National Military Medical Center where he died of complications from a brain injury.

want to take it day-by-day, but you also need to give your attention to the objective.

I continued to patrol the same area seeing the same things. I could notice a rock out of place, which gave me an added sense of security. I couldn't help but think the enemy was conditioning us, hoping we would become apathetic or lethargic while on patrol. For most of us, it was not an issue of boredom. It was an issue of being tired. I was tired. I was ready to take a break.

My block leave crept onto the radar. I was more than excited to go home. As an energetic twenty-one-year-old, I was most concerned with buying my first beer and hitting the town. I had heard the stories from other fellows who had been home. I was anxious to have a few of my own. I contacted my best friend from my hometown and told him I would be home soon. He assured me he would throw a kegger "in my honor."

Despite the Groundhog Day feel of our operations, I was not sure if I was ready to be taken away from the family I had here. I didn't want the mission to continue and not be there to help out. I felt guilty. We all shared that sentiment in one way or another, but there was not a damn thing we could do about it. The orders were to go recuperate. Closing in on seven months deployed, when the time came, I packed and headed out, hoping the family would be the same when I returned.

June 10, 2006 –

I was prepared and packed, waiting while the rest of the guys were raiding a location where the troops were ambushed in the early hours of the day. There were no casualties, but I had a remorseful feeling while waiting for the helicopter at the LZ. I wanted to be there. I wanted to go home. I was torn. I sat waiting for my ride, listening to gunshots surrounding the base. It was that time, let freedom ring.

1st Squadron, 61st Cavalry, 506th Infantry Regiment, 101st Airborne Division at Camp Virginia, Kuwait. Comanche Company is center of the formation.

Comanche Company at FOB Rustamiyah

The view of Route Pluto from the Paint Factory

Jisr Diyala and the sewage pooling in the streets

Tyler on the gun while DeLay scans for targets on top of the Baathist resort hotel

The Al-Huda Husseiniya mosque in Jisr Diyala as seen from a turret

Tuwaitha Nuclear Complex in the heart of our AO

Jeff taking a breather

The author

Schrader (left) and Notaro (right)

Sorbello

Burns

Moving toward an objective along the Tigris River

Jisr Diyala and the riot as seen from a guard tower overlooking Main Street towards the market

Author's photo of the gate to Rustamiyah from the last patrol of the deployment

Part of the reunion crowd at the museum

June 12 to July 2, 2006 –

Home. Enjoyed it. All good things come to an end, and I had to return to Iraq. I'm not sure a part of me ever left.

Catching a UH-60 Blackhawk helicopter ride to Baghdad International Airport, or BIAP for short, I soon found myself sitting around the terminal waiting for a plane to take me to Kuwait. At the sprawling airbase, there were many other soldiers being shuttled to and from the many American installations around Iraq or rotating to the United States.

I ran into a couple of buddies I knew from other battalions. In particular, I met a friend of mine, Dobbins. Before my time in Comanche, he and I were in the same squad in Second Battalion. It wasn't until one early morning while doing pull-ups that I got solicited for a position in the brigade scouts. I asked how my old squadmates were doing, particularly my friend, Buckley—who I was disappointed wasn't on leave with us since we grew up only a few minutes' car ride from each other. He reported they were well and told me that he would relay my greetings.

Dobbins also told me that his company commander was to replace my CO around the beginning of July. It was news to me. I was less than enthused with the update. I had grown to admire our company commander but understood it was inevitable to change leadership. We'd swap out first sergeants in the summer as well, adding another significant loss to the feeling of team.

Dobbins and I waited for our next ride and debated the future of Iraq, changing topics after thirty seconds. We watched people scurry around the flight line and took turns predicting travelers' occupations by the condition of their uniforms and gear, which was a more enjoyable way to pass the time.

Together, we caught a C-17 flight to the dusty emptiness of Kuwait. From there, we flew a 16-hour commercial hop to the motherland, stopping in Ireland and landing in Atlanta, where we would chill in the USO until our connecting flight to our final destination.

Leaving Dobbins to head home, I flew from Georgia into my small local airport. On the plane, no passenger dared to ask me anything, not a word. I am sure they smelled the glory of a few days without a shower. We descended towards our destination and broke out of the cloud deck. I looked out the window, amazed at the emerald cornfields. The Midwest is forgettable to many, but to me, that day, it was the most beautiful shade of green I'd ever seen.

The airplane taxied into the terminal. I grabbed my assault bag usually filled with ammunition and a radio, now carrying a shaving kit and extra socks, and walked towards the front of the airport. Rounding a corner, I could see my mother, my grandfather, and more extended family. They held a banner that said 'Welcome Home' and I couldn't help but feel a bit sheepish. It was a nice gesture, but the fanfare made me uncomfortable.

We walked out to the parking lot, and it was apparent that Mom had had a tough time saying no. The vehicle was crammed full of people. I squeezed in the back of my aunt's sport-utility vehicle without complaint. I didn't mind. I felt like I was getting ready to ride out of the FOB in the back of the RG-31. I scanned the road like I was doing just that.

On leave, I visited as many people as I could. I'd come across people who knew little of what was happening across the world, and they'd ask how it was. I'd answer in general terms to end the discussion of the topic and move the conversation along to more pleasant things. Besides, I doubt anyone wanted to know. It wasn't so horrible I couldn't mention it, it was just that I didn't know how to chat about it without sounding uncaring or cold—not a characteristic that lends itself to being the life of the party. I spent time with my mother and father, even squeezed in a trip to my grandparents' farm.

It was there that I sat watching the local news with my grandpa, the after-dinner tradition. The newscaster started the evening's stories by announcing a soldier from the area had been killed in action. I sat there with a sense of disbelief as they read the name: Corporal Ryan Buckley. I was unsure of how to react. Nobody said a word. I stood up and walked outside when the time was right. It was calm with a warm summer breeze. The sounds of the farm reminded me I was safe.

Although I was 7,000 miles away, the war wasn't far from me. It was surreal. My mother called out, asking if I wanted pie. I took a deep breath and rejoined my family to make the most of our time. In a few days, I would have to go be a part of the storylines I watched unfold on the news from the safety and comfort of my grandparents' living room.

Before I knew it, with some great memories in tow, I was loading onto a plane destined for the Middle East and a war that, for many, only existed on television. Stopping in Atlanta, I walked into the USO. I found friends I'd journeyed with a couple of weeks earlier and we set about wagering the number of hours until we were patrolling the streets of Iraq.

Not long after, Dobbins strode into the lounge. He took a seat next to us, and we waited to hop on our flight to Kuwait. Knowing he was returning to Second Battalion and without much thought, I told him I was sorry about Buck. His eyebrows wrinkled. I felt a sinking feeling in my stomach. He hadn't known.

The communication blackout had limited anybody from informing him. Ryan was in his squad, in his own fire team, as intimate as soldiers can get. Delivering the news of his death made me feel shameful. Not that there is any good way to break bad news, but doing so at the airport right before our return flight stung of heartlessness.

Dobbins looked as if he was swallowing his emotions, so we walked onto the balcony overlooking the hundreds of passengers hustling along in their travels. I apologized, and in silence we watched the travelers meander through the terminal, oblivious to the prices being paid halfway around the world. Dobbins shook his head in disbelief, mentioning that he'd had a bad feeling when he left. There were no tears. We knew what was to come.

Then, we did what soldiers do—we put it behind us and continued mission. At that moment, that meant getting on a plane and going to combat, knowing that the fate of Ryan Buckley could be ours as well. Returning to BIAP and the war, Dobbins and I shook hands, caught helicopter rides to our forward operating bases, and prepared ourselves for war. I never saw him again.

May 29, 2016 –

Notaro's truck made the sharp turn, tires shrieking, into the battalion parking lot right outside the headquarters building. He pulled his lifted 4x4 into the vacant commander's parking spot, throwing it into park as the tires nudged the concrete parking barrier. He hopped out and took a few strides to the entrance pathway walking with a sense of purpose and conviction. I pulled into the spot next to him, looked at Kat with a raised eyebrow, and climbed out to see what his hard-charging entrance was about.

"Explain this!" Notaro knife handed the ground. "Where the hell are the stones?" He looked around as if somebody knew where they had been moved. In fact, the most sobering thing concerning our arrival was that the sign identifying the current tenants to the buildings was no longer 4th Brigade Combat Team, no longer the Currahees, no longer our squadron. It was some unit unknown to us. Our history was fading not only with the memorial markers' removal but our absence from the training grounds we had dominated years ago. This used to be Currahee country, and today it is owned by another unit.

Jeff walked to him. "Well, things are changing."

"No, man, no." Notaro puffed. "You don't just remove these things."

"What do you do with them, Frank?" Jeff asked. To hear Jeff call him by his first name, a former senior NCO, cut to the core of Notaro. Jeff had used his name to redirect his anger. It didn't work. Notaro's face hardened.

We recognized the scowl that gave way to sharp, widening eyes as if he wanted to spear his words into Jeff. The vigor to which we had grown accustomed while serving alongside him had returned. For some reason, it was welcomed. It was Notaro as we knew him, as he was remembered, as if he was in uniform standing outside headquarters. We felt a familiar feeling. At that moment, it was if we could sense Zayas' tough veneer hiding his gregarious underbelly or Weirs' tight cropped haircut as he stood at parade rest, making him look every bit the soldier but hinting at his country-boy approachability. We were back.

But they weren't there; neither were their granite monuments, and that pissed off Notaro. "You give the monuments to the community, the family, the damn base museum, Jeff," he said.

Jeff nodded. These were options he hadn't considered when engaging Notaro. "Well, we can hope they went to one of those."

Kat stepped behind me, and I felt her non-kinetic nudge to speak. "Their names are listed at the Currahee Iraq monument at the museum, for what it's worth," I said.

"Not good enough." Notaro turned and marched into the headquarters. "I gotta know, man." Ignorant of what he was planning, Jeff, Burns, Kat and the rest of the reunion followed him to investigate. He swung open the double doors and stepped to a counter behind which three young soldiers sat on staff duty with eyes glazed over. They jumped, startled by the clamorous entrance of a fiery gray-bearded retiree. We had prearranged our visit, but it wouldn't have mattered—his entrance was jarring.

"Can we, can we help you guys?" The nervous NCO out front challenged the visitors. The three soldiers stood, not knowing the protocol when addressing a crowd of retirees, veterans, and the like. They put down their spit bottles for the tobacco they weren't supposed to have and gave us their full attention. They hoped to give us what we needed so they could return to their staff duty malaise. But what we were looking for, they couldn't give.

"Gentlemen, let me ask you this question." Notaro leaned into the counter, resting both hands shoulder-width apart, ready in case he needed to hop over to investigate further. "Where the hell are the granite memorial stones this dude right here dug holes to place ten years ago?" Notaro asked, pointing to me.

I laughed at the absurdity. "How would they know?" I offered to deflect. Notaro may as well have asked an employee at the Post Exchange where the stones were.

"Who's the battalion commander?" Notaro asked. They answered. "Write it down, please," he ordered, even though the name hung on a placard in the front of the building and in front of his parked truck. "Look, gentlemen, these guys here..." He waved his hand across the group that was busy examining the pictures on the walls, the war trophies behind glass, and the awards plastered in the hallways, none of which contained the word 'Currahee.'

"These guys are veterans from the unit that was here before you. We trained in these hallways and classrooms, humped to these ranges, and went to war from these buildings." Notaro leaned back. "We lost guys over there. Two guys had granite stones in the ground outside with their names on them. I want to make sure they went somewhere they would have appreciated, y'know?"

"Roger that," the staff duty NCO said. "They haven't been out front since I've been here."

"That's what I'm afraid of," Notaro said. He took the small paper with a name he didn't intend to call and jammed it into his pocket. He stepped from the counter. "You gotta look out for your guys, man. Gotta make sure they get the right recognition. No matter what."

I peeled my eyes from a plaque listing soldiers I didn't recognize winning awards I hadn't heard of. "We have," I muttered.

"How so, man?"

"Our guys are going to forever be a part of the Fort Campbell museum," I answered. The group rallied around the counter, completing their inspection. "People will see their names as they come to visit and learn the division history. Their names will greet them, 'Blood does not define brothers.'" I slapped Notaro on the back.

"Neither does a stone sitting outside some other battalion. These guys wouldn't take care of our brothers the same way we would." Jeff extended his hand. "No offense."

The NCO shrugged, not debating the accuracy of the statement.

"Damn, man," Notaro said. He calmed and resigned to reality. "I'm glad we got those bricks. We need to record that history, and those guys are a huge part of it."

"Without a doubt," I said. "We've made sure people will know them."

"That's it, man," Notaro admitted. "People are going to forget what happened, like what we did."

"Nobody is going to forget anything," Eric charged. "It's if we learn from it that matters." The staff duty soldiers behind the counter fell back into their cheap office chairs. Eric cracked open the door. "Let's go."

"Let's move!" said Kat. She charged out, hoping to lead the posse and break the tension to coax the event along.

"A beer sounds pretty good." Sorbello smirked and followed Kat's lead. "Enjoy the staff duty, boys!"

Jeff, Eric, and the rest flowed outside. I waited to grab the door from Eric to lead Notaro to the exit.

"Yeah, thanks for helping us out," Notaro said. "Take care of yourselves."

"No problem, sir," the NCO said. Confident that they were relieved, I smiled at the soldiers from a different decade doing the same work we had done a few years before.

"Don't call me sir," Notaro uttered as he walked out the door to rejoin the reunion. We found out a year later the stones had made it to the families of the fallen.

July 3, 2006 –

Just returned from mid-tour leave, and we're heading out. It was like I hadn't left. The mission is another OP set on Route Corn, the route north of Jisr Diyala along the river, which turned into a hot spot while I was gone. Ambushes, IEDs, the enemy had even blown up a building our team had used the night before hoping to degrade our surveillance site availability.

We got to an orchard on the northwest side of Jisr Diyala, un-assed the RG-31, and ran for a piece of cover before taking a knee. I heard a rip. Son of a gun. My pants split from the groin to the knee. Unreal. I must have enjoyed mid-tour leave. We snaked into position. It was going to be a long night and morning with a cool breeze without any underwear.

We watched a few guys on a rooftop across the Diyala River. A house at our twelve o'clock was circled with dogs. The tenant, frustrated with the barking hounds, came out and shot a dog in the middle of the night. No doubt, the dogs were barking at us hidden a short 100 meters away from their house. Poor dog.

The new company commander, the one Dobbins informed me of, tagged along. I'm sure he was evaluating how we did our business. We humped through the orchard, looking for exfiltration as the sun rose. Jumping creeks and breaking brush, we made it to the edge of the grove. The platoon giving us a ride home called, and they wanted to meet us in the market. My pants are ripped and it's daylight. Great. I did the best I could to avoid an international incident. We loaded into the RG-31 and headed to the FOB. Happy Independence Day!

I must have enjoyed a bit of gluttony over my R&R. My pants had had enough. After dismounting from the vehicle, I took a knee, and my pants ripped right along the seam. Not wearing underwear has its benefit, but in this situation, I would've welcomed a good pair of briefs.

I crept through the orchard, paying careful attention to the wait-a-minute vines and branches to avoid a surprise stab. Soon enough, we made it to a small clearing and determined that we had a decent enough position in some thicker foliage ahead. I whispered to my teammates that I was exposed. They were puzzled. I pointed to my rip. They chuckled in a quiet, sniper team hiding in the bush kind of way. Tyler toyed with his optics. He commented that things look smaller under night vision. I responded with the most professional sign language I knew.

The mission aside, the test was our exfiltration and recovery. Second platoon was in the Jisr Diyala market a kilometer or so away and requested we rendezvous as they patrolled the busy intersection. The morning market was abuzz with vendors and their shoppers. We emerged from the small orchard and formed into a wedge formation. My rifle was slung low and I risked a slower reaction time, but the wound to my pants was covered. No Iraqi was shown the crown jewels, and we maintained the coalition status quo.

We made it to the market and climbed into the RG-31 with some other platoon members. Pulling away to return to FOB Rustamiyah, I proudly showed them my wounded pants. Everyone got a good laugh as the driver negotiated the traffic and the gunner yelled obscenities encouraging compliance. After spending a couple of weeks in the states, I was home. The laughter faded, and faces turned stern, scanning for signs of the enemy. With a strange sense of comfort, I fell into the seat and hoped we didn't hit a bomb.

July 4, 2006 –

Rolled to the company area after the patrol and got told to change and head to formation. I'm getting promoted. What a great way to celebrate the 4th of July!

Becoming a non-commissioned officer was, to me, a vote of confidence by the senior leadership about my abilities as a soldier and leader. The council of elders had met earlier to grill me on all things Army, all things infantry. The squadron's first sergeants gathered alongside a table with a single chair on the other side rapid firing questions designed to test my knowledge and ability to handle the pressure. I was motivated not by the pay and responsibility increase, but more so from the fear of letting them down. Somehow, they gave me a thumbs up. It was humbling.

With their blessing and some Army promotional accounting, I was pinned as a Sergeant a few months later. My peers and I took the charge seriously and knew the level of accountability and responsibility we assumed was extraordinary. The company had several approachable NCOs for me to draw lessons from, and I was fortunate to take advantage of their insight.

A few of us were promoted on the same day, the Fourth of July, including Davis, who stood next to me in line to receive our stripes. We stared out at the company formation with heavy bags under our eyes from the night before. The new CO led us off with a rousing speech on freedom followed by the first sergeant giving a talk on the origins of Independence Day. He described the Founding Fathers leading us through America's precarious first moments with the assistance of a few outstanding NCOs.

We moaned a dull Army groan and came to attention when the orders were read. Beaming with fraudulent motivation, we were dismissed. Davis and I marched off to celebrate with turkey bacon and eggs to show off our newly acquired chevrons to the Pakistani cooks. Walking back, we remarked on the significance of our promotion to one another. We were NCOs. We were tired.

5.
ASSAULT RIGHT DOWN

July 14, 2006 –

Tonight, I drove a truck in support of a dismounted patrol through a neighborhood east of Wild, across from Wardiya, called Ja'ara. We lumbered along Pluto and made it a few kilometers south of the Route Pluto bridge. BOOM. Call it, contact IED. I suppose the triggerman got nervous, or he didn't time it right because we got lucky. It blew a crater knee deep and tossed cement chunks across the street. It was bright and loud but misjudged, the center of it missing us by a few feet.

We got away with only minor damage to the trucks. We stopped and checked it out, called it higher, and continued to Ja'ara. The dudes dismounted to go patrol, and as a driver, I got to hang out, waiting to respond in case they got in a fight. They didn't. It was a pretty chill night.

July 15, 2006 –

We received a tip that insurgents were planning an attack on a neighborhood mosque. We formulated a plan and moved out. Cruising for a half hour, we soon negotiated the canal roads north of Jisr Diyala. One of the trucks manned by a mortar team got a flat tire. Great. We're stuck in Jisr Diyala while we fix the flat. We could have driven it out, but the platoon leader didn't want to risk the damage to the vehicle.

I disembarked and organized some security. As we sat collecting sweat by the quart, a sizable gunfight a few kilometers or so to our south kicked off. We couldn't maneuver on it but made a radio call to inform the operations center. It was Mahdi-related, but it was not at the mosque.

The tire was fixed, and we continued rolling towards our predetermined position. Once there, a crowd of people had gathered, infuriated about the firefight not far from the mosque. The group was worried, but we assured them the POB were taking care of business. 2nd platoon is doing what they can to make deals to keep this place calm, but it was tense. We needed to honor those agreements and needed to leave the area.

The truck started running rough and we pressed on to get out of Jisr Diyala before we were stranded there. These trucks are getting worked overtime. It's time to call it. Maneuvering our way onto the hardball road, we crept to the FOB where the truck coasted into the motor pool before dying. How lucky is that? Even more fortunate, no attack on the mosque.

Jisr Diyala developed into the worst part of our AO. It was a dense neighborhood of soft brick and plaster buildings stacked on top of each other. The mosque minarets dotted the skyline over houses that, at most, were two-stories, a couple of businesses had a third. Living spaces were compact.

The area was a geographic bomb of ethnic tensions, as the Shias and Sunnis were living on opposing riverbanks. The bridge that linked the two had a heavy police presence, but that did not stop the death squads from coming over to accomplish their gruesome missions.

Rolling out of the FOB, we traveled into the area and routinely met a volley of rocks, bricks, and trash. The constant threat of violence from a growing sectarian divide cultivated a sense of fear and spread the roots of resentment towards American forces. Even the most oblivious knuckle-dragger felt the tension.

Still, Jisr Diyala was home to a robust marketplace that lined the street right off the bridge. Our trucks hopped curbs, zigged around shoppers, and zagged around panhandlers hawking black market cigarettes. The men yelled at each other over the din of cars and motorbikes, while women carried large amounts of grain and produce over their heads, their eyes cautiously peeking out of their black burqas.

It was like a scene from a movie, but one crucial sense was missing. The smell here was overwhelming. The side streets contained puddles of sewage, the cooking, using whatever fuel available, was constant, and the fly-infested sliced-to-order goat meat hung from reconstituted rebar.

Compounded by the one-hundred-twenty-degree heat, the market was a menagerie of sights and sounds, amplified by a potent amalgamation of odors. The confluence of the Tigris and Diyala River was but a rifle shot away from the neighborhood. Everything met and mixed near the Jisr Diyala market, and the stench of violence was no different.

July 17, 2006 –

I volunteered as a gunner for a truck to the Jisr Diyala Neighborhood Advisory Council meeting. These shindigs are essentially a meeting between our bosses and local leaders to discuss the tragedies of the day. The convoy cruised through the market to check on the Iraqi police at the river checkpoint. It was all good, so we circled the wagons in the Tuwaitha parking lot.

In no time, we welcomed the inevitable arrival of local kids. They squeezed through holes in the fences as the leaders strolled out to conduct the meeting at the police station across the road. We joked around and handed out stuff to the kids. In an hour or so, the officers and senior NCOs returned and we packed it in for the FOB.

On Route Pluto, the Iraqi Police flagged us down and showed us a cache they had found. It turned out they had watched some guys go into a junk pile and leave. They went to go see what they were looking at and found a dozen rocket rounds. I was not sure why they let them just walk away if they were suspect. We made it to the FOB without incident.

Later that afternoon, sometime around 1430 or so, I heard an explosion in the distance. WAM! A rocket landed 5 meters outside my room. I jumped out of my chair and crawled to the other side of the room. I heard the cries for a medic and went outside to a crowd gathered around some dudes laying on the ground. Their wounds weren't too severe, and they got fixed up and hauled off to the aid station. Later that night, another indirect fire attack and another casualty.

Indirect fire became a sport, a dangerous game. You have zero control over where it lands, so we developed the attitude that it was like a game show. Like a demented type of Plinko, drop a mortar or Katyusha rocket and let it bounce through a series of nails into your position. If you won, your prize was not a welcomed one—it was death, or serious injury. We were a giant target, and the skies rained indirect fire so often that we were conditioned to the falling metal. It was hard enough to stop the munitions from making it into the city, let alone prevent their launch.

Still, we dipped, we dodged, we ducked, we played the game waiting for it to impact. Once it hammered home, our faces contorted sometimes followed by a maniacal laugh covering any comprehension of what was happening. The dust settled. We opened doors and came running to see if anybody had won the game and needed help with their prize. The steel rain was drenching us in apathy. We did our best to find and kill those responsible, with some success, but many times the attackers fled unmolested.

It was aggravating. These weren't targeted artillery fire or coordinated mortar attacks by trained professionals—a much more frightening scenario—but rather, these were attacks so wild and unpredictable that we complained about them as a nuisance. The falling, haphazard projectile was not controlled, so we grabbed some cover and knew that just because it impacted 200 meters away doesn't mean the next one wasn't drilling you a nice new hole in your head.

Control was an illusion and exerting substantial energy towards what you cannot control led us to walk the FOB with a tinge of lunacy. The leadership knew this. When we got a decent point of origin, the brass would unleash the hounds and we'd improve our condition, but never control it. Often, the next round of indirect fire struck minutes after we made it to the base. It was a cat and mouse game, and instead of spending our time chasing them around the house, our energy was best spent finding out how they made it out of the barn in the first place.

July 19, 2006 –

The sniper teams headed out to do a mission near the Tigris in one of the towers surrounding the Tuwaitha complex. We crept there in a slow, near idle crawl, weaving through the Tuwaitha checkpoint on the outskirts of Jisr Diyala.

When we climbed the tower, there were some Iraqi dudes at the top and with Bob, the interpreter, we had us a nice little chat about the situation, living conditions, the Jisr Diyala neighborhood, and so forth. They decided they weren't going to hang out with us anymore, so they gathered their guns and walked to a shack off the road 50 meters away.

We spent the rest of the night harassing each other when the call came to pull off. Nothing happened all night, not even a few gunshots in the distance. It was disturbingly serene.

Huddled in the tower that night, with Bob translating our conversations, we got to know more about the Iraqi Police. It was easy to make them scapegoats when things were not progressing satisfactorily. Challenging their commitment was effortless. But it wasn't easy to understand them, to see things through their lens, to appreciate the tremendous sacrifice they and their families were making to improve their lives and the lives of their countrymen.

As dirty of a word as empathy is in the infantry, I empathized with them. They told us of how they wanted peace in the country, how some nefarious individuals had penetrated their ranks and committed evil, how they struggled when they discovered their enemy was their neighbor. Their lives had crumbled since 2003, and three years later, they continued to live in a warzone.

For most volunteers in the national police force or the Iraqi Army, chances were pretty high that they would be killed executing their duties. They sat in exposed guard shacks along the highways, easy pickings for the insurgency and militias, and did so with inadequate training compared to American standards.

As a result, and in conjunction with a complicated web of cultural influences, they often refused many offensive actions and deferred to the American military because of our technologic advantage, our equipment, our logistics, and most importantly, our warrior culture divorced from their tribalism and religious intricacies. More often than not, we obliged but took them by the hand to help them progress towards an independent military and police force. Although they didn't fight like us, they were our partners.

Guys like Bob, our terps, were a central part of this partnership and were significant targets for the enemy. Our success and combat capabilities depended upon our interpreter's ability to communicate back and forth between the Iraqi military, police, civilians, and coalition forces. Without them, the cultural and language barriers were insurmountable. We learned much from them and I respected them for their service.

Bob was killed in Iraq not long after our departure, being tortured and murdered for his involvement with American military. His death was unfortunate, but tragically not unique. Interpreters and other civilians who aided our efforts, and by extension the efforts of their nation, many times met gruesome ends at the hands of a ruthless enemy. As they climbed down from the tower, I watched through my night vision the dozen Iraqi policemen move to their next position, wondering how many of them might survive this war, if any.

May 29, 2016 –

After standing in the company area at Fort Campbell reminiscing about being late to formation, the resulting remedial physical training smoke sessions, the general one-person-poops-we-all-wear-the-diaper-approach to military discipline, we were ready to head to Nashville to the reunion proper.

"This was home," I told Kat. "This was where we became a sort of family."

"Was Notaro the dad?" she joked.

"More like a crazy uncle." I laughed.

"I heard that shit, Paul!" Notaro said as we worked our way into the parking lot and to our waiting vehicles. Notaro's truck still sat in the battalion commander's spot. "We'll see you there, man." I gave Notaro a quick wave and we split up.

In a sort of convoy, we hit the road and headed for the main gate, peeled onto Route 41 to Interstate 24 and the 45-minute drive to our hotel. Arriving there, we had an hour or so before we would rendezvous at the Veterans of Foreign Wars Post, a short drive from our lodging. While the others hung out resting from our busy morning, I cleaned up and collected the diaper box with war mementos.

"Think you're going to let others have a look?" Kat asked, referencing the journal.

"I'm nervous," I answered. I leaned over, fishing it out of the box packed away in a corner. I flipped open a page to a picture of me holding a foam dart shotgun my brother had sent me during the deployment. I had used it to clear the command post of red-eyed soldiers on duty in the earliest hours of the morning. "I don't want to let anyone down."

"What are you talking about?"

"Well, you heard Notaro," I said. "I don't want to let anyone down. Sharing my perspective on these missions makes me worry that others think I'm too sentimental or think I'm too soft."

"Since when have you ever worried what others thought of you?" Kat said as she brushed her teeth. "Ya n'ver 'ave before," she said without removing the toothbrush.

I deciphered her speech. "These guys are different. They set the bar high."

"No." She spat into the sink. "You set the bar high. These guys could care less."

"Let me explain." I stood and stretched out my arms. "There is this unwritten rule. You don't seek the limelight…"

"Stop." She pointed her toothbrush at me. "You think this is about you? What's in those pages is the story of all of you.

Yeah, through your eyes and your pen, but it ain't your story. They were there too, y'know. They were a part of the same stuff, witness to the same story. Take a chance, share the pages, and others will share theirs. It'd do somebody some good."

I sighed and returned the journal to the box. Kat made a point, but it didn't help. I felt that my perspective wouldn't do justice to the soldiers of company C, the Comanches. The tribe's acceptance meant much to me. The journal presented an obstacle, and I struggled to even acknowledge why it was a hurdle for me to share the story that they knew anyway.

There was no need to tip-toe around it like I had been doing for years since returning from Iraq, but it was like some sort of default reaction I fell into any time the topic surfaced. I could tell a story or two, but I couldn't describe to anyone what it felt like or meant to me personally—Kat and the Comanches included.

Pressed for time, we made our way to the VFW. Opening the door, we entered with soft, timid footsteps, heading in the direction of television sounds from another room behind a set of propped open double doors.

"Well, 'ello, darling," the bartender said, welcoming us in. "That's your room behind you." She pointed to the room we had entered. "We are excited to have y'all this evening."

"We are excited too," I said. "Do you mind if we move some tables around?"

She didn't have any problem with it, so Kat began shuffling about. Shortly, Jeff and Kara entered the room, exchanged greetings, and joined in, pushing tables around and adding chairs where they were needed.

"This tall one should be set right here," I said, holding a tall table for a centerpiece. "I got those pictures of the memorial photos you guys brought. They'll be placed front and center." I went over to the box and pulled out photographs of two of our fallen—Zayas and Weir—and set them on the tall table in the middle of the ballroom's stage.

"Rightfully so," Jeff said. His gaze locked on to the pictures before sinking to the floor.

"The grog will go there." I pulled one opposite of Jeff's table. "I got the mementos to put here."

"Fantastic."

I pulled out some of the old newsletters from the deployment and stacked them on the table. A copy of the Meritorious Unit Citation signed by General Petraeus recognizing our contributions to the fight that year, a Fort Campbell courier paper writing about one of our missions, and a few photographs evened out the spread. I propped a few letters on the picture frames—one from the first company commander, another from my former platoon leader, both unable to attend. Another message was from our old squadron commander wishing us a proper and memorable reunion. All of it was intended to stir discussion of times we shared.

"That's it." I scanned the table and took a long breath. I kneeled, reached into the box, and grabbed the last conversation piece: the journal. Jeff stepped behind me. "I was unsure if I was going to put this thing out for you guys to thumb through, but Kat talked me into it."

"What is that?" Jeff inquired.

"It's my journal from the deployment. Stupid little notes after the patrols we went on. Every patrol and my reactions to them, I guess."

"Dude, you kidding me?" Jeff asked with a hint of surprise. "I didn't realize you brought it. That's amazing. The guys will love it."

"I'm skeptical." I remained unconvinced.

"I know so. Look, man, it's been ten years. It's time we reflected, and this thing will help. We can let the armchair quarterbacks write the stories of the politicians and generals and stuff, but the average dude on the ground, that was us and..." Jeff pointed to the journal. "This was us. We executed the same patrols. Don't keep the history to yourself."

"My concern is that sharing my views, we'd disagree or that my experiences don't measure up." I stopped talking and digested my words. I was searching for validation of my role in the tribe, that I had served the team well. Or maybe I was coming to terms that I had left the Comanches but never joined another tribe stuck in some sort of societal purgatory. Or even worse, had I learned the wrong lessons? Maybe warriors were not supposed to envisage life after combat. Maybe once you're a warrior, you will always be a warrior. And maybe that's fine.

Unlike our missions, after which we discussed how to perform a better bounding overwatch or use better communication, we hadn't held a personal after-action review or debrief of the deployment when we returned and certainly didn't discuss how our time deployed fit in the overall picture of the Iraq campaign. We spoke in generalities. We received medals sometimes contentiously awarded. We got some badges and a combat patch that declared us warriors. We got the shiny things that said we went to war but we didn't get the things that matter most. We didn't get that it was okay to be uncertain about the whole thing, that it was okay to shed your armor and look on it not with a sense of nostalgia but with reflection. It was okay to turn experience into insight.

"Leave the damn thing out for the guys to look through and you'll see that they will appreciate it." Jeff grabbed the journal and put it on the table. "You'll see."

Kat, hearing the conversation while placing chairs around tables, yelled from across the room, "I told you so!" I set the pages in a spot off to the side and prepared for a night of revisited memories.

July 22, 2006 –

Davis and I were put in charge of a truck while the other team conducted an observation mission. I volunteered to drive. This was the first patrol that I had forgotten my good luck charm. We cruised to the intersection of Wall Street and Pluto and positioned ourselves north of the traffic circle.

It got dark and we moved to park alongside a bunch of scrap metal outside a shop. We unloaded the team for their mission. They infiltrated towards their position and, on their way to the target house, they found some 60mm mortar rounds.

After finishing that, they arrived at the house and discovered a group of squatters inside. These Iraqis are part of an increasing exodus from areas rife with sectarian violence. They spent the night dealing with them and looking for bad guys. A whole lot of activity was going on across the river with the other units doing sweeps looking for the enemy.

We chased after some guys but lost them in the pursuit, so we chilled out. How bizarre this whole thing is. We are so removed from our other lives here. The clock struck 6, so we met our compatriots and crawled to the FOB. Mission complete. I was relieved to return to my little four-leaf clover pendant.

Superstitions were indeed a part of our time in Iraq. There was comfort in doing a little ritual or having a lucky charm that stayed constant. Few other things remained so. Whether it was a piece of home, a religious trinket, a photo, or some other knick-knack that provided luck or a sense of fortune, we had our own ways of dealing with our future outside the wire. For many, it was a repetitive thought or action.

Rolling to the headquarters and getting the latest from the intelligence personnel on duty, our team leaders spewed out a brief of our objectives, and we'd mount up to conduct the mission. In our own little ways, we prepared. As we locked it on and rolled out the steel gate through the Hesco Barriers and concertina wire, I'd grab a little pendant given to me and tell myself that whatever happened, happened. Accept it. It was brazenness bordering ignorance, but that's what I told myself.

Then, depending on my position within the convoy, I'd charge the M240B machine gun or otherwise ready myself for the job at hand. For some reason, the ritual of grabbing the small pendant and saying the words, regardless of how I left the base, brought solace to me while simultaneously feeding my ferocity.

With our peace made, the gun trucks hopped over a bridge outside the base to greet the constant swarm of Baghdad traffic. I adopted the most intimidating posture possible and swung the turret around pointing a machine gun to part the sea of taxis and jingle trucks. We were rolling targets and needed to maintain a safe separation for mutual reasons. They didn't get blown up next to us and we didn't get blown up by a car bomb. Keeping the traffic away protected all of us, and so did my pendant.

July 24, 2006 –

Neighboring units are continuing their sweeps across the river, so we positioned ourselves by the Tigris around Route Gator to see if we could catch anybody attempting to flee. We rolled to Wild and backtracked alongside the riverbank. We dismounted after we found a suitable house to occupy.

With the three of us at it again, DeLay, Davis, and I crept around the house to find a way in. I did. It was a window. I climbed some metal bracing on the exterior of the building and held on to a pipe to lower myself into the building. Once in, I realized I was alone. I listened and scanned the industrial-looking room. It had to be some sort of pump room. I whispered an all clear, and the guys followed.

We cleared the rest of it, made it to the top floor, set some trip flares, and hung out. The other team was having some problems finding a hide site with a suitable field of view. They were lounging in some bushes, waiting for the sun to retreat to continue movement.

It soon came across the radio that they had been compromised. A local national with an AK-47 had stumbled upon them. When confronted, Wright snatched the AK from the flabbergasted old man. They escorted him to his house and questioned him.

Across the river, the area-denial artillery was intense with the King of Battle dumping shells into a location across the river. It was a kilometer away, and it shook the cement building we were hiding in. We felt it in our chests. Friendly targeted artillery—I wouldn't want to be on the other side of that. I'll take the insurgent and rocket fire any day. We pulled off at midnight and met the other team that had made a friend.

Risk has its rewards. Startling the old man who was unsure of who was by the river, Wright grabbed the rifle from him. Instead of viewing him as an insurgent and ending the discussion there, Wright opened a dialogue that led to the targeting of other insurgents in the area. Honor bound for sparing his life, the old man we called 'Farmer Joe' worked a deal to help identify members of the Mahdi Army he knew had infiltrated the area. We took it with a grain of salt, but it was a step in the right direction. In fact, dozens of other leads developed. The Mahdi were infiltrating much more than we had initially assessed and seemed poised to engage in extrajudicial killings of their Sunni neighbors in Wardiya and Ja'ara.

To his credit, Farmer Joe repaid his debt by risking his life and naming a dozen Mahdi fighters moving throughout the area.

The gamble with his and his family's lives to help the nation's security efforts was noteworthy. The sacrifice was great and penalty swift for those colluding with the Americans. Snatching that rifle may have led to snatching several enemy fighters. It may have even saved a score of Iraqi civilians. Still, as a Sunni, Farmer Joe gave up his Shia neighbors. We'd need more than sectarian angst to prosecute any targets he offered, but it was a start.

July 28, 2006 –

I had a day off. That was nice. Now, I'm back at it. This time to do what we thought was an OP of a route where two IEDs were found during the week. Little did we know, when we got a few hundred meters past the Route Pluto bridge, the squadron would call us to the FOB to escort a wrecker to 1st platoon. It turned out they had rolled a HMMWV.

We met the wrecker and its crew to accompany them to the rollover accident site. The driver of the half-sunk truck had run it off a small canal bridge and overturned it into a sinking still-water mire of muck containing the sewage from the nearby village. They survived with minor injuries. My old roommate, Oliver, was part of the crew. He was in the back seat and had a hell of a time getting out of the vehicle as it filled with water.

They escaped with no time to spare and scrambled for cover. The team was exposed for some time, being the last truck in the convoy, before being recovered by the remaining 1st platoon vehicles. We got the wrecker to the site right outside Wardiya, and within an hour or so they had the truck upright and out of the canal. While we were escorting the tow vehicle to the FOB, another call came to return to the scene so we could scour for any items lost in the rollover. This was the proverbial shit sandwich, and we're about to have a picnic.

Like so many things, at the heart of it, the accident was the result of miscommunication. The soldiers were driving blacked out, using their night-optics to navigate the narrow dirt roads off Route Wild. The platoon leader came across the radio directing them to turn their lights on once their truck crossed the bridge. Oliver's truck acknowledged this command, but the truck preceding them prematurely clicked on their lights, drowning out the night vision of the driver for a split second. With spotted, nebulous sight for the briefest amount of time as they made the turn onto the bridge, the driver steered toward the edge, and the cumbersome HMMWV had no problem rolling right off into the canal.

The rollover drills we practiced were effective. The gunner was not ejected from the overturned truck. In the foul water of that ditch containing the unfiltered excrement of the local villagers, the heavy up-armored vehicle sank deep in the filth. The driver and truck commander climbed out, and the gunner slithered out too, but disoriented and in the pitch black, Oliver was stuck as the rear passenger. He unsuccessfully attempted to work free the window and the heavy door. That would have been hard enough to do in the daylight, not to mention in the night as the truck filled with water. The truck commander, extending his saving grace of an arm, helped Oliver, who was breathing through a pocket of air, to safety.

Yet, that was not the end of their ordeal. The patrol was spaced out so that one IED could not attack two vehicles—a common tactic. When Oliver's truck overturned into the canal, it was out of view of the other HMMWVs in the convoy. The other vehicles continued north on Route Wild without noticing the submerging truck's absence. It was several minutes, when seconds counted, before a gunner noticed the missing HMMWV. They turned around and retraced their route looking for their teammates.

The stinking, drenched, and distraught guys had a few weapons between them in the middle of hostile territory, which was a situation they were familiar with but in this case, there was one critical difference: they had no radio.

Hoping no enemy took the opportunity to gather themselves a trophy, they opted to move towards an Iraqi Police position for assistance. It was a risk, but so was sitting exposed by the brown water of the canal. As precarious as the situation may have been, Oliver and his crew were recovered without another incident. The fun, oddly enough, was only beginning.

July 30, 2006 –

The engineers were called, and they brought in some heavy equipment to go to work on this ditch. The canal was dammed and a backhoe dug out the soil for us to sort amongst looking for sensitive items lost in the HMMWV accident. By sort, I mean walk through the mud with sticks to poke through it, hoping to strike a lost piece of equipment. We made our way out of the FOB after rotating security duty at the accident site.

Then, we were tasked with escorting the engineers to BIAP after we account for all the missing gear. We arrived three hours early and helped the platoons shift through the mud madness for another 6 hours. We sweat like it's our job before the last item was found. Everyone cheered as if we had struck shit-covered gold—but it's just a helmet with a set of night vision on it.

The engineers trailered their equipment, and we discussed with them our path to their home at Camp Victory—the sprawling base next to the airport. Making the turn onto Route Wall Street and cutting through Jisr Diyala, we were soon on Route Irish. It wasn't long before we came across an IED concealed in a dead dog. We pulled our convoy along an

*adjacent street able to see the bomb and waited for the
Explosive Ordinance Team.*

*Two engineer troops rode with us, and one of the
friendlier guys confessed to me that he was here to drive
bulldozers and backhoes, not deal with dead dog IEDs. I didn't
know how to respond, so I apologized on behalf of the enemy.
When the detonation happened, the engineers were startled. In
the following silence, we sat there feeling bad for the dog.*

*We rumbled on and, making it to Camp Victory, bid the
engineers farewell. Words from the squadron was that we were
to hang tight and carry some guys that were returning from
their mid-tour leave, so we had a few hours to kill. We
would've had to wait regardless due to an IED killing a dude
on Pluto closing our return route until it's declared safe for
transit.*

*With the time given to us, we got to eat fast food and visit
the largest Post Exchange in the theater. I went after typical
junk food but procuring those things made me feel so out of
place and strange. The PX made me aware that we are like
some war tourists on an all-inclusive vacation except I had to
pay for my slushy and beef jerky.*

*The time came to make our way home, so I got the
speakers jamming and I saddled up in the turret but didn't
make it to the gate before I got yelled at for sitting improperly.
Maybe the master sergeant didn't like our music selection. We
were out for 20-plus hours and tired, but I locked on the focus
as we roared out the gate.*

*We continued our tourism through an alien city with the
curfew in full effect. Tall buildings looking dead with no lights
on, no people on the streets, and the gentle breeze made
Baghdad feel like it was vacant of life. We greeted the familiar*

smell of sewage and turned the corner into Rustamiyah without incident. Placing the pig, the M240, into the rack in the CP, I was bullshitting when the new CO crashed the party. I'm out. I'm tired anyway.

Camp Victory, the giant forward operating base next to Baghdad International Airport, may as well have been the moon. The base was very different from Rustamiyah. It was like a small city hidden behind tall concrete walls with guard towers. In the center of the camp, the Baathist elites' former palaces around the man-made lake looked magnificent but out-of-place among the contractor-provided trailers and US military equipment. The roads were dotted with people walking around with bright, reflective belts around their waists and bus stops shuttling them around the installation.

The base had been built for a different mission and with a different culture. That is not to say that FOB Rustamiyah was so desolate or that we didn't have everything we needed and more, but this was different. Our base was indeed comfortable, but Camp Victory was America in the Middle East. This was a base built upon billions of dollars of US government contractor money awarded in amounts never seen before in the history of war. As we made our way further into the base, it became even more apparent we were out of place.

After dropping off the engineers, who I expected to tell their buddies about their time in South Baghdad and the dumb infantry guys combing through poop, we pulled into a gravel lot next to the liberties area. We took the guns off our beat-up HMMWVs and locked them in the cab. We soon noted the conditions of the other trucks running around the base. They were clean and in good order. Each truck was the same color of tan. Next to them, our greenish machine looked tough and full of character. We'd complain if it ever mattered. Besides, at the moment, trading in our truck would've seemed like a betrayal.

I had slept little the last couple of days and mulled over the idea of finding some shade but didn't want to lose the chance to eat some fast food and purchase beef jerky. The platoon leader turned us loose with a time to rally. He told us to, "Go get fat, but don't get into trouble." We promised only one of those things and ran off in search of the spoils from a contractor's war.

We first made our way to the PX and, arriving, we were stunned. You could buy a flat-screen TV or order a Harley Davidson to be delivered to your home in the States. They had a ton of beef jerky and chewing tobacco—stuff that was in demand at Rustamiyah, so I loaded a basket with goodies and prizes for future favors. Then, I turned a corner and saw it. They had slushy machines churning their sugary, awful drink and for some reason unknown to me, I was determined to drink one.

I grabbed the biggest cup at the table and eyed the machine to decide which color looked the most refreshing. The Iraqi clerk barreled around the corner and told me that they needed to churn for 20 more minutes before they would be ready. Joined by my brothers-in-arms holding baskets filled with Americana junk, we looked at each other, shrugged, and flopped onto the floor, right in the aisle. We plunked down weapons, undid holsters, and otherwise relieved ourselves of the accouterments of an infantryman's war and sat waiting. We didn't realize it was an issue until we noticed people stepping in between our legs to get through to bags of chips and magazines. Nobody dared to tell us to move either because of the crazy look we had in our eyes or the combat worn gear hanging off our bodies. Heck, it also could have been the smell.

After consuming the ice-cold drink and stocking up on supplies, we ate fast food. I had a hamburger and fries. It was heaven on a bun but also made my stomach a bit uneasy. I joked that those who would soon be sitting next to my rear end in the turret should do so with caution.

It was time to rally at the trucks after waiting around for a couple of hours. I got the gun ready and cranked some tunes on our makeshift radio. The air was on fire outside so to cool off, I sat with my feet next to the gun and my butt resting on the turret lid. This was the best way to ride around the FOB, and I had done it several times over on the other side of the city—far from the rest of the Army and Air Force.

The sun eased behind the large concrete barriers and another night approached. We drove onto the road, searching for the gate to the battlefield. Slowing at an intersection with the radio blasting away from our tiny two-inch speakers, a Master Sergeant, walking to his Kellogg, Brown, and Root air-conditioned trailer, launched into a tirade, yelling at me to stop. I was leaving the base to face the Baghdad night on Route Irish, notorious for IED strikes, so I acted like I couldn't hear and we accelerated away while the NCO continued his outburst. He was attempting to do the right thing, but I was not in the best frame of mind for correction of proper turret posture. Besides, I had promised the platoon leader only one of those things.

Once out the wire, since the curfew was in effect, the streets were empty. It was bizarre driving around the alien city of seven million with scarce lighting surrounded by high buildings I knew slept hundreds of people. The singular human presence on the night streets was the police at checkpoints placed at the occasional intersections. Cruising through a city with a population three times the size of Chicago without any vehicle traffic is an experience. The effect the war was having on the locals was evident, and it was quite impressive that the streets were so empty.

The small police force could not have stopped them from flooding the streets. This was willing participation in the reformation of their society. They respected the government curfew decree, or they didn't want to be shot by the Iraqi police. Either way, the people adhered to the rule of law. Back in the US,

I think it would take much more than the government telling us to stay indoors to make the streets of a major city as empty as they were on this Baghdad night.

The scene made us feel ripe for an attack, and we were alert, but we made it to Rustamiyah without incident. With a tremendous letdown, we settled in for the rest of the night. I stowed my gear and related the experience to those burning the midnight oil in the command post. I told them of the strange planet of Camp Victory and the dead dog IED delaying our arrival. The latter bored the already bored soldiers. They wanted to hear about the slushy and the PX. I told them, but the discussion was cut short. The company commander roared in to point at the map and shooed us out, so I turned the corner and went to go find my bed. It's funny to think that a dog carcass rigged with explosives was no news, but getting an awful iced drink was noteworthy.

August 4, 2006 –

Word came in the morning that we were to do a mosque monitoring mission. We were tasked with patrolling the vicinity of a mosque within loudspeaker distance and to respond if there was any attack. We'd have the interpreter listen to the message broadcast by the Imam to gain the pulse of the neighborhood.

We convoyed to the north of the traffic circle, right at the intersection of where Pluto and Wall Street meet. We chilled there until 1100. I was the gunner again, so I sat in the sling watching all the people as they drove by on their daily grind. They stared at you. I stared back.

We chugged down Wild past the Wardiya mosque. There was a group of old dudes hanging out on the road and we got to chatting. They invited us to eat. Soon, we found ourselves enjoying a small feast: chai tea, watermelon, grapes, and flatbread. I got tapped out of the turret and stuffed my face. The dude in charge was a lawyer and knew decent English. It's not common that we met an Iraqi that speaks our native tongue so well out on the streets.

We gave the kids the candy and MRE goodies while handing out the two soccer balls we carried in the trunk. There was much rejoicing. The family looked happy. It was refreshing. At last, we departed and made our way to Rustamiyah. I hoped the family stays safe, but with the Mahdi active in the area, I'm skeptical. No rest. We're tasked for a night mission.

August 5, 2006 –

Did an OP at a house at an intersection off of Route Pluto. After getting dropped off, we walked for 400 meters through the moon-soaked dark. The dogs were barking. There wasn't a soul on the road. We maneuvered through the shadows like a sniper team that had spent 9 months in Iraq. It's times like this where I like to take a step back and see what we are doing. It's times like this where I realize how dangerous this is and how I won't forget my adventures here. Three dudes, surrounded by a population that wouldn't mind if we lived or if we died. I love this feeling. It's like we are animals—predators waiting for their prey.

Once we reached our target, a vacant building, we nudged the door, but it's stiff like it's shored up, so we pulled off 100 meters away and took cover in the ditch. The dogs barked and barked and barked waking anyone nearby. We radioed that we were going to find another place to do business. No dice. Intel reports the house is vacant—find a way in.

I reasoned that we made as large a signature moving with the feral dogs barking as we do kicking down the door, so we made the sprint and stacked on the door. Somehow, I end up doing the kicking. One...two...boot. Boot again, the door swung open. Rushed inside. Stopped. The house was occupied. We searched for hands. Shouted. Nobody was armed.

About 20 or so squatters were huddled in the house. The children cried. They thought we were kidnappers or the like. What an awkward situation. We walked right through the house like we owned it, in the middle of the night, to clear it before heading to the roof to do our work. What would you do if, at 3 in the morning, guys booted in your door, rushed in and through the house, before walking out onto the roof to look for bad guys until the morning? It must be quite the experience from the other side. I am sure when we are long gone, they will tell their grandchildren about it. Or maybe that's just me—I'll tell my grandchildren.

We got on the roof and watched an otherwise peaceful Iraqi night. Some sporadic machine gun fire to the west in the Jisr Diyala area but not much that earned more than a shrug. I sat in the doorway that led to the roof so I could look at the family huddled below. I watched for cellphones and whispered to remain quiet. I put my hands in the sleeping gesture to suggest they go back to sleep. The kids calmed. Candy helped.

About 5 in the morning, it was time to leave with enough darkness to mask our movement. We walked right out of the house, through the squatters on their migration, and made our way to the extraction point. Nothing significant in the way of action, but it gave me time to think about what the occupation must be like for the other side. Time to think about the lasting impression we have made in their lives, and mine.

After looking for the best approach to
abandoned house, we took some cover to collect (
moment. Hiding in a ditch 100 meters from t
focused our night vision and debated our course of action. _
we'd go. We stood and got to a full gallop, heading for the door.

Bursting in, I started clearing and looking for threats like I
was trained. It took a tenth of a second before I realized the
situation and took a bewildered step. I continued to scan for
targets amongst the occupants. I pointed my weapon until we
saw the hands we needed to see. The women shrieked and
covered their heads as they tried to hide. Others waved in the air
with surprise, but I'm not sure who was more confused.

The site of the displaced people, squatters, was saddening.
One elderly man lay on the ground with an amputated leg—
either from diabetes or from the war. The large, what I gathered
to be, family rested on the first floor in what would be the living
room or den, huddled around a flickering lantern.

Stepping between their legs and bodies, we filtered through
the mass and cleared the remainder of the shoddy masonry that
constituted the home. We got to the roof and assembled our
equipment. I plopped down in the threshold of the door and,
with the view downstairs unimpeded, kept an eye on the family
to make sure they didn't call on a cell phone or leave the house.

It was a vivid moment for me: face-to-face with the true
victims of the war. We gathered the snacks we carried, including
some of my goodies from the country's largest PX, and
distributed them among the squatters in the lone act of comfort
we could offer. The offering calmed the frightened children.

After the patrol, we discussed why we had seen so many
more squatters moving around our area of operations. Our sister-
team had come across a group a fortnight ago. We didn't have
time to question these folks but assumed that to uproot your
entire family, a significant threat must have guided their actions.
Was it the Mahdi Army in the area, death squads, foreign fighters,

ɔunni insurgents, crooked Iraqi police? All of them? It was difficult to narrow the source without more information, and we entertained the possibilities.

Regardless of the circumstances influencing their withdrawal from homes long established, I was appreciative of my status as an American citizen. I was grateful to be lucky enough to be born in the United States. As I sat in the chow hall, eating powdered eggs and toast, it was difficult to relate to their situation. I wished we'd improve it.

August 8, 2006 –

We got launched as the Quick Reaction Force to join a mission in a southern portion of our area of operations. A SOF raid to capture some High-Value Targets between Salman Pak and Jisr Diyala netted two caches that we were to secure. At the squadron headquarters, we were met with the sniffing dog and metal detectors. After leaving the FOB, we took some backward route and reached the outer cordon of the raid held by some Bradley Fighting Vehicles of a unit from the 4th Infantry Division. We got to the site, tapped them out, and secured the premises.

Before they left, we helped load the detainees into a Bradley, and off they rumbled. It was 127 degrees outside. We were melting. Wright walked along the outer edge of the farm continuing to search after Navy EOD had taken the two discovered caches of weapons for destruction. Luck was with him, and he found another cache, DeLay found another, then we uncovered another.

We discovered tons of weapons, RPG rounds, mortar rounds, and grenades. The place was an entire armory of insurgent gear. The stockpiles of weapons could arm a small company. We called EOD, and when they arrived, they were unhappy they had to return to the heat. Once we showed them our find, though, they were blown away they had missed so much.

As EOD gathered the weapons, we continued our search. I walked into a livestock pen and poked the roof covering the sheep. Machine guns were in the thatch. Score.

I grabbed a metal detector and began sweeping the ground around the edges of the farm. Every time I put the earphones on, I felt the temperature skyrocket. I knelt in some hay and took off my helmet to chill. I felt a bit woozy. The heat and humidity by the river were dangerous and were exacerbated by the body armor oven strapped on us.

We got some intelligence visitors, and they questioned the family left at the farm. More goodies were found. We crawled back to the FOB with zero water left. So many weapons were stockpiled in the backyard of our AO. What were they preparing for?

Hands down, this was the hottest day I have ever experienced. After we loaded the detainees into the Bradleys, the ramp went up and they pulled away in a trail of dust. We were left to secure the site. Amongst this heat, we committed as best we could to drink water and do what needed to be done, but it was a losing fight.

Putting on the headset to the metal detector increased the temperature ten degrees in an instant. Feeling a bit light-headed, I sat on a haystack to regain my composure. We ran out of water after several hours and continued to melt with more work to complete. Our efforts, initiated by a professionally relentless Wright wanting to poke around more, uncovered a gold mine of weapons missed during the initial raid.

Many of the weapons and ammunition were concealed in blue jugs dug into the ground. Some were hidden among the dung and roof of the livestock pen. We spent time playing with the arsenal before the explosive ordnance disposal team returned to take custody of the materials. The detainees had packed quite an amount of firepower. It was an impressive assortment of weapons—AK-47s, PKM machine guns, RPGs, hand grenades, web gear, rocket launchers, even bolt action rifles.

It was chalked up as a solid victory until we realized it was amid our area of responsibility. It begged the question—what were we missing? Of course, it was a success that the weapons were captured, but how did this armory get here? We were careful to not think that winning a battle would win the war. With our presence sporadic at best, the enemy could move the stuff in without our knowledge, and the attitude of the locals must not have been sympathetic to our cause. Otherwise, this armory and safe house would not have been here.

The temperature rose, but so did the signals that the enemy was planning to bring the heat. They were moving into our sector to target rival factions to undermine any security gains we had achieved. Working with the local leaders including those from the Mahdi Army, like Abu Ayatt and his deputy Abu Sayf, we had secured quiet compliance affording the Iraqi government and police precious time to build security apparatuses, administer local services, and establish the rule of law.

As long as the militia stayed on the sidelines, we were able to concentrate our economy of force operations against the Sunni insurgency, foreign fighters, and death squads proliferating across the nation. Like the troubled water flowing by Jisr Diyala, you can only swim upstream for so long before the current rips you in the direction it intended to carry you in the first place.

6.

THROUGH THE SKIES OF BLUE

August 15, 2006 –

Mission for today: conduct a dismounted patrol of Wardiya. During our departure, 2nd platoon had taken casualties in Jisr Diyala. Specialist Zayas took shrapnel to the face from an improvised claymore. Everyone is eager to take the fight back to them, but operations in that area are put on hold. Further complicating the situation, the bridge crossing the Diyala on Route Pluto was destroyed by a truck rigged with explosives. The suicide bomber blew a hole straight through the middle of it, rendering it unsafe to ferry us across Route Pluto.

It was a well-targeted attack to delay our response time. Now, we had to drive clear around the FOB on the opposite side of the river, cross at Jisr Diyala, and take Wall Street to Wild. It added substantial time to our battlespace commute and also ruffled feathers as we had to skirt the outsides of Jisr Diyala to get anywhere in the area. Our AO feels like it's being targeted due to its advances in peace. Nevertheless, 2nd platoon had their hands full.

While we eased towards the fiery Wardiya, the Iraqi police at the checkpoint right at the end of the Tuwaitha berm dashed into the middle of the road. They pleaded with arms outstretched for us to stop. As we pulled alongside the road at the top of Route Wild, it was obvious, somebody was in a fight. Machine gun blasts echoed and smoke plumed above the trees to the west. The police were taking fire from areas of Wardiya near the river and wanted us to lead them in. The past week or longer there had been rampant murders and house burnings in the area, but we had arrived too late to do anything to stop them. This time, it was different.

Iraqis police were taking cover 200 meters in letting me know that somebody wanted to scrap. We were going to oblige them. I readied the M240. Let's dance. Fogle hammered on the HMMWV accelerator, and we sped towards the sounds of the battle. My pulse quickened. My knuckles were white. We were taking fire across the front. Where from? Keep it moving! Bullets snapped overhead. We came to a walled compound on the left side. Runners! A group of fighters spotted us and fled. Gotcha! The dismounts opened doors and ran to the wall of a compound. Everyone drew down. Enemy in the open. Rat-tat-tat-tat! Pop pop pop! Boom!

Tyler and the dismounts were surrounded by a cloud of dust. I need to move now! Move me forward right now! The truck lurched ahead. Lowered the machine gun. Rock and roll. I eyed through a haze of dust and tall reeds. Enemy fighters in the open. Rock and roll.

In a fury, the other truck rammed the gate, and the dismounts flooded the compound. We charged into the compound to join the assault. Rolling the HMMWV in to provide cover, we found one dude hit in the pelvis, and he was strewn on the ground bleeding, screaming, and to us— hilarious. The medic stripped off his web gear and patched him up. He was damn lucky!

As we tended to the enemy wounded, I started taking fire from the east, but I knew the Iraqi police were in the general vicinity, so I didn't fire into the blind. I kept an eye out. No rock and roll. Heck, it could have been the police shooting at me for all I know.

The rest of the team continued pursuing the enemy through the reeds as we loaded the dude shot in the butt cheek into the truck to head to the FOB to get him aid. As soon as we cleared the Iraqi cordon, the police unleashed a barrage into the area to cover our return and suppress any ideas of a counterattack, but the enemy had withdrawn. It was over.

To this day I'm not sure if we had stumbled upon a death squad that had crossed the river or a group of militiamen hoping to challenge the Iraqi government forces encroaching on their turf. In this instance, it didn't matter. It was time for a fight. And it was one I recall clearly. I remember so distinctly how fluid this fifteen-minute firefight progressed, even though it felt like time stood still.

The compound was as big as two football fields with a pond in the middle and a couple of ramshackle barns on the northernmost side. Reeds and overgrown grasses sprouting from metal implements of an abandoned farm provided ample concealment for the enemy within. To add to its defense, a five-foot-high wall made of a clayish substance surrounded the compound. It was a decent place for a defense.

Making our advance, the rifle fire snapped around us. We maneuvered our steel beast alongside the wall, unloaded our dismounts, and edged into a position where I could unleash the pig. I yelled at Davis in the gun turret ahead of me to move forward. I realized I was standing while I was yelling at him when I heard the crack of a shot, and I fell behind the gun. The trucks inched forward, and I peeked around a tree into the compound.

The dismounts were busy leveling their weapons over the wall as they unleashed targeted volleys from their rifles.

Dressed in typical street clothes and making their way around a bed of reed grass, the insurgents were firing on our dismounts who had scrambled up on the clay barrier. While they were concentrating on returning fire, the incoming rounds struck the wall right in front of Tyler and the dismounts producing a cloud of debris and dust. The team returned an overwhelming amount of fire spiced with an unmatched rage at the enemy.

When Davis' gun truck rammed the gate into the compound, the insurgents were firing and had continued making their way around the pond through the reeds that surrounded it. I took my cheek off the machine gun and glanced at Tyler as he picked his M14 off the wall in preparation to storm the compound.

I yelled to ask if he was okay. He roared in the affirmative, but the blood soon hit his lips. He stuck his glove in his face, and his eyes widened. He realized why I had asked. A deranged kind of smile spread across our faces. The incoming rounds, striking the wall right in front of Tyler and zipping right by us, had chipped off a piece of the wall, rocketing it into his face and causing a small gash to bleed in a surprising stream. He was lucky. He followed the truck into the compound, and I went to the gun.

Turning my head to the fight, I caught sight of another three of the enemy through the vegetation and took aim. I looked straight at them and, for an instant, locked eyes with one. Time froze. They were young, one in a white tee shirt and jeans, staring at me as if we were communicating through eyesight, or maybe he was fixated on the machine gun in front of me. They were clawing to get away through a thick growth of bushes.

With a natural sense of mission, I trained the machine gun on the corner of the compound and the waiting enemy. It was my moment to claim the title of economical victor, three for one burst, when the judicious mortar section sergeant strode into my view, focused on another group of Iraqis who were escaping in the opposite direction shooting through the reeds. I was furious and shouted at him to get out of the way, but it was too late. The shot was spoiled, but the fight drove on.

We gave chase. Our truck lumbered into the compound, pulling alongside the pond area where one kid lay bleeding from his backside. He had a web gear harness containing several AK-47 magazines and grenades, and one had taken a bullet to the top, discharging rounds. To his luck, none of the rounds entered his body. As I waited to snatch up the wounded man for questioning, somebody, either those three kids or the Iraqi police, was shooting at me, but they were not accurate. I was intent on finding them and dumping a hundred rounds in their direction. But I found no satisfaction.

Our team bandaged the kid to make the trip for interrogation and medical care. The remaining members scoured the rest of the area following blood trails, and, satisfied the enemy had withdrawn or were killed, we blasted towards the FOB and the aid station. Having heard the radio chatter, a team was waiting for us, and we pulled next to a plywood sign with a red cross spray-painted onto it. Like a battlefield poet, and with a grin, I yelled, "We got one!"

During this engagement, I was aware of so many things. My senses seemed supernatural in the face of these ghosts caught in the open. My brain received the necessary information and translated it into action as fast as it could, but it still wasn't enough. I let a few get away, and that will forever be frustrating. But we had stopped the attack and maneuvered well. I had solace in the fact that none of our guys were hurt—even Tyler's smile was just as chipper as before.

May 29, 2016 –

"Wow, this is quite the operation you've put together, Paul," Eric said, walking into the VFW hall for the reunion. He strode over to the table and casually looked across the assortment of mementos I had brought to encourage discussion.

"Eh." I shrugged. "Thought it might jog our memory."

"Bro, this looks amazing. I feel like I'm reuniting with a long-lost family," Sorbello said as he swaggered up and leaned on me. He was the most social one of the group, and even during a hard time, we could count on him to maintain our spirits.

"Maybe we are." Eric was peeking at the letters from his fellow officers who had been unable to attend. His presence was a testament to his no-gap leadership. He stared at the journal tucked away behind a framed picture. His brow wrinkled. "I'd like to share some stories tonight."

"I'm sure we can make that happen," I said, nodding. In truth, it was what we wanted to happen, needed to happen, but we wondered who'd go first. Eric would again lead the way after the event kicked off and other Comanches arrived.

That didn't take long. Soon, the VFW ballroom burst alive. Fogle, Wicker, Oliver, Schmidt, and their wives, the Burns brothers, Notaro, plus others coming for the reunion proper muscled opened the doors. A-Rod had driven from distant Michigan. Arroyo, Antonio, and more trickled into the VFW, hoping to find something they weren't sure they were looking for but somehow missed.

My heart swelled as the soldiers that had watched my left and right filed into the reunion. The group settled and picked seats around the tables. I opened the evening with some comments on how this came to fruition and how grateful I was for their attendance. I turned it over to the VFW Post Commander to say a few words followed by Oliver's spiel about the history of the 101st as he created a grog for the occasion.

Drinks were distributed, and we launched into a few words regarding the warriors lost.

"...so, to that, I say here-here." I toasted to the pictures sitting front and center to the crowd—Zayas and Weir.

"Here-here!" the crowd responded.

Zayas had been a pillar of the enlisted troops in the company. Hailing from Dorchester, Massachusetts, a city that later named a street corner square after him, he had joined the Army later than the typical soldier. He was more mature at a warrior's age of 29, was a devoted husband and father of two, and was also a dedicated soldier. When it came time to compete for the coveted Expert Infantry Badge, Zayas was one of eleven who had earned it from a pool of 80 eligible. He also had revealed that he believed in his mission, noting that he saw his own children when he watched Iraqi kids play. He wanted to help.

"Now, I'd like to hand it over to Eric to tell a story I think we'd like to hear," I said. I moved to the side and took a seat next to Kat.

Eric stood, walked over to the center of the room, nodded, and put his thumb in his pocket with a beer in his other hand. "You know, I've been on a lot of deployments. But this one…" He paused and looked to the crowd and for the right words. "It was tough. It was special for a lot of reasons, not the least of which are those warriors behind me. Y'know, I remember when Zayas got his first purple heart." He motioned to the photographs. "That dude…"

"So do I!" Sorbello interrupted with a boisterous bellow. "Zayas got wounded the day Jisr Diyala went to hell!"

Eric smiled. "Let me tell you how it went to hell." And so, he did.

Standing at the front of the room, Eric began:

"I was to go on block leave. It was August the 15th. The instant of the detonation is clear as a star-filled Iraqi night. The patrol was against my will and better judgment, and I knew it had the potential to go bad, but I understood the rationale for the order and tried to be as noninvasive as possible. The moment I looked at that car, turned my head, and faced the blast is frozen in my mind. With a single explosion, the relationship and agreements we'd developed shattered, and they'd never be whole again.

We had made a deal with Abu Ayatt and the Mahdi Army. Our company was running this whole thing mafia-style. We had agreements cut with the major players, and the Ayatt deal was the one that was sitting in the balance. In Jisr Diyala, it was better to let Abu Ayatt control his people and quell the violence instead of us kicking the hornet's nest.

The plan was to allow things to quiet for another week, then open communications with the militia and negotiate peace between them and the Sunnis. The results were speaking for themselves. Relative to much of the country, we were maintaining the harmony between the factions.

Then, the day before I was scheduled to go on block leave, I'd been ordered to do a dismounted patrol in Jisr Diyala. I talked it over with the company commander. We decided the safest place was the main street since it was congested with shoppers and it was doubtful the militia would attack us among their own people in the market. So, we went.

We left at ten in the morning and got to JD 45 minutes later, taking it slow on a direct approach, looking as inconspicuous as a coalition convoy could. We moved along the main street, turned around, and positioned the trucks for security. I made a call over the radio, and we dismounted the team together for a bit of talking with a few vendors we'd been working with in the months prior.

After a few minutes, we moved across through the divided median to the other side of the street. Once the trucks shifted a hundred meters to cover us, we continued patrolling. My truck, with Kelley driving and Zayas in the gun turret, was in front, and parked within the divide, facing west to overwatch an intersection. As we moved, a vehicle careening around a corner to our south caught my eye. I watched it for a few seconds until it turned into a driveway. I turned my head toward the shop and was greeted in contemporary Baghdad fashion.

Boom! Everything disappeared in black smoke, and a stinging wave of heat hit my backside. I assumed it was a car bomb and accepted that initial thought. It took a second for the smoke to clear while the soldiers were taking cover. I spun around and called for a status update as I moved to a nearby wall, took a knee, and scanned the street for a triggerman or potential shooter. I was swift to reassess, and it was clear that it wasn't a car bomb, but rather, an IED that had been buried in a trash pile in the intersection, underneath the rear driver side of my truck. I sprinted to the HMMWV to check on Kelley and Zayas while calling for a medic.

I wasn't the first to the truck. Doc needed zero direction and set about his tasks like a professional. Glancing through the door, I saw Zayas and Kelley were both unconscious. Kelley came to right away. His face was smashed where he'd been slammed into the steering wheel and dash, but Zayas was still unconscious, and his face was covered in blood. I left Doc to work on him so I could get an assessment of the rest of the guys and send a report to the CO before the enemy accomplished anything else.

I looked around and saw the guys doing what they needed to do. The NCOs were putting guys into security and scanning hard for threats or enemy to kill. Langford was bleeding from the ears. Before the dust had settled, a crowd gathered around a wounded local. His stomach was split open laterally across the center, exposing a bunch of his intestines and organs, but if he

229

were sewn together, he'd survive. Nothing was punctured. It was time to button up and move out with the casualty in tow.

In minutes, Kelley was wide awake and functional. Zayas was bloody but manning the gun in the turret. They had the truck turned around and ready to go. Though it had a few flats, we knew we could get to a better place to swap tires. We couldn't move the local national casualty with us, so we commandeered a small pickup truck and loaded the man with his bandaged stomach and told the driver to get him to the nearby hospital.

A large crowd had gathered. I was angry as hell about this whole ordeal, so I took the opportunity. I walked in front of them and with great anger, told them, "Do you see this? This is the Mahdi! This is what they do to you, the Iraqis! You see that none of my men are hurt, only Iraqis. And, we help you! The militia is the enemy of the people!"

Despite my broken Arabic, I think I made the point. There were a lot of shocked faces. I told the trucks to start moving. As the driver began rolling the HMMWV, I ran to it and jumped in for a hasty departure. No sooner had I shut the door than rocks and bottles bounced off the hood. I scanned around and identified a crowd coming from the direction of the Al-Huda Husseiniya mosque.

The guys were watching the increasing number of Iraqis looking for weapons. We had to clear a way out. The crowd didn't cooperate with our initial request for them to move. I fired a few rounds ten feet over their heads—I was not screwing around at this point. It was effective. With each passing second, the risk was increasing. The situation was deteriorating at a rate so unexpected we needed to withdraw and regroup before any further deliberate action.

We took the back way out of Jisr Diyala and parked in a perimeter to change tires and reassess the casualties. The fury hadn't left me. While the boys worked, I grabbed the terp and dialed Abu Ayatt. To my surprise, he answered. I exploded with words of anger, which the interpreter translated with him on speaker phone. My blood was on fire, and I intended to return to the heart of the city straight to the Al-Huda Husseiniya mosque and start crushing people, beginning with the Mahdi guards.

As soon as I was collected enough to start listening again, Ayatt launched into excuses that it was Sunnis who'd detonated the IED. I told him it was impossible for a Sunni to emplace and detonate an IED in the neighborhood without being intercepted by the militia. That was ludicrous, and he knew it. He also stated that we'd violated our agreement, which I could not deny, but nonetheless, the IED was unjustifiable.

After a few minutes of heated arguing, he insisted he would find the person responsible and hold him accountable, which would likely result in the death of any unfortunate Sunni in the area to the south in Wardiya or Ja'ara. To avoid this, I gave him conditions to meet or we'd begin more targeted raids: he must hand deliver the responsible party, unhurt, and call me. Upon this, I'd contact the police and arrange a detainee transfer. I was fighting mad, and soon we were ordered to return to base to regroup before dealing with the growing crowd in Jisr Diyala.

With orders received and another deal made, both Zayas and Kelley were back to normal. Zayas was in the turret, face bloody, but smiling and looking like a warrior. I talked to him for a bit, and he said his bell was rung, but he was okay. He'd keep manning the gun. I loved him for that. It was the kind of determination that made us exceptional. We rolled to the FOB and got the guys further checked out by the medical team. We were seething with anger at the shattered deal and fragmented peace. Abu Ayatt, the head of the snake, had to be removed. His days were numbered, and soon we'd return to that den of vipers."

I looked across the room as Eric told his story. Significant others sat in silent contemplation, brothers-in-arms nodded their heads in remembrance, and Kat grasped my hand. It was the first difficult war story told during the reunion and Eric telling it drove the words straight into our chests. For some, it may have been the first time they'd learned what happened. For others, it scratched at a scab they wished had healed. Anger seeped out of the sore.

"It's funny. I opened Paul's journal and flipped right to that page," Eric said. He shrugged his shoulders. "I thought you should know, even though it sounds like you guys had your own fight on your hands." He tipped his baseball cap toward me.

I answered from our table off the side with a north and south head nod. A sense of uneasiness came with the idea that somebody else had read parts of the journal and broadcasted it to the others. I knew they were going to look at it. That's why I put it out. The fact that it had led to discussing a tough topic made me tense.

"I gotta say, I was proud to see Zayas back in that turret. You guys were so damned determined. Even though I didn't say it, I wanted to thank you guys. Thank you, guys, for your dedication, and when things got tough, thank you for looking after your buddies, like you continue to today." With that, Eric raised his glass and toasted.

Having Eric lead off the evening of storytelling, reminiscing, and camaraderie reestablished his position as a leader, not in title but in reverence. During our time in the deployment, as a junior enlisted soldier, we were seldom privy to the entire workings of the platoon or company. More often than not, you have your lane, and you stay in it. What others are doing doesn't concern you.

The value Eric added was his viewpoint. He knew the broader actions of the Comanches, and he understood the intent of the commanders on a much more intimate basis. During the reunion, Eric provided context to so many events that the soldiers, now veterans, didn't recognize a decade later.

"You know it did go to hell. Not only in Jisr Diyala but the whole damn country, man," Notaro said at a volume loud enough for the entire group. "It's no fault of our own. And it didn't come out of the blue. Shit got crazy."

"That's the truth, Notaro." Sorbello shook a finger in agreement. "Every time we went out, we were ready for the next fight. This wasn't no simple route security. I wanted to get in there and bust skulls. By the end of this thing, the whole damn AO was on fire."

August 21, 2006 –

I'm tagged as a gunner for another patrol of Wardiya and Route Gator along the Tigris. Crossing the new metal bridge, we rumbled to northern Salman Pak and turned off Wild, heading along the river. This road made me nervous. As our engines idled southbound on the pavement and turned onto the dirt road, we took in the damage from the recent violence.

Driving under thick foliage shading parts of the road, we saw some of the trees were smoldering from the fires. The war had arrived. Yesterday, the POB had a battle in the streets. Death squads are roaming the area intent on cleansing these villages of rival sects and the police had battled to stop them.

Things are going sideways. The charred remains of POB pickup trucks littered the road. Most of the hulks had been pushed off, but some had been left to burn where they died. The POB lost 8 trucks, each with several occupants killed. Death was everywhere.

We're directed to stop by a house. 1st platoon developed a working relationship with its residents. As our convoy neared the house to drop off some aid, we apparently scared off the enemy. Armed gunmen had arrived moments earlier to burn the house and told the residents to leave or be killed. Our loud, rumbling diesel engines had saved their home for another day.

I sweated until I dripped, sitting in the turret, keeping a lookout, listening to the sounds of phantom bullets and bombs while our guys dropped off the goods and questioned the hysterical family. The mother kept hitting herself in the head, wailing and flailing her arms into the sky in a disturbing dance of mourning. I didn't understand it.

It was time to go. It looked like a storm was blowing in. We paid a visit to Farmer Joe's house. The leaders talked, and he said he knew the whereabouts of some kidnappers in the area, so we headed south to investigate. We cleared the street of smoldering pickups by edging them off the road with the bumpers of our HMMWVs and made it to the residence Joe indicated was the kidnappers' safe house, where we took photographs.

While we sat, a mortar barrage booms in the distance—less than 400 meters away. Wardiya is getting rocked. A lady came running down the street, bleeding, crying her eyes out, asking us to help her children, but our hands were tied. We were trying. We contacted the POB to help with the casualties and raced to find the point of origin of those mortars.

The storm arrived. A sandstorm whipped sand into the air, turning the sky a haunting orange. We idled into Wardiya. Quiet. Did they use the oncoming storm to cover their withdrawal? The place was a smoking ghost town. The mortarmen had vanished in the haze.

Turning one corner into Wardiya, we saw a truck being loaded by a family. They were going to slip out of town during the sandstorm. The kids were crying. Get out while you are alive, I suppose. We drove south into a more residential district and tossed out soccer balls across compound walls to the families seeking shelter from the stinging wind. We looked for any suspicious activity, but even the dogs are lying low.

We called it a day and headed to Rustamiyah. The gaping hole in the middle of the bridge remained but the engineers had constructed an interim solution to help us get across. It was a one truck at a time trust exercise. Back at the FOB, I took the pig off the turret and it was caked with dust—the perfect ending to the day. This place is in trouble.

The VBIED that had blown a hole straight through the bridge was a large dump truck with explosives packed in the bed with sandbags layered on top. This construction technique forced the explosive energy downward out the bottom destroying the bridge beams spanning its width. For a week it wasn't safe to traverse, but the engineers soon arrived to remedy the situation. You could peer over the fifteen-meter chasm into the Diyala River as you drove over the creaking thing.

The insurgents weren't fools. They knew that the bridge was a choke point for coalition traffic and, if destroyed, would lengthen our response from the FOB. By the time we could travel to the far-reaching areas of our AO—say JD, Wardiya, or Ja'ara—the enemy could withdraw. The insurgents targeted the bridge so they could conduct their sectarian killing unabated.

Within a few days, the dedicated engineers' furious construction efforts allowed us to again cross the Diyala a single truck at a time. We were thankful to them to not have to extend our trips throughout our AO by a couple of hours and be subjected to more time on roads littered with IEDs. No doubt, the engineer's efforts saved lives both Iraqi and American. But the choke point still gave precious time for the enemy to withdraw.

Even with the faster commute to the battlespace, Wardiya wasn't improving. Families and policemen were targeted methodically. For every Public Order Brigade pickup truck we pushed off the banks into a final resting spot as a reminder of the bedlam, there was a carcass of a house smoldering nearby. A family had been displaced or killed.

The Iraqis with the means to flee packed what possessions they could and left, sometimes under the orange glow of a sandstorm. The enemy was cleansing the mixed neighborhood along sectarian lines and targeting the POB to demonstrate the government's inability to protect the masses. Reports indicated that even the police were involved in civilian bloodshed. The violence was systemic. Each time we entered an area, we found more remnants of the carnage, but not those responsible.

August 24, 2006 –

Time for another visit to Wardiya. Once there, we cleared more truck skeletons off the road. The POB trucks continued to be burnt to the ground. More death, more destruction. Bullet casings at least indicate somebody had been fighting back.

Houses further and further away from the river are being burnt. A woman confronted us screaming for help. They beg us to rescue them each time we go there. Our answer is the POB. We talked with another family as they were packing their house and they said the same thing—the death squads are getting too close. We told them to work with the POB.

We did this over and over. They need help, people are getting killed, and we aren't around to stop it. That said, we can't stop it if you don't tell us who they are or where they went. If they want help, they need to work with us and the POB, but nobody offers us a single tip. The enemy is too close, and dealing with the Americans can be a death sentence. It's an exhausting, not to mention frustrating, cycle of violence.

The Iraqi women, who could be most spirited in their cries, were so distressed their bodies quaked with emotion. Wardiya did not resemble the area from a few short months ago and looked like a complete wasteland. Burnt hulks of trucks, walls riddled with bullet holes, houses smoldering, and vehicles being loaded with a family's personal items were as common as the scattered pieces of trash strewn across the streets. I sat and watched through night vision as an emotionally-drained family loaded a jingle truck in the middle of the night with tears in their eyes. They and their relatives had lived in this area for as long as they could remember but had no choice. They had to flee or they would die.

I was just a young soldier flirting with adulthood. These sights did little to faze me. I was desensitized to the sufferings of the Iraqi people. It was easy for me, as I had little experience in the real world—no mouths to feed, no attachments, and no concern for anyone but my tribe. I was detached. Other guys had wives and kids, and I think it made them relate more to the family struggles of the Iraqis, but they too distanced themselves from the local citizens' plight.

The callousness was necessary to do the job required of us. Thick skin is like armor for the soul. Nine months into this thing, we may as well have been an Abrams tank. The slings and arrows of misfortune did little to dent our resolve nor erode our sense of duty. We'd keep patrolling, but knew we'd have to stay put to make an advance.

August 25, 2006 –

I volunteered for a patrol to support a raid on several Jaish al-Mahdi members. We convoyed to the area near the traffic circle and waited as a QRF for the platoons. We were there 2 hours before we were called in to assist.

We hit a couple of locations and took some detainees. We worked our magic and this time found the necessary paraphernalia for a mortar team. On a nice rug, we laid out our find, including a batch of cell phones. One of the captured phones had a video from some dude discussing how he killed 4 more people today and later found out that they were Shia, not Sunni. He shrugged and laughed. Heartless.

EOD arrived, collected our mortar find, and we departed. I sat on top of the roof of one of the target houses, looking for somebody to kill as a family sat huddled together below, not speaking a word and wondering what I was doing there. I didn't care. The cell phone video hardened me further. It was difficult to believe they didn't know they had a murderer in their midst.

I was called to take charge of some detainees before we got them loaded. I stood outside, watching the military-aged males, telling them to shut up every once in a while, so they couldn't invent a better story for the interrogators. I took a knee and locked eyes with each of them. For a moment, we studied each other in muted concentration. The women and children wailed as the trucks roared in to load the detainees. Your fathers and brothers are murderers. No sympathy. Get back in your house.

August 26, 2006 –

Despite being part of a sniper team, we haven't done much sniper stuff in quite some time. We are sent on mounted patrols with the mortar section. They are great dudes to be out on the streets with so it's fine, but I feel like we need to do some work around the area to catch these murderers in the act.

Today, we are to do another patrol of the area surrounding Wardiya and Ja'ara. Route Pluto was a mess with several explosions in the last 24 hours, so we took plenty of time clearing our way. We hit Jisr Diyala and skirted south along the river hoping to come in from behind the villages. We talked with some people and confiscated an AK. A few small arms rounds came at us, but I couldn't tell from what direction. I felt the tension in the air.

We kicked in a few doors looking for named individuals but found none so we clambered into the trucks and drove into Wardiya. The place is barren and shops are closed up. It was time to move north. We made it to the traffic circle when I heard and felt an explosion. It rattled my heart. It was 2nd Platoon on Route Wall Street a few hundred meters away. I saw the dust. EFP. It's around 2300 hours. Specialist Zayas KIA.

May 29, 2016 –

"Our AO wasn't special. It had been smoldering for a long time. We blew on the coals, got a flame, and tried to put out a fire," Burns spoke up. Everyone listened. He circled the last ounces of his drink around the bottom of the glass, glancing out occasionally to break his trance. "Like Notaro said, the whole damn country was falling apart, and we were keeping it from burning to ash. Those deals we made worked, but we had to go in there sooner or later. Every day we went out, there was more murder and sectarian bullshit. They needed to know who was in charge there, and it wasn't the militia or the insurgents."

"That's right." Jeff tapped his hand on the table. "Nobody attacks us without paying."

"Hell yeah, man," Notaro echoed. "We did get in there and whoop some ass. The squadron commander wasn't screwing around. He sent us in there to take the head off the snake. The place was a pit, man."

"I get that. The fact is, a snake without a head is still a snake." Eric took his hand out of his pocket like he was engaging in an escalation of force. He knew that we had been hungry to seek and destroy the enemy. He had also understood we were the hammer when the task required a screwdriver. It was a tough sell to a group of infantrymen who were trained in the violence of action.

"You see, we could control these guys since we knew everything about them. I knew that if we'd decapitate the snake, another head would grow back. We needed to make sure we could control the next head. Our mission was to secure the area for the Iraqis to stand alone, bring as many of us home as we could, and that was the way forward. We needed to keep it from being the tens of us against the hundreds of them. It'd happened in other parts of the country."

He was right. In 2004, the First Cavalry Division was sent into the slum headquarters of the Mahdi Army—Sadr City—and became engaged in a furious firefight known as Black Sunday. Some of the militiamen we faced in Jisr Diyala were veterans of that battle, which had left eight Americans dead and fifty-one wounded. The militia suffered over 500 casualties.

Eric knew the potential for that to happen in our area—a second home of al-Sadr's faithful—was high and those numbers meant Second Platoon, the sole unit responsible for Jisr Diyala, could be swallowed up with little improvement in the area. The situation was delicate, but when the time came for force, our response promised to be overwhelming. The facts were immutable. We couldn't tolerate murder for the sake of the rule of law. The whole company would soon bear down on JD and its militia loyal.

"Eye for an eye!" Sorbello snarled, standing to take the floor. Born of love, even though we wouldn't admit it at the time, our motives to get at the enemy were rooted in our devotion to one another. Many of us wanted to get at Ayatt and his henchmen because they had gone after our guys. "The mob pushed us out, but we had to get back in there."

"We did!" Notaro barked. "We went right back in!"

"How could I forget?" Sorbello swallowed and cast his eyes to the floor. "Y'know bros, I…I lost one of my best friends that day. That warrior…"

"Zayas was one of the strongest members of the tribe." I searched for words but knew I wasn't equipped for the task. "That warrior saddled up after shrugging off his wounds from ten days prior and strapped it on to help the team." My voice trailed off as I sat in my chair, remembering a radio call from ten years ago. It ended with three sharp letters: K-I-A.

Back then, I had briefly slumped into the turret sling, stunned, but taking control of my faculties, I popped back into position behind the gun, ready to grease any target I could spot through my night vision. I had failed months ago to secure the perimeter and spot any triggermen, but I was determined to not let that happen again.

Second Platoon had a task none of us wanted, but all of us had a part. On their eastern flank, I stood ready to assist. Nothing could have been more satisfying than spotting those responsible for the detonation and lighting them up. A fire burned inside of me, inside of us, but we found no such relief.

Second Platoon completed their work as consummate professionals and we worked back to the FOB. A medevac helicopter was en route, and a group of the guys walked to the landing zone next to the aid station to see Zayas off. The sergeant major and others carried our deceased warrior brother to the awaiting Blackhawk, and we offered our final respects. A salute to the fallen was the most anyone could muster. Anger boiled underneath. It was compounded the night of his memorial service.

The first sergeant called the last roll call, and we stepped to the rifle, boots, helmet and dog tags of the battlefield cross and said a soldier's farewell. As the service concluded, our large group filed out the door of the chapel in a quiet shuffle.

Momentarily breaking the somberness, a rocket whined through the sky as a token of our enemy's condolences. The projectile was hesitant to find a suitable place to mourn but finally chose to slam into the gravel right outside our chapel. Rocks whistled by. A heavy mortar barrage, which had been tipped off and targeted by a local national within the base, rained down upon us. Those of us caught in the open sprinted between impacts from cover to cover as the air filled with a familiar sea of sparks and curse words. Nobody was injured. The barrage did little but harden our resolve.

A decade later, Zayas was remembered as a founding member and central figure to Comanche Company. The group discussed the night of the attack with a vigor we didn't know we still had. Some hurled verbal spears to an enemy from a far off, distant land. Some redirected the group with shouted toasts to the fallen. Some stood in silent remembrance of a fellow soldier known by everyone as a charismatic pillar of the unit. All remembered the details of a night they couldn't forget.

"That shoulda been us to carry him to the bird," Sorbello said to part of the group that had drifted into a side conversation. Tears never shed wetted his eyes. "I shoulda carried him." The reunion had taken him to a place he hadn't visited in a decade. He was sharing a sentiment that had, before this moment, existed solely internal. He was in Iraq. He was among his brothers-in-arms, his tribe. I walked over to him and led him to a corner of the VFW hall. The group continued their discussions, pardoning our absence without notice.

"No, no you shouldn't have," I told him. From the edge of the room, we stared together at pictures of our fallen friends given the place of honor in the center of our reunion. "That shouldn't be your last memory of him. Remember him for the soldier he was."

Sorbello took a deep breath. "You're right. He was a hero, bro. A believer in the cause. It couldn't have happened to a better guy."

I looked across the room at Eric, who had taken a seat at a table facing the pictures. Eric had been ordered to take his mid-tour leave and thus wasn't present when Zayas was killed. He had learned of the death of one of his soldiers after getting married on his short break. I knew that he had taken it hard that he was absent. As a leader, he had responsibilities, but as a soldier he had orders. He had to go home. Eric's words came to me, and I turned towards Sorbello. "You can't change the outcome, but you can change your outlook."

7.

KEEP YOUR EYES ON THE JOB TO BE DONE

August 28, 2006 –

We assumed QRF at midnight and are activated at 0128. I threw my gear on and scrambled to the truck. I got the pig situated and grabbed some water. They got another location on Abu Ayatt, the militia leader living in Jisr Diyala. We checked last minute gear and readied ourselves at the squadron headquarters.

The whole company was in on it. We rolled to an Iraqi outpost and joined a platoon of POB troopers. We met with the SPTT. The SPTT are the Iraqi handlers, and word is that we can't action on this target without their assistance. Taking first Pluto, turning along the river on route Corn, we then booked it south to Jisr Diyala.

Sitting north of the bridge, we spent a couple of hours hoping for another indication of his whereabouts. No dice. Packed it up. While we were turning around, we received a call. Somebody gave us a tip—he is at a mosque! Move it! We cordoned off all exits and called the bosses for permission to enter the mosque. Multinational Division-Baghdad granted the request faster than expected, and we were given permission to kick in the gate.

It was chain locked. I sat behind the M240 waiting for a gunfight. Making quick work of the raid, our guys nabbed 10 guys and attempted to establish positive identification of Ayatt. No luck. He was not in the group. A radio call came across the net. Quick. 1st platoon was just outside a building and had spotted some guys making their way across roofs trying to escape, but it's not going to happen. They got him. There he was—Abu Ayatt, the bastard in the flesh—cowering on a rooftop corner, no less.

It soon became apparent that our time in JD was limited. A large crowd formed and were chanting anti-American vitriol. There was to be a riot on our hands. We took off like bats out of hell under cover of Apache helicopters. During the debrief, it was reported that minutes after Zayas was killed, Abu Ayatt got a text message saying, "The watermelon has been delivered." He had directed the killing of Zayas.

May 29, 2016 –

Jeff strode to the front of the reunion crowd, energized by Eric's speech. The group was intermingled among the round tables of the VFW hall in informal debriefing sessions rousing about the days of old. Jeff shouted for their attention. He got it. "You know, when people ask me about Iraq, I tell them about the one thing you can't see on the TV or find on the internet— the smell. Images can't capture it, and words don't do it justice. And I know foul smells; I lived with Endris for a year."

He got a gentle laugh and a few shouts of agreement. "That place smelled like garbage," Notaro remarked.

"It did. Garbage services were nonexistent. It was awful. It was more than trash. It was a perpetual toilet." Jeff's eyes focused. Smells are potent keepers of memory. A hush fell over

245

the crowd as we recalled the smell of a country lacking in standards of sanitation. Everywhere, human excrement floated alongside the streets. Stepping into the death water, by unwelcome chance, aggravated the smell. The pools of muddy sludge sucked the boot off of your foot as if the raw sewage was a weapon devised by the insurgency themselves.

"The night we got Ayatt in that toilet of Jisr Diyala, I'm pulling security at the crossroads of a literal shit creek. It's daytime and well over 100 degrees. The not so floral scents of a soiled diaper have infused the air. I'm liberating my boot from the suction of the sewage and losing. When I break free, and as a trickle of sweat burnt my eye, I regain focus and remembered what I'm doing in the middle of this shithole," Jeff recollected, and his face twisted with disgust as if the sewage mud was still stuck to his boot, if only sticking to his memory.

Jeff continued, "I was pulling security on the southwest corner of the cordon's perimeter. We were spread thin, and the next soldier was no less than 30 meters from my position. With my patience wearing thin and my determination reduced after pulling off an arguable victory with a poop puddle, my eyes snapped to activity on the second story of a building above me. I witnessed three individuals jumping out from the side of the building on the corner outside our perimeter like some stuntmen on a movie set."

Continuing the story, Jeff launched into a sermon complete with interpretative dance. His arms and legs were most animated as he reenacted the angry scene of the capture. Knowing that the company was already spread thin, Jeff was prompt to radio his observation, and several others rushed over to respond. They pulled at the front door to the building, but it wouldn't budge. One of the responding soldiers, a stout dude named Allen, proceeded to kick the door with the force of a pissed-off mule. The metal door budged only an inch with each kick until the bottom corner curled inward revealing that the door was reinforced with rebar. Allen, the ox, broke some of the steel bars free, and the door gave way.

"What if the door was booby-trapped?" Jeff confided to the group before moving forward with his recreation of the chase. He shrugged. "Screw it. We had to move. Time was of the essence, so we had to enter. We'd take the chance if we wanted to get these guys, so we did," he rationalized. "Now, the squad-sized team scurried through the doorway and advanced through the building, clearing the corners and moving up the stairs. Adrenaline was pumping, and the misery of being in my earlier predicament was gone. Poop puddle be damned. Not knowing what we'd find, we made our way to the rooftop of this building, but I think everyone had a sense of what was about to happen."

Jeff spoke with hands knifing the air as if he was clearing the building. He continued, "The rooftops were arranged no differently than the people of Iraq styled their streets, y'know. They are littered with junk and trash. Making our way to the top, we fell hot on the trail. Established at the top of the rebar-doored building, we jumped from one rooftop to the next with a speed that surprised even me."

Jeff paused. "Then, on one roof, we felt it. Somebody was there. Rounding a corner and noticing some fabric sticking out from behind one of the rooftop water collection tanks, a rifle found a hiding man huddled with a pistol holster emptied in hopes of being taken alive and not viewed as a threat," he said.

Jeff's excitement faded, but he continued with a matter-of-fact demeanor. "Without hesitation, the team jumped on the hiding individual, and a brief wrestling match ensued, resulting in the custody of a middle-aged male in a white dishdasha. There was no doubt that we had captured our target. His thick beard was a dead giveaway. It was Abu Ayatt."

Jeff went silent. We had decided. Inaction is an action. The head of the snake was coming off. Conflict is full of choices and this was no different. Keeping the head on the snake meant we were able to keep the peace and avoid conflict, but removing the head meant capturing a criminal responsible for murder and attacks on coalition forces.

We knew the potential for violence increased if we eliminated either Ayatt and Sayf, but criminals can't go unpunished. The moral dilemmas throughout this war were plentiful and not relegated to the few, but to the many. Like so many things, what was done can't be undone. All ranks involved had to choose different outcomes. We chose violence. We chose aggression on behalf of those defenseless souls on whom the belligerents preyed. We chose to strike and Ayatt was captured—the snake's head was removed.

The reunion didn't cheer as they hadn't ten years ago. Upon capture, there'd been no time to celebrate. The platoons, facing a growing riotous crowd, had to get Ayatt out of there before his friends came to fight for his release, resulting in more local nationals' bloodshed. A HMMWV pulled curbside to extract the prisoner, and he was thrown in for a one-way trip to the FOB. It wouldn't take long for the crowd of Mahdi sympathizers to begin throwing rocks at the rest of the cordon and coalition forces in the area, but with the head of the snake removed, the remaining elements withdrew. It was a small victory. It was justice.

"Screw that snake!" Notaro roared. "That son of a bitch attacked us. He deserved to be shot."

"Absolutely," Jeff said. "It didn't work out that way. He was unarmed. He wasn't dumb. It happened so fast. We got him, and we got the man who had killed our friend."

September 1, 2006 –

Time for some route security again. We're letting things cool off a bit. We stuck to the main roads. Tensions are high, and each time we roll into a neighborhood, we are met with a hail of rocks and bricks.

A local came to notify us of unexploded ordnance, so we called the POB to take care of some bombs in the dude's backyard. We watched a gunfight between the guards in the Tuwaitha towers and some dudes in the trees. We were told to not butt in. The Iraqis have it under control.

We patrolled along the Tigris and circled to Jisr Diyala to push through the market. The shoppers and vendors stared, but nobody wanted to dance. I wouldn't make a good partner, anyway. We checked out a couple of possible IEDs on Pluto and convoyed home. There are two more months left in this place.

One may not think that being stuck as a gunner for these missions was a good thing. I remember thinking that it was the best position in the truck, but it was still in the truck. Being on your own two feet was a relief. You could fight back and avoid hazards on your own initiative. You could see more and be closer to the people. On top of that, the death toll from IEDs was increasing. Being stuck in the truck made you a giant rolling target. Taking out a HMMWV was a big deal for the enemy and the best chance to collect American casualties. IEDs were going to blow off your leg, pepper you full of metal, or send you flying out of the turret.

There was a collective sense of casualty aversion to a mission that was not going to be over in the timeline we assumed. The grunts knew the risk. The reports of IEDs became so common that gunners put one foot in front of the other as they sat in the turret sling so when you were hit, maybe you'd lose one foot or leg, not both.

You can't eliminate risk, only mitigate it. Risk aversion flows from the top down. The soldiers on the ground accepted reality and sometimes reality sucks, but it doesn't make it any less real. There was a savage mood and a cheerless attitude flowing through the company.

The Comanches wanted to address the root cause. They wanted to get after the enemy. They wanted to mitigate it through violence on a population many viewed more and more like the opposition. We also knew among the civilians were those who would help us find the insurgent and Mahdi threats. Many adopted circular reasoning—to save some, we needed to kill some and to kill some, we needed to save some. Identifying which ones to kill and save was the way to break the circle and see any movement towards success, whether on foot or from the turret.

September 4, 2006 –

We finished a patrol and quick-turned into another mission at 0530. We had to take Pluto northbound and swing around to the west to get to Jisr Diyala due to the Route Pluto bridge being shut down again. We cruised through downtown and came upon the bridge in JD. Traffic is hell with the rerouted vehicles gumming up the two-lane crossing. We attempted to butt our way through and push north, but it's hopeless.

Regardless of the pandemonium, it was into JD market we go. We got a half kilometer from the bridge and walked ahead of the trucks pushing dudes out of the way. The heat was stifling. We made it through and patrolled around a whole lot of disarray.

Wardiya was burning to the ground. Ja'ara was fighting off a growing sectarian tide. Each neighborhood was continuing its decline. We listened to rifle fire enveloping us but couldn't pin its source.

Soon, we found ourselves having to make our way through JD to get pointed downtown on our way to the FOB. The people grew even angrier, but so did we. Get out of our way! Despite the curse words and fury, we made it to Rustamiyah without a scratch. I liked that.

I took a nap but was interrupted by incoming and the cry for a medic. I stumbled out of my bunk and took a look around. Dombroski was running with his aid bag. Some dudes caught shrapnel in the foot and hand and leg and whatever. They dragged him into Notaro's room for treatment. One lucky bastard. Nothing too serious. Notaro was pissed about the blood. Hilarious. I went back to sleep.

September 6, 2006 –

Today, we took a route that meandered alongside the Tigris on the opposing bank to the JD bridge. The route has so many potholes from IEDs that it rattled your teeth and shook your bones. The road was terrible. We got to the bridge and again had to fight through traffic to cross. I'm sure any observers were letting their dudes know we were on the way and with this traffic, we couldn't respond in time to stop any attack.

We checked out a hole some locals had been digging. We scared them off, but they were innocent. There are pipes stacked nearby and they were digging for irrigation but thought they'd get shot. We investigated some Iraqi police checkpoints and took off into a small village in the eastern part of our sector. There, we questioned some natives. They didn't have any concerns. Good. It's the one quiet place in our entire area of operations.

251

Not that our stuff is out of control—we are faring much better than Anbar or other areas, at least according to the chow hall news. Our dealing with the militia, though, is declining and they are progressing further into crime and murder. We convoyed to the bridge and linked up with 1st platoon to beat our way through the traffic.

We made it in one piece but can't shake the feeling the Jisr Diyala situation is simmering and ready to ignite. Every time we fight through the traffic, we are making no friends. The Route Pluto bridge needs to be fixed again so the traffic into Baghdad can resume normal operations. Incoming fire while I write this.

September 9, 2006 –

The quick reaction force I was assigned launched on a recovery mission for a suspected downed drone. We're told to return to base after it's safely recovered. The heat was intense out on patrol, so the radio transmission to return was welcomed. Later that night, we were stuck in the motor pool changing fluids on the HMMWVs. We finished and were shooting the breeze.

Incoming! We endured another batch of indirect fire. It caught me off guard. One landed right in front of me. I saw the sparks and felt the concussion with a wave of heat across my face. People were running and crawling off their trucks for a nearby bunker. The rockets screamed in, slamming in the tightest shot group to date. Wright takes a small piece of shrapnel in the forearm and pulled it out with a multi-tool and a headlamp.

I watched for wounded and thought I saw a guy get hit. He staggered upright and ran for cover. Lucky. Eight or so people were sent to the aid station for injuries. One died. Later, I found a piece of shrapnel in my neck. It was a little metal shard. It felt like a small campfire burn. Damn, that was close.

It was the most intense indirect fire attack I remember, and it was one that changed my passion for the game. Dropping the hood of the truck, we were going to drive from the small parking lot of the motor pool to the company with a pit stop at the chow hall. Nobody heard the launch like the typical barrage of rockets or mortars we'd grown accustomed to hearing. As soldiers leaned over engines and dudes greased tracks on their turrets, listening to a dusty radio tucked on top of a workbench, the rounds caught us by surprise.

Wam! Wam! Wam!

They were Katyusha rockets falling from the skies like whining footballs of death. Sparks zipped across the motor pool and showered the trucks with hot, yellow flakes of metal. In favor of immediate cover, I yelled to Davis to get into the truck and he agreed, though he smashed his head into the thick steel armor from a helpful nudge I gave him to get inside. I apologized and sat in the rear driver side, watching the barrage continue.

Within a few seconds, several rockets impacted the area around us. The projectiles made the whoosh-whine sound as they entered their terminal phase of flight. One, in particular, struck the metal roof of a building right next to the motor pool and our truck. It sent shards of aluminum spraying around us. I felt the shockwaves and heat from each impact.

Looking out the window, I noticed a soldier climbing out of the turret in an attempt to make it to the safety of a bunker. A rocket crashed into a jersey barrier right next to him, spewing concrete fragments for several meters as he tumbled from the top of the HMMWV to the ground amid the continuing shower of sparks.

I tugged on the door handle and got one foot out of the truck when another soldier sprinted past him on his way to shelter. Stumbling around, he got up, wobbled, realized soldiers were rushing around, and, coming to, staggered off in the same direction as the crowd. I broke out laughing in a sort of idiotic way. I was happy he was all right.

In that lull, I poked my head out and saw a few people on litters being put on the six-wheeled utility vehicle to take them to the aid station. They were wounded, and the medics were treating a few on the scene. There was a lot of yelling and confusion. We sat in our truck and, with nervous laughter, chalked it off as a close one.

I crawled to the driver's seat and when the time was right, drove us the 200 meters to the company area. It was there that I noticed the small piece of metal in my neck. I came to a conclusion about the bravado-filled sport of indirect fire that night as my naïveté was blasted away—this game sucks.

Of course, the game became hotter than ever in our sector, but the tribe carried out their missions with little fanfare. The briefing before a patrol consisted of a few words from the non-commissioned officer in charge and a few expletives from the men. Most of the curse words were directed towards the routes selected. Some people hated certain roads more than others because of their experiences. Some disliked their truck assignment because it was falling apart, but most cursed because they were tired.

We did our damnedest to fight the complacency but wanted to get at the enemy and not be relegated to doing the route security missions assigned. Leadership wanted to let the conditions in Jisr Diyala cool. The soldiers understood that our hold in the area was increasingly tenuous but wanted nothing more than to attack the problem at its next acrimonious root—Abu Sayf.

8.

WE'RE THE SOLDIERS OF THE HUNDRED-FIRST

September 13/14, 2006 –
Firefight in Jisr Diyala. Weir KIA. No entry required.

"We went back and got those assholes!" Notaro boomed. Most of the reunion-goers were sitting, but Notaro stood. Discussing the topic of Ayatt's capture made tensions that had smoldered under the layers of our being boil to the surface. We fell right into September 2006. We had been infantrymen stuck in a nation unraveling, and when you are confronted with chaos, you can become chaotic.

"I doubt anyone can forget that," Jeff said. "It was the worst engagement of our deployment."

"Whatcha got written about that one, Endris?" Notaro asked.

"I felt like I wasn't going to need to write that one down," I replied. I wanted to redirect the conversation and shifted to Eric. "Sir, as the platoon leader, it's best left to you. You had the pieces, after all."

"I did." Eric took a swig from his mug and shook his head. He put his thumb back in his pocket and scanned the crowd. Eric knew the topic was unavoidable. He knew the reason for his attendance was to do this. "We missed our chance to properly

255

debrief this thing as a unit—at least outside of the professional context. We redeployed and splintered. Well, here we are. It's best to get this outta the way."

Eric began telling the story of the night we locked horns with the enemy.

"I arrived at FOB Rustamiyah in the midnight hours on the 6th of September. The first order of business was to get updates from the team. There was plenty to be done, and many things were in motion or in limbo, demanding immediate attention. It was obvious we were not done with Jisr Diyala. Abu Ayatt was the decisive target there, but many other key Mahdi leaders needed to be dealt with—otherwise, they'd replace him. The local militia was in a state of frenzied disorder without a directive leader at the helm. They had no direction and no restriction.

The next targets on the list were his deputy, Abu Sayf, and his religious advisor, Sheikh Majid. There was concern that an unknown Mahdi leader could come in and take the lead, whereas our planned method would have manipulated those already in the local militia system. However, if properly executed, this operation would create breathing room for the local government in the form of some domestic security and freedom from intimidation.

We planned and conducted a platoon mission to confirm the suspected location of Abu Sayf and a raid to capture one of his aides to lead us to him. On both missions, we received sporadic small arms fire. On the raid, as Schrader returned fire, one round from the enemy clipped the butt stock of his rifle and ricocheted off of his American flag patch, leaving a baseball-sized bruise on his shoulder. If the flag patch we wore wasn't bulletproof, then

Schrader was. It was evident that the militia understood that we were serious about lethal targeting. The pressure was building.

Three days after I returned, we got the order. As details were disseminated, thanks to Lieutenant Colonel Winski's leadership, we conducted excellent rehearsals. We did the doctrinal sequence of briefs, back briefs, rehearsal of concepts, and platoon level rehearsals utilizing sand tables and a variety of terrain models, imagery, and small mockups. We were pulling out all the stops.

As we'd done during past squadron level operations, we reorganized the reconnaissance teams, attaching an extra man from the platoon headquarters element to increase our manning to six personnel per squad. That was the entirety of what we could muster, but we were confident. The rehearsals we conducted were the key to the soldiers all the way to the squad leader level understanding the essential details and timings of the operations, resulting in a smooth execution, even when the plan changed.

The Iraqi Police would be used as a perimeter for this operation. They'd provide outer cordon five kilometers from the center of the operation—the Al-Huda Husseiniya mosque. Pattern analysis and our combined intelligence picture indicated that Abu Sayf and Sheikh Majid were to meet at 2300, as they did each night. They must have felt pretty secure in Jisr Diyala or depended upon a widespread early warning observer network to conduct their meetings in the mosque. Their complacency, not ours, would be their downfall.

That night, with our checks complete, we staged, ready for departure from the FOB. We departed at an hour or so before their meeting. First Platoon would stand by at a checkpoint two kilometers to the south with a direct approach to the center of the city to support Second Platoon. They were tasked as the reserve if we deemed we could isolate and assault organically. First Platoon left well beforehand to conduct a patrol as a red herring and get into their position. Their route required them to drive south towards Salman Pak, and turn north to assume a position in northern Tuwaitha, along the Tigris River out of sight and sound of Jisr Diyala—terrain we all knew well.

Our route was based on deception; my primary concern was hitting an IED on the way in and never reaching the objective. Leaving Rustamiyah already created a large signature that an operation was underway. We were sure that if the militia was aware we were conducting an operation, they'd place some reinforcing obstacles in the form of IEDs. However, the infiltration route worked, and we entered Jisr Diyala without incident along a narrow dirt road from the north. In a seven-vehicle convoy, we drove under night vision as we came into the central portion of the city. We slowed to a crawl, and our senses sharpened. We entered the den of vipers.

We made it to the street of the mosque without encountering any IEDs, although the CO was passing reports that numerous roadside bombs were found around the exterior of the neighborhood—no doubt emplaced due to the increased activity. He also informed us that First Platoon had a suspected IED blocking their passage to reinforce from the south. It was the first indication the enemy was prepared. We were at the rally point short of the turn to place us in direct line-of-sight with the epicenter—the Al-Huda Husseiniya. We conducted a short halt to check conditions.

As made clear during the planning, we intended to be on this road for as long as it took to locate the target, then veer off and conduct a dismounted infiltration to maximize the enemy's confusion. We planned to bring the vehicles in support of our flanks. After the communications check and conditions check with our assets and forces on the ground, we radioed that we were departing the rallying point and requested radio silence. It was time.

Kelley turned on our lights. The lights were taped and blue-tinted, so we didn't look like a HMMWV without closer examination, and we needed a few moments of confusion to keep our force disguised as long as possible. We took the turn and proceeded at a walking pace. The street was 20 feet wide; there were cars parked on both sides and just enough room for us to drive in the center. We'd taken this road many times, and it was assumed that the militia understood our intentions based on the force posture in the area.

We drove at idle speed, waiting for confirmation of our target. About three minutes later, with my vehicle 200 meters from the mosque, we got the call. Confirmed. No sooner than our brains could process that transmission than a car alarm went off next to us. Accompanying that alarm, a bright orange ball lit the mosque at the bottom of the street. It was an RPG. The projectile streaked a few feet over the convoy impacting to our right rear on a residential building. I called out, 'RPG!' The radio came alive. As soon as the noise of the impact subsided, we were engaged with small arms fire from every rooftop in every direction. It was safe to say, and I stated soberly, 'I think we are in a firefight.'

In that instant, I keyed the radio to raise the squad leaders on the net to no avail. The frequency was saturated by the company commander and first sergeant attempting to relay a situation report. The windshield and hood of the HMMWV were receiving impacts from the incoming direct fire. Kelley was giving fire commands to the gunner, who was returning fire to our front. Bob, the interpreter, was as small as he could make himself, hiding unarmed behind my seat. Things deteriorated to mayhem in less than a minute. We had no communication, but it was clear by the two-way small arms fire that guys had already dismounted and were fighting. I had to join them. This was not ideal, given the narrow street, but they weren't going to fight without me.

I informed Bob that we were dismounting and expected him to follow. I took a breath and opened my door. Bullets splashed off the door and the wall to my right. The wall was close, so I could open the door against it and create a barrier against the incoming fire. Bob dismounted, shut his door, and together we ran around the rear of the truck to take cover, leaving my door open to cover us. You could count on Bob. He was as brave an interpreter as they come.

We took cover behind the truck, and Higgins' squad was maneuvering to us. Our cover behind the truck proved to be useless, as we were taking fire from the front, rear, and both sides. As we crouched behind the truck, bullets skipped up the street from behind us. Higgins sprinted into my position. He took a knee next to me behind the truck and asked for some direction.

His squad was dispersed amongst available cover in the street, returning fire at a rapid rate. From visual recognition and team radio chatter, I gathered that two squads had dismounted and were maneuvering to the front with us. I put my hand on Higgins' shoulder, and he fell over forward—I thought he lost his balance while he thought I'd pushed him. Later, Higgins found a bullet that would have hit him in the dead center of his spine if it hadn't been stopped by his body armor. Nobody had shoved anybody. Body armor works. Our option at this point was to close with and destroy our enemy.

We bounded forward across an intersection and signaled Kelley to move forward with us, which he did with the last remaining engine life of the vehicle. We maneuvered to the street under direct small arms and RPG fire to within 100 meters of the mosque, returning fire on the way. We made entry to a building on the south side of the street and gained rooftop access. I went in and saw an Iraqi family huddled on the floor on the first level. I motioned to them to stay low and not move, and they complied. Kelley and the other vehicles inched forward, securing the intersection, blasting at the enemy with precision and conviction. They were aggressive, and I liked it. At this point, I raised the CO on the radio and relayed the situation.

With a base of fire established and communications relayed, I returned to the street. I saw the squadron headquarters element drive around the corner to our north to take a position near my vehicles that had deployed to side streets.

As I was waiting for Higgins to report his field of fire from this rooftop, Lieutenant Colonel Winski strode down the road, stoic amongst the gunfire, searching for the CO. The repose in which he conducted himself lent great affirmation to the character we thought him to be. The squadron commander asked where the CO was, and I pointed to our rear. Winski nodded and walked away amongst the fire. We fed off his composure.

About this time, Higgins reported that he did not have a line of sight into the mosque from this position, so we'd have to move. It was the right decision, and we maneuvered closer to the Al-Huda Husseiniya.

A lifetime of twenty minutes had passed. We continued pushing farther up the street to find a decent vantage point to gain fires on the mosque. Every spot was a bust, so we kept moving. Higgins eyed the street to spot his next position, and we bounded to it. As we continued to advance, we huddled behind a vehicle and a stack of pipes in the street. With this cover, we unleashed a barrage of return fire. As Higgins breached the courtyard, several RPGs arced through the street towards us.

Keck, trailing the advance, dove across the street to avoid the incoming projectiles. He attempted to clear the pile of pipes. To vault off the top of the tubes, he reached his hand onto the apex to hurdle him over. The RPGs impact disrupted his maneuver. He missed and slid his arm between two of the pipes resulting in a serious arm break upon landing.

Keck told me he was injured. He'd hurt his arm—I did not see what had happened, and I thought he'd hurt his shoulder pushing a door open or hitting a wall. I told him to wait until we got into the building so we had some cover before we'd take a look. It turned out to be a compound fracture with a severe snap in his lower forearm. Thirty minutes later, I talked to him as he was loading magazines in the back of a truck, using his one hand to de-link 7.62 ammunition and stuffing it into a magazine for one of the rifles running out of ammo. I asked him how he was doing; he said, "I'm fine sir, I took some ibuprofen."

As Higgins' squad got into the house, other squads conducted a similar maneuver to the north. I spent a few minutes running back and forth to be sure they were on line and had good fields of fire onto the objective. At this point, we had established a solid base of fire on the Al-Huda Husseiniya mosque, and we were dominating it with direct fires, gaining the initiative. We had eyes on the sprawling labyrinth of a compound surrounding the mosque. We were in positions with adequate cover and support by fire. I was happy. That was when I called for First Platoon.

Listening to the radio, I determined First Platoon's approach path was as planned. They arrived fast from the south. The clock was ticking, and we were consuming an enormous amount of ammunition, having already cross-leveled ammo once, spreading the bullets to who needed them. I had to explain to First Platoon that we had decent support by fire positions and were ready for an assault force to flank the enemy, but communications were an issue. The net remained saturated.

There was little choice. I took an M249 SAW gunner from Higgins' squad and bounded south with him a few blocks to join First Platoon. It was a hectic move, and we were taking a significant risk out on the flank alone, but we had to get to them before they blew past our current position or we would not be able to flank the enemy. I had no personnel left to send or take with me. It was the two of us, and we charged through the street, desperate to ensure we rallied with them.

A few blocks south of my platoon's position we saw First Platoon's vehicles approach, and I used an infrared laser to signal them. We linked up, explained our situation, and surmised the best route to flank the enemy. We both knew the ground well and felt that it was a good plan. We radioed across the command frequency more for awareness rather than approval but got neither. The CO replied that he wanted First Platoon to hold and ordered me to find the target.

Although I saw the logic in this, I knew that at this point our best bet to capture the target was to clear this objective and kill the enemy as they presented themselves. The fight had become high intensity, and precision targeting was not feasible under the current conditions. We also had one casualty and were bound to take more from direct fire. The CO made it clear that we were to find Abu Sayf.

However, it soon became apparent that we would be unable to locate him using our intelligence collected beforehand. Understanding this, and to limit any further collateral damage, we were ordered to withdraw. This was a tough pill to swallow, and it would take significant risk to get this done with depleting ammunition. We'd be exposed.

Notaro took the lead on recovering a vehicle, which had been disabled by small arms and RPG fire. He was furiously preparing it for a tow. Notaro, without fear, stood in the street under direct small arms fire—with multiple RPGs fired at him— for fifteen minutes and connected the vehicle to his to pull it out of the fight. As he did, we prepped for a phased exfiltration as best we could. Just as we were stepping out of our northern forward dismounted position, the enemy took the opportunity and maneuvered on us.

Our fire on their positions had ebbed, freeing the enemy to emplace a machine gun to the north in a warehouse that overwatched our location. As our withdrawal progressed, the enemy engaged with cyclic firing, pouring nonstop lead into our position, making it utterly untenable. Serendipity was with Notaro. He had just finished his work and was towing the vehicle out. Timing is everything.

I was dismounted and had checked with Schrader to see if we had accounted for men, weapons, and equipment. He acknowledged in the affirmative, and I ran to my HMMWV. The squadron commander's element was attempting to suppress the enemy machine gun but were unsuccessful. They didn't have the position. We needed to keep the fire on them as we filed out. Our gunners were up to the task.

I bumped into Winski on my way back; we nodded to one another as we both took cover for a moment behind a vehicle. He was an out-front leader, and his presence among the troops was reassuring, but I was not concerned with anything except getting in my truck at that point. The whole platoon was waiting for me to remount so we could leave, but I needed protection from this fire. So did Winski.

Soon, during a break in the shooting, we ran to our trucks. I told Kelley to start moving, and I navigated for him. I was waiting for a status from the others as we raced through the city under fire, but the radio transmissions were broken and the frequency was crowded with a steady stream of radio calls. At that instant, Schrader transmitted a message I could not understand. I waited for the radio to clear and within a moment, I received his sobering transmission. "My gunner's been shot in the head. We are working on him; we need to get back now!" It was David Weir—the gunner that had stepped in for Zayas, the man who had covered our withdrawal.

About the time I received that transmission, we were getting onto the paved road and we asked the bruised trucks to give us their all. Within twenty minutes we were at the FOB and Weir was under the care of our surgeon. The wound was critical. Somehow, the team had kept him alive during our exfiltration. Everyone in the truck was covered in blood. I watched him in the aid station until the aircraft arrived to take him to the Combat Support Hospital. As he was loaded on the helicopter, he looked stable, but he had a weak pulse. We were hopeful.

About forty minutes later, while we were detailing the events of the evening, compiling reports, and learning to improve, we were told that Weir went into cardiac arrest during the medical evacuation flight and died before he reached the US head trauma center in Balad. Weir was killed by the same enemy that had killed Zayas three weeks earlier. It stung. On this mission we hadn't gotten the target; we didn't even go onto the objective. We did kill twenty or thirty enemy fighters, but if you asked any of us, the mission was not successful. Sayf and his militiamen lived for another day."

Nobody wanted to admit that it was a failure, but we knew it wasn't a success. Killing the enemy takes you only so far, and our leaders knew that. We were limited by our guidelines to curtail civilian casualties. The Americans, restricted from entering holy sites, witnessed several mosques develop into safe havens for militia and insurgents alike. We were reliant upon the Iraqis. It was frustrating but necessary. We wanted to drop a 2,000-pound bomb on the Al-Huda Husseiniya and declare the game over, but we couldn't. Leadership had orders and so did we, but that didn't make it any easier to take. Our discipline held steadfast.

We sat around our circular tables in the VFW remembering the bitterness lingering ten years later. We had done the right thing, but sometimes the right thing sucks. Eric had summed it up as a failure. We didn't get Abu Sayf. We did kill a significant number of fighters as overhead pictures showed later, but winning this type of war isn't accomplished by killing more of them than they kill us. You have to kill the right people for the right reasons. You have to bring overwhelming violence of action to the target selected so the enemy can't maintain composure. You have to keep them off balance.

Attrition doesn't work in this context. Body counts haven't worked in the past, and they didn't work here. These weren't uniformed members of a nation-state. They were guerrillas, insurgents, militia, civilians motivated by radical ideology— powerful ideas of martyrdom and redemption. The fight was against emotion, against an idea which is not changed with violence alone. The war on terror demands a more holistic approach that leaves the clear victory and ticker-tape parade elusive. The results were victories smaller and less celebrated than those expected from past experiences.

I broke the silence. "Eric, I think I speak for the group." Kat squeezed my thigh. "It may seem like a sort of failure, but I think if you look around the room, there are some faces here that would not have been if it wasn't for you exposing yourself to that fire and directing the team through a pretty intense firefight."

"Hell yeah! I thought I was going to die that night!" Notaro boomed. "When you told me to get that truck, I was like, damn you, leave that piece of shit!"

"I had orders, Notaro. You and I know that we weren't gonna leave a truck for the enemy to take photos in front of," Eric asserted. "Plus, if there was anyone I was going to sacrifice to recover the truck, it was you, Notaro!"

The room exploded in laughter. Notaro grinned from one side of his beard to the other. It was true. Eric had marched up and down streets among a barrage of rifle and RPG fire to relay commands, get the guys in better positions, and ensure we maintained the initiative. Without his bravery and commitment, the fight might have turned sour. We joked, but underneath, we knew the right calls had been made.

"Eric, sir, I know after that went down, many of us were spiteful. I was angry. I wanted to crush as many of them as we could, for Zayas and Weir. But Paul is right, I owe you. It could have been so much worse." Sorbello stared at the pictures to the front. "I mean, we lost two damn fine Americans. Those heroes kept us from losing twenty."

"You don't owe me a damn thing." Eric narrowed his eyes and took his thumb out of his pocket. "You think I was the first out of the trucks? No. You think I was laying the blankets of accurate and lethal fire? Not like you guys. You guys were the ones out there taking it to them. You guys were the ones watching each other's backs. Like Keck, bone sticking out, but loading mags to make sure the fight continued, you guys were the ones who brought each other home. You guys were the ones that kept it from getting worse. You guys did it."

"That's right," Burns stated. We listened. "It was the team. I was damn proud of you guys that night. Everyone was doing their job. That's what kept it from getting worse."

"Remember, though," Jeff piped in. He realized that even though that firefight was tough, and Abu Sayf was sustained by an increasing number of militiamen, we had brought the fight to his front yard. "We went back in, we got him. Weir covered our withdrawal. And we made those dudes pay the price!"

Weir, the fire support specialist who had joined the company after Zaya's death, was welcomed to the Comanches with open arms. He too was a founding and prominent member of the squadron. From the hills of southern Tennessee, the Rocky Top country boy had had a lifelong dream of serving in the Army. When his remains made their way to Cleveland, the city's citizens lined the streets waving flags for his arrival. The county declared September 20th as 'Sgt. David Weir Day'. His death electrified the patriotism of his hometown and sharpened the dedication to the mission of his brothers-in-arms.

The fight was far from over. We were going to regroup and charge into Jisr Diyala and rip Abu Sayf from his militia protection. We continued to conduct missions while, in the interim, the leadership drafted plans for our next large-scale operation. It wasn't the only show in town. We had other areas to patrol, but it was the fight we wanted.

Sayf's capture may have been in the name of arresting the descent into anti-governmental and sectarian violence, but it also had shades of redemption. We wanted the militia leaders gone but knew Sayf was more valuable alive than dead. If we were going to remove the head from the viper, we needed to know all the snakes in the pit.

September 16, 2006 –

Jisr Diyala is a no-go area. We are coordinating a massive sweep-and-clear mission. In the meantime, we visited Wardiya to see how much the violence had progressed. There was little change. The enemy was busy in Jisr Diyala. We drove to the riverbanks and picked up Farmer Joe. He told us he would again identify insurgents living in Wardiya. We gave him a mask, threw him in a truck, and off we went.

He pointed out a few houses deep in Wardiya itself, and we soon found ourselves at a dead end. We didn't have any working power steering so getting the trucks turned around was a pain. If Farmer Joe led us into an ambush, we'd follow him as long as we didn't have to change directions. We took the information from Joe and were most discrete in his return. Let's see if those tips amount to anything, but we'll do that later. We returned to the Rustamiyah in time to catch a few mortars smashing into the base.

September 17, 2006 –

The sniper and headquarters elements are tasked with a new mission. We are to depart for a city northeast of us further into the Diyala province called Nahrawan. We were to reconnoiter for some future operations we've got planned but made it a few miles before radioed to stop. One of the trucks took a dump. The trucks are in pretty rough shape, but our mechanics are champs.

We took it to the FOB, did a quick fix, grabbed some fuel, and rolled out for a routine patrol instead of the Nahrawan expedition. We got to the outskirts of Wardiya to investigate Farmer Joe's claims and make it within communications range of 1st platoon. They had taken a few rounds and were assisting the police. The POB was duking it out on Route Wild. We joined them, but they had the situation under control. A few sporadic bursts from a machine gun, but the returned fire from an Iraqi APC makes short work of it.

We are directed to let the POB action on the targets given to us the day before. We went to see Farmer Joe with food and goodies for the kids. We told him thanks, and we took off to negotiate our way through some defunct neighborhood before hitting Routes Wild and Pluto. Some engineers were doing route clearance ahead of us, so it took us forever at 5 mph but better safe than sorry, I guess. The bridge was operable again, so we let them clear ahead, and we chilled. As we sat, a sister unit called in an IED strike on Route Wild. The bomb was put in right behind us.

The insurgents had pushed to the fringes of Route Wild from the sanctuary of the Tigris River. Soon, they would be burning homes on the other side of this two-lane highway in Ja'ara. It was a bit riskier for them to cross the road since coalition and Iraqi forces cruised up and down it on patrols. They also knew that coalition forces used the buildings as observation posts. We had conducted a dozen OPs along Route Wild in the past and would've loved to spot them toting an RPG across the highway. Still, they were pushing further and further into rival sect turf, murdering any opposing them. It was a violent sectarian Sykes-Picot division of neighborhoods.

In an attempt to stop this, the police established positions several hundred meters towards the Tigris to build a buffer between the congested highway and the roving insurgent death squads. It did little to stem the violence. We knew that many of the police had ties to the Mahdi Army and other insurgent groups. With so many areas slipping away into the violence, our patrols consisted of damage control. We acted upon any tip, chased phantom shots, investigated any remote house, but had little to show for it.

The rest of September continued this way. We'd leave the FOB and travel to an area, engage the local leaders, and toss out a few soccer balls. The holy month of Ramadan had started, and we were skeptical that the violence would decrease in observance of the Muslim holidays. We were briefed on the cultural relevance of Ramadan and did our best not to eat or smoke cigarettes in front of the observants as they fasted or have any outwardly insulting interactions.

It made no difference. Jisr Diyala and its inhabitants were not welcoming to our presence despite our cultural sensitivity. Nothing stopped the continued assaults between rival groups in our sector. We felt it, but the air was electric in September. Our area of operations had a current running through it that charged the militia. It was clear we needed to remove their power source. It was time to get Abu Sayf.

September 29, 2006 –

In preparation for a squadron-wide raid, we set out for an observation post on the outskirts of Jisr Diyala. We returned to our roots. We took the back way into Tuwaitha off Route Gator, along the Tigris. We dismounted and climbed into the weeds.

After negotiating some obstacles and crossing a giant open field, we were in sight of the guard tower where we were to position ourselves. The problem was that the tower was near a dozen Iraqi security guys. Time to be sneaky. We closed in, moving five meters a minute. The dogs caught our scent and barked like hell. We trudged off adjacent to the road, but that wasn't going to work either.

A couple of trucks with PKC machine guns crossed the checkpoint and entered the compound, which was unusual. We waited until they left and circled around a metal shed and came in from a different angle. We dodged lighted areas and made a 20-meter dash across another open field before entering the tower. Success, we didn't want to tip them off that we were gathering intelligence for the raid we'd planned.

We spent two hours pulling observation without any significant actions. A few unarmed men walking about past curfew, but the darkened, shattered buildings made it too damn hard to tell if there was more activity. There were so many places to hide.

The town was pretty quiet. I expected more—a roving patrol or at least a spotter. Time to leave. We got our gear together and made it out much quicker than we made it in. We hit the roadway and forced marched the 500 meters or so to the pickup spot.

On our way out, we paid the guards a visit. They mentioned they thought they heard some noise to their rear. We told them to check it out, and we drove off. We hit Wall Street, which borders Jisr Diyala and Tuwaitha. The road hasn't seen much coalition traffic as of late. I was bummed we didn't have more to report, but reporting nothing was reporting something.

October 4, 2006 –

It was time to head to Jisr Diyala. We were supposed to do this 48 hours earlier, but our informant reported that Abu Sayf had skipped town. We've been spending hours studying the layout of the city, the plan, the contingencies, and rehearsing concepts. In the sand table room, they made a model city labeled with impressive detail. We coordinated with the Iraqi Special Forces to see where we could best augment them and cover our guys.

Due to the Ramadan holiday, the plan was changed late from sweep-and-clear to a more precision raid of a set list of target houses to apprehend any high-value targets and remove any possible caches. The mood was tense since the last time we went into JD our company had been ambushed, but we felt ready. We weren't the only ones—reports of armed militia patrolling the town and even making fighting positions let us know they were prepared too. Although we saw no indication of this during our OP, it wasn't unrealistic.

We could surprise them with our massive force and keep them from organizing any resistance. The time came, and we had a job to do. At 0445, we rolled out the gate, and I clenched my pendant for luck. We crossed the bridge and hit the route along the Tigris to enter Jisr Diyala from the north.

As we neared the target areas, I looked out the window and could see other elements crossing the bridge and coming from the opposing side of the river through our already emplaced cordon. The execution brought a tear to the eye, or maybe that was just sweat. Dozens of HMMWVs muscled into position with the skill of a unit that had spent close to a year deployed.

It was impressive, but it wasn't long before it dawned on our targets. The speakers from the mosques began blaring warnings to the locals that the Americans were coming. A few random tracers flew into the air from inside Jisr Diyala. It was from the rifle of a Mahdi fighter scaring the citizens to act as obstacles and deterrents to the impending raid. Their early warning wasn't early enough.

Our convoy turned onto the market street. Opposite us, a kilometer west on the other side of Jisr Diyala, 2nd platoon had infiltrated via Wall Street to narrow down Sayf's location. Before they could do so, we got a report that one of the cavalry troops hitting their first target building near the outer cordon had captured Sayf without resistance. What luck.

No slack, though—we continued to prosecute the other targets, but with the satisfaction that our primary target was apprehended. We made it in without hitting an IED. Dumping off near our target building, we cleared a house, scaring the family to death, and claimed a rooftop to overwatch. I expected at any time for hell to break loose with enemy fighters showering bullets from PKCs and blasting the occasional RPG.

The platoons booted in doors and conducted their work with a methodical madness. We scanned for any response and found unarmed women and children crying and shouting as

273

their husbands and fathers were pulled from their houses and arrested. Our sources indicated they were complicit in murder. No remorse. I got a radio call telling us to hit another building, so we raided the house pulling a named individual from his roost. He was coming with us.

We handed the detainee off, and it was time to withdraw to Tuwaitha. Making our way behind the perimeter of the nuclear complex, I saw a line of 40 dudes with blindfolds on and hands zip-cuffed. We had apprehended them without firing a shot. The militia was caught off-guard, and our mass, surprise, and maneuvering had denied them the ability to organize a response. Beautifully planned and executed.

I sat outside the ad hoc detainee collection point listening to the radio reports of militia members fleeing on foot through the fields to the north. The decision was made to release the Strykers that had come to lend a hand, and with them, we sent some detainees with a military police escort back to the FOB. We sat waiting to collect and escort more of the captured individuals when we got word a mob was forming.

The locals were furious. They overran and killed the police at a checkpoint near the market and ignited tires in the streets to cover the city with black smoke. They sought to storm Tuwaitha, but we were ready. The company took positions in the towers and along the fence. Everything possible was used to beat back the crowd minus lethal means. Our guys couldn't engage those shooting from behind the tire fires for fear of hitting unarmed civilians.

It was a full-blown riot, and there wasn't much coalition forces could do. We let them rage, providing a few warning shots to let them know to stay a healthy distance away from us. Upon our leadership's request, the Strykers returned, but the mob leaped onto their vehicles, ripping off gear strapped to the green behemoths as they pushed into the crowd. It didn't matter but soon enough the sight of these green caged demons sent people into the side streets and the crowd lost its momentum.

We returned to the FOB after the rampaging crowd dispersed. We were supposed to return that night, but it was canceled. Nobody was allowed into Jisr Diyala for another 24 hours. The police were sent in to try to quell the city. Good luck.

May 29, 2016 –

"We went in there and got those dudes." Jeff's words sparked. The electrified spirit of the riot returned. The thought of the day we took down senior leaders of the Mahdi Army in Jisr Diyala itched like a rash he couldn't scratch. "That riot, though, was insane."

"There must have been a few hundred people, maybe even a thousand," Notaro added. "Glad we had Tuwaitha to fall into." The intensity of the riot sent the soldiers looking for cover with not a moment to spare. A fusillade of bricks, rocks, and glass projectiles came screaming in from smoke-concealed rioters. Jeff had taken a position in one tower of the facility and had a front-row view. Others sat inside the gate hoping the crowd didn't overrun their positions, or force them to blast the unarmed Iraqis away with lethal means.

"We had been tasked to remove somewhere around 28 insurgents, but I think in total we detained near 40," Jeff said. He sat at a table discussing the events but may have well been standing. The room shifted their attention to his recollection. "We had to zip-cuff a dozen other guys who kept interfering with

275

our operation. If you try to protect your insurgent friends, you get insurgent prizes."

These militiamen, though, had established themselves as prominent citizens. After we had captured many of these members of the community as part of our combined operation, the remaining religious officials and Mahdi sympathizers, who may have been one and the same, blasted messages from the mosque bullhorns inciting violence on behalf of their removed neighbors. As the soldiers kneeled behind the gate, a barrage of rocks and debris flew at them, thrown by a growing, angry mob of Jisr Diyala citizens trying to provoke a reaction.

Jeff adjusted his seat behind him. "I never admitted it before, but a blink of fear flickered within me. Higgins, Langford, and the rest of the guys took positions in the tower or outside the gate." Jeff motioned with his hands to indicate the relation of the positions our teams had established. "It didn't seem like we had enough people to stop them. I thought they were going to run right through the gate."

"Fear doesn't mean scared," Notaro said. He was across the room, but his loud voice didn't have a problem making it to the other side. "And even if you were scared, courage doesn't exist without fear."

"Ain't that the truth," Burns said. "As long as you stood your ground, you did what you needed to do." Burns toyed with an empty glass. "Fear or no fear, you kept it from getting worse."

The rioting crowd advanced towards the Comanches and the supporting elements within Tuwaitha. The Jisr Diyala locals rallied around flags and burned tires to mask their movements or conceal shots of opportunity. We demanded they stay away over a bullhorn, but it was futile. The roar of the crowd drowned out any message we broadcasted. The mosque speakers added to the din. With limited options, we planned to defend ourselves and did what we could to disperse the crowd.

"How many damn smoke grenades did we launch into the crowd? At least ten. I can't believe they picked them up and threw them back. It had to have burnt the hell out of their hands." Jeff continued. "That's when old Notaro here decides to make me go deaf."

"What are you talking about?" Notaro asked, with a lack of concern but genuine interest.

"You don't remember? You grabbed the shotgun and blasted a group with less than lethals when they tried to climb over the wall. They must have been 50 meters away, but the barrel was five inches from my head."

"Ha! Oh shit! I forgot about that!" Notaro thundered. "That didn't do a damn thing either. It slowed them, but it wasn't going to stop them."

It didn't. It wasn't until the Strykers returned that the crowd got the hint. The soldiers from 172nd had their tour of duty extended and we were glad they had—if only for one selfish moment. Their herculean eight-wheeled armored fighting vehicles crushed along Route Wall Street, closing on the crowd that was growing and inching closer to the troops powerless to stop their advance.

"If it weren't for the guys from the 172nd, it would have been a far tougher situation," Jeff commented. "I'm grateful." The Strykers veered around the corner and faced the mob. Their vehicles steadily pushed into the crowd. The Iraqis pulled gear from the Stryker's exterior, a few climbed its RPG cage, but harmlessly fell off as it shuffled forward. The rioters tangled with our new friends in town but soon submitted. The enraged demonstrators dispersed. The damage was done.

The fire burned hot, and high black clouds of smoke filled the air. Reports of murdered civilian bodies soon made their way in from the Iraqi police networks. It was probable that the executions were being used to incite violence. With the crowd on the ropes, the company slipped out of the Tuwaitha complex and returned to the FOB to deescalate any further rioting and turn the operation over to the local police.

The situation in Jisr Diyala and relations with its inhabitants were declining. However, our mission was a success. We had taken Abu Sayf without a lethal shot fired, arrested and removed a significant portion of the leadership without using deadly force, and slipped away from an uncontrollable riot.

It wasn't a shock that there were unconfirmed reports of death within the city, which may have been Mahdi extrajudicial killing of those unwilling to confront the Americans or thought to have rendered aid to our cause. Even if we had reports of this before moving into Tuwaitha, our drive into Jisr Diyala to stop the murder would have resulted in more death—particularly of the innocent crowds coerced into the streets. Solutions create new problems. There are no good decisions.

Withdrawal, our best course action, meant avoiding any wanton destructiveness that reentry to the city would bring. We had defanged the viper at limited expense, but what was not well understood was whether another set of teeth would sprout in their place. Regardless of whether the militia was wounded, or the leadership removal would slow their ability to challenge the legitimacy of the government and its policing power, the area was in turmoil with the citizenry stuck in the middle of the fighting. This we could not refute as thick plumes of black smoke hung over Jisr Diyala and we returned to FOB Rustamiyah and another couple of months of patrolling.

9.

WE'LL FIGHT 'TILL THE BATTLES WON

October 6, 2006 –

It feels like we are on the backside of this thing, but I'm worried to let that feeling creep in. It doesn't matter if it's day 1 or day 361. Things happen.

Today, we go out to do another mission of mosque monitoring. Jisr Diyala is a mess. Lots of extrajudicial killings to the south so we traveled to the mosque in Wardiya so the locals could pray in peace.

We found a decent position but soon moved closer in case we couldn't hear the mosque's loudspeakers. We circled wagons on the soccer field in Wardiya proper and waited. Kids were out playing and a couple of children let us fly their kite. Another kid walked to me with a busted finger, and I sent him to the doc to get treated. Not one kid threw a rock at me today. It was nice.

We cruised by the mosque, and it was empty. Wardiya was calm, almost peaceful. I don't think I heard a single shot fired. Is the enemy hiding? Do they know we are coming and don't want to play? The loudspeaker stopped, and we left to cruise Pluto to conduct some routine checkpoint assessments next to the bridge over the Diyala. Everything checked fine. The guards were jovial. Having moved on from their checkpoint, we halted before rejoining the disorder of Pluto traffic. I sat watching from behind the gun.

But then it happened. To my two o'clock, a crazed, small pickup plowed through the checkpoint and accelerated straight at us. I spun my turret to the speeding truck as fast I could and readied myself for more rock and roll. My first thought was that it was a VBIED. I leveled the gun. Finger on the trigger. Heart rate. I yelled in broken Arabic to stop. No response. I needed to kill them before they killed my friends. There's not much distance. Decision. I eased on the trigger.

Son of a...! I released the trigger with a few pounds left before the fury. A car bomb rarely has more than one driver. That hesitation was all it took. The truck slammed on the brakes skidding sideways in the gravel. As the dust cleared, I looked closer and saw a few bodies in the bed. One is looking at me, and blood was pouring out of his mouth. He blinked.

A lady in a black burqa was covering another man in his underwear. She rose to her knees and shouted at me. I slouched into the turret and with an astonishing twist of nonchalance, told the guys, "Hey, I think we got some more dead bodies here." The guys inside the truck were puzzled after hearing my shouting. I didn't have time to explain what had happened. "Umm, I guess they might be alive." My indifference didn't help, but our guys quickly went to render aid to the four bodies.

I spotted a Bradley a block away and had them radioed for assistance. After treating the wounded civilians, the POB loaded them and took off for the hospital. We hopped on Pluto northbound to the next checkpoint. The traffic was a mess. Police were shooting into the air trying to move vehicles. I yelled at the cars to get off the road and made it to the FOB alive. Pointing a pistol sometimes moves cars faster than

pointing a machine gun. Getting close to the
deployment. I don't want to take any more chance

Looking back, my actions are vivid and carry a sense of internal urgency. Parked on the lower portion of an L-shaped bend in the road, I was in the turret of the rear vehicle of the convoy, focused on the engineer's metal bridge funneling cars across the river on our left flank. The Iraqi police at the bend in the road waved us through, and we had taken a short halt before maneuvering onto the busy traffic of Pluto. As a truck came barreling through the checkpoint, the Iraqi guards came running out of their shack, waving it on. It was a car bomb. I was sure of it. The truck was less than 150 meters away from us after making the turn. A building had blinded me to its approach, so I didn't see them until they were on the final dash towards our position. My throat tightened.

If the truck was going 40 miles an hour, I had less than three seconds to make the decision. I lowered the M240. One second gone. In the background, I saw the frantic Iraqi police officer waving to get my attention. I looked down the barrel into the cab of the truck. Two men; one with a red scarf around his head, stared back. I hesitated one second. Car bombs are normally solo rides, but I didn't want to take a chance. I remembered the first sergeant's words. I interpreted the variables fast enough to slow my trigger pull. It's not a bomb, but they could be armed. To my relief, the truck slammed on its brakes, sliding sideways in the gravel and broken asphalt.

The reason for their haste became unmistakable. I saw the bodies tumbling around in the bed. A woman was holding onto four bodies as best she could as the truck screeched to a halt. She belted out an agonizing wail as she, and the bodies toppled in the truck. One body came to rest on its side. It looked at me. I made eye contact. His skin was a paraffin wax shade of pale, wicked by a crimson string of blood from his mouth. The body blinked at me. He wasn't dead. He was alive.

Over ten months of combat had hardened me, and the other guys like me, to the suffering of the Iraqis. My reaction was tempered by the understanding that this was a violent place, and there wasn't anything to be gained from getting worked up over a few victims of sectarian violence in the bed of a pickup.

We had become callous, the wildness inside us no longer. It was external and consuming, but the mission, or our sanity, required it. The human condition after war is a haunting where veterans hunt for the ghosts of their former selves, sometimes not wanting to find them because they demanded recognizing the change they underwent from their experiences. But they must. In life, change is undying.

It's easy to not see those Iraqis as people anymore, and it's more difficult to see them as human. I sat back into the turret strap, wondering if I had made the right call. As I scanned for targets, I concluded that I had done my best, but I was angry. How dare they interrupt my peaceful patrol!

As suddenly as the truck had appeared, my rage evaporated. It vanished with the thought that we had to get back to base. We got the victims bandaged and hauled away before continuing our mission. That night, instead of being mad about the constant discovery of violence and not its perpetrators, I sat around the chow hall table, thankful for another hot meal and another day alive.

October 8, 2006 –

It's a brand-new day, but the same old sunrise. We crossed the Route Pluto bridge and continued south looking for the usual bombs and whatnot. We hit the traffic circle and banged a left out into the boondocks. We were curious and dove off onto some back roads we had not taken before.

282

We turned left, then right, then left, and hopped some ditch and then climbed on some other dusty road. After those rough roads, we came upon a housing complex for the Ministry of Oil. It was the cleanest looking place I have seen in Iraq. We kept a healthy distance from the outer walls and decided it was best to not interfere.

We made our way to civilization and pulled over into a little shopping area along a busy road. Everyone played with the kiddos, and I bought some junk food to give them. The whole team handed out the few pieces of candy and whatever we had. The soccer balls drew a massive crowd. The kids lost their minds over those things. The platoon leader was two steps from being trampled.

A little kid late to the party saw the handouts from across the road and wanted in on the goodness. The kid chose to run across the street but made it two steps in before an orange and white taxi cab slammed into him. The driver smashed on the brakes, but it didn't matter. The kid flew backward 10 meters before tumbling to the ground. He stood and didn't know if he wanted to cry or run away, so he did both. He limped away with a bum leg and injured dignity. The medic caught him to check him out, and he was fine. Then the radio went off. IED blast on Pluto. Go secure the scene. Roger. Let's get the hell out of here.

May 29, 2016 –

Realizing that we could use a beverage, and we'd been telling stories as a group for over an hour, the reunion took a pause. Looking around the room at the growing family of Comanche veterans, spouses, and family members, I knew the group was enjoying the renewed camaraderie and storytelling of the days of a tribe since disbanded. It was as if we had been waiting for a day to discuss these topics and it had arrived. Instead of a day, we needed a full weekend to digest the experience. Maybe a lifetime.

"I'm glad we did this," I told Kat. She remained seated as I stood to stretch my legs.

"I'm glad we did, too. It's clear that the best support you guys have is each other," Kat said.

"Who says we need support?"

"Haven't you been listening to these stories? You guys are like a family. It's amazing. You guys each support a different point of view. As you look back, it's clear that each of you has internalized it differently."

"It's interesting," I said. "I've gained so much more perspective on the whole thing. I've wanted to learn from it, personally and historically, but something about being with these guys helps make sense of it."

"I know you have. It is also why you journaled as a twenty-two-year-old."

"I was twenty-one."

"Whatever. The fact is, after ten years, it shows how much you guys cared about one another, even if you were only twenty-one."

"Eh, these guys are okay." I smirked and lifted my mug. "Speaking of twenty-one, I'm going to go exercise my legal right under the 21st Amendment."

"Get away from me, nerd," Kat joked with a bit of truth.

I walked into the VFW bar attached to the ballroom. It was smoky, and a dozen or so older veterans were sitting around the bar top polishing off some cold domestics. The young bartender was busy pouring drinks for other guys from the reunion, so I grabbed some real estate next to a man who, judging by his age, was from the Vietnam era.

"How's it going?" I mumbled as more of a greeting rather than a genuine question.

"Fine, and you?" the man asked. He wore jeans and a flannel shirt with the sleeves rolled to the elbow. He wore thick glasses underneath grey hair tucked into a worn trucker hat.

"Great. Actually, really great." I gave him a genuine answer. The bartender came over and asked for my order. Cold and domestic seemed like the right answer.

"What you guys are doing in there," he said, "my generation should have done years ago. Getting everyone together and all."

I searched for a decent reply but found none. "It's good to get together and talk about some of the things."

"I'm sure it is."

There was an audible pause in the conversation. It was quiet but loud enough for us to feel it.

"Three things are certain for you guys: taxes, death, and discharge," the man said breaking the quiet. He didn't look at me but stared ahead, transfixed on the apparitions of times past, or just the sports highlights on the television. It was hard to tell. "What I will say is not certain; people aren't going to know your war. They aren't going to know what went on over there. What happened to you guys. It was the same about my war. It took time."

"I am sure nobody will know what happened in our dusty corner. I'm certain."

"Well, I'll ask you this. What good does that do anyone?" Again, I had no answer. "No matter how uncomfortable it makes you. Get over it. Share. Find a way to share, and in doing so, you'll find a way to move on and grow from it."

"It makes me a bit nervous," I revealed to the man I knew nothing about, "and I'm not sure why."

"I know why," said the assumed Vietnam vet, turning his stool to face me. "You're scared."

"That's probably true," I confided, surprising myself.

"The question isn't about being scared about sharing a story. The problem is whether you can handle the results." The veteran ended his sentence with a sip of beer from his glass, returning his eyes to the television or that apparition of times past.

He may have been right. I smiled, bid the man farewell, and dismissed myself. For an instant, I tried to decipher what the old soul had told me. What results? What did he mean? I had to ask. I turned to the Vietnam vet. "What do you mean by result?"

The man smiled a warm, gentle grin. "The sheep isolate the sheepdog because it looks like a wolf. That is until they hear a midnight howl." Standing, the man threw a few dollars on the bar. "Answer that howl. Then, return to the flock—it's already heading to the next patch of grass." The man waved to the bartender, nodded at me, and made his way to the exit. I was confused by the man's cryptic verse and screen print t-shirt poetry. I wrinkled my brow and realized I hadn't gotten his name.

Rounding the corner to rejoin the reunion, I made my way through a set of double doors and walked to the table of memorabilia that had drawn a few reunion-goers. Jeff had pulled up a chair and was reading to the group as a father would to a child. My stomach knotted. I waited for the spears cast in my direction. Their approval, the approval of the greatest tribe I had ever known, meant much to me.

Notaro spotted me. "Look, Paul, you can't change anything." He pointed at Jeff and smiled. "All sorts of fingers over this thing." Notaro's eyes lowered to Jeff, who turned a page and combed through its contents.

"I wish I had done more to record our time there," Jeff commented without unlocking his eyes from the journal. "I've already recalled so many things I'd forgotten, at least in the details."

I was anxious about my fellow tribesmen thumbing through my memories of the patrols we so often shared. I preferred to confine my thoughts to words on pages I'd felt compelled to collect years prior. Language is a tool I was not well versed in using, and I couldn't convey what a year of patrols meant to the Comanches without some judgment. "Well, it's not worth much, but I wanted to find some meaning and learn from the events of that year," I offered. I was defending the merit of the journal to no one but myself.

"You did more than that, man." Notaro eyes broke from the pages again and sharpened as if he knew I was downplaying the value of what was in front of him. "This isn't your patrols, man. This is our patrols, our missions. We were there. You made sense of our story. If the rest of it seemed senseless, so be it. Talking with you guys just opens my eyes to what happened, y'know."

"I'm not sure I provided any answers to any questions you had," I said.

There was a moral ambiguity behind the whole thing and skepticism of how the year played into the larger conflict. I wanted to remove that and seek personal lessons learned to process our deployment apart from any geopolitical context. In doing so, I had chipped away the armor built during training and hardened in combat, lifting the necessary defenses of war. Yet, a potential for a lifetime of uncertainties lingered.

"I get it, we get it." Burns moved around the table beside me. "This was a complex war. There were so many variables from top to bottom. It's easy to get lost in the middle and worry how the year ended."

"That's right. We spent 300 odd days fighting and doing the best we could. There's nothing more anyone could ask," Jeff said. He turned a page. "It's a shame it'll be forgotten."

"By who?" an incredulous Notaro asked. "Hell, man, most people had forgotten before the thing ended. Only a few try to understand our experience." Oliver, Wicker, Fogle, Antonio, and other reunion attendees made their way around the table. Oliver wrapped his arm around my shoulders, drawing a smile from Kat from the fringe of the room. Jeff soon found himself at the center of a circle. The journal became a beacon, a North Star leading us to discover parts of us our closest family and friends had never seen.

"That doesn't matter," Burns answered. "The approval you need is that of your fellow soldier but, most of all, approval of yourself."

"Allowing people to know or remember our story and seeking approval isn't the same thing," Jeff said. He hadn't looked away from the journal. "It's learning from our history and sharing it with others."

"Agreed," Notaro responded. "Heck, I'm not exactly a hundred percent sure what happened across the country when we were there. I only know what happened in our little part."

"What happened doesn't matter on a personal basis. The results won't provide justification or validation," Burns suggested. "Our nation sent us to do a job. We did it. What comes after is up to us, up to yourself, and nobody else."

Burns' words blasted me like an IED on Route Pluto. As Eric had said, you don't choose the outcome, only your outlook. I felt as if I needn't have worried what was written in my journal, but only about what it provided me. The war was contentious, and it may have ended poorly in 2006, but I had absorbed much from spending a year deployed to Iraq. I learned how I dealt with intense stressors, my morality, empathy, and most importantly, about my character as a person. All it took was an understanding and willingness to look upon my experiences and learn without worrying about any other person's perceptions.

Eric joined the group around the table. "Reflection on combat is important for all veterans to do. And sometimes that means looking to your brothers to help you. Turn the page to January 15th." Jeff obliged the command. "This is the day I joined Comanche. I walked into the company area and could tell how tight the team was. It was incredible. There was a large degree of self-reliance, but also a sense that each soldier could depend on each other. A few weeks into the deployment, you guys were going out with a sense of purpose. It didn't matter why we were here, only that we were. Now that we were, our obligation was to win—whatever that may look like. And that's it. You are here. You are veterans of war. It doesn't matter how you got here, it matters only that you are. Figure out what that means to you because I know what it means to the team. It's the same thing it meant on January 15th. We are a tribe, we are a brotherhood."

Eric's comments were met with a hushed calm. The title of leader is only assured when the appointment is ratified in the spirits of those that are led. Eric had secured the title. His points were well-taken.

"Finished?" Jeff asked. He flipped to mid-March and continued reading. "Where was I?" We chuckled at his challenge to his former boss. "Ah, here we go. You guys remember when the whole company went across the Tigris River in zodiacs?"

A few answers came from the circle, and the group continued reminiscing. The entire group added perspectives that made the journal entries come alive and reignited the bond we shared from those mutual experiences. The discussion radiated memories of life tucked away in the creases of our minds, digging further than the superficial judgements we had long ago deduced. The journal became a compelling, outright commanding tool to unlock our most reflective thoughts on the events we recounted as a group in that VFW hall. We began to understand.

As the night went on into the darkest hours of the morning, we discussed, with these experiences behind us, what we had drawn from them. Many accounts and conclusions about our experiences varied, but most were universal. We recollected harrowing times and why we needed to use those experiences to ground ourselves amid a busy, noisy life. We recounted the aggravations of our operations that took two steps forward, and one step back, forcing us to accept it as necessary for success.

Our dissatisfaction with not having the quick win was overcome by understanding the context of our fight. Certain things will always be out of our control. We revisited the anxiety-inducing travels on roads like Route Pluto. Knowing the next bomb may be for you never stopped us from doing what needed to be done. We relived how our part of Iraq succumbed to bloody sectarian violence and how we were numb to its descent into civil war. That numbness many still felt but now recognized its existence. Aware, we marched on.

We reflected upon the loss of our fellow soldiers, Zayas and Weir, and others that we lost in the ensuing years, and determined to live a life worthy of their sacrifice. Their spirit would live on through us and those they affected. They were among the ghosts that guided us. Live, they demanded.

We learned and began to understand more in that night than we had absorbed in an entire decade. Sharing the journal's contents reminded us of memories we otherwise may have relegated to the oblivion of our minds. The journal had helped unlock something we had thought forgotten.

Yet, those entries were just words. The camaraderie-stirred discussion and the collective revisiting of memories mattered most. It was our fading past that needed refreshing. We saw so many events of our deployment from different angles and internalized them even more differently. It was these lines of memories woven into a knot cut long ago that needed tying back together. A story needed telling.

The VFW staff hinted at the fatigue of holding the place open for several hours past their norm, so the reunion withered. Kat grabbed my hand and together with the group, we made our way into the brisk Tennessee morning air. Like our long trip towards Omaha, we didn't welcome it, but our reunion operation had come to an end, although not without achieving its objective. That night we reminded ourselves of so many things but none more apparent than that even after a decade back from the war, we watched over one another, we maintained the brotherhood of combat, we depended upon each other. The Comanches were still a tribe.

October 24, 2006 –

We went out to do the same patrol that we always do. The mission consisted of another run to check Ja'ara, east of Wardiya. The platoon leader's HMMWV got stuck in sewage water but made it out covered in fecal matter. We helped some old dudes push-start their van. We were going to head north towards the FOB but spotted some punk with a pistol, so we stopped. We detained the kids for a moment and searched for the gun they had thrown in the grass, wasting time.

About 10 minutes later, 2nd platoon had made contact in Jisr Diyala and we were going to aid in the fight. We tore through the streets. Entering JD, we could hear the sounds of a prolonged engagement. We pulled into the market and proceeded to cross the river into the next area of operations.

The fight transitioning to foot, 2nd platoon was dismounted in pursuit of the remainder of the enemy they had spotted. The car next to us was bloodied and bullet-ridden. During the firefight, 2nd platoon had caught some dudes fleeing across the river and riddled their vehicle with bullets. Two of the detainees were wounded—one with a grazing shot to the head. By the time we got established, the fight consisted of a few sporadic bursts of machine gun fire.

I wasn't quite sure the origin because the enemy had fled into the thick vegetation along the river. Ghosts again. It was soon evident that we weren't going to find any more signs of the enemy, so we packed it in. We rounded up the detainees for the return trip to the FOB, which we made before we had another riot on our hands.

Jisr Diyala was a hotbed of enemy activity. As Second Platoon went after some dudes, they bolted across the bridge. Unleashing hell, the soldiers unloaded on them, grazing the driver in the head. The car spun in a circle. A few of the enemy dismounted and ran for the trees along the riverside. Our guys were in hot pursuit.

Joining the fight, we edged into a blocking position and took custody of the militiamen who weren't fortunate enough to get away or had been shot in their attempt to flee. The car was riddled with bullets. The gunner had done a crack job blasting the windshield. The detainees lay on the ground, the mud caked on their faces, with bandages over their wounds and zip-cuffs tying their hands.

Off in the distance, the popping of rifle fire continued with the occasional burst of enemy machine-gun fire underscoring the fight we had yet to conclude. I watched Berry, a brawler from Second Platoon and a hard-charging Texan, bound from position to position, hunting the enemy like each bullet shot was personal and directed at him as an insult. I spun my turret towards the bridge and watched the growing traffic jam created by our clash. You couldn't fight a battle in Baghdad without spectators.

The scene was ripe for another attack, or potential civilian casualties, so we moved fast to collect the wounded. The remaining fighters had fled to the south through the dense vegetation along the river, but it was time to move before another riot was on our hands. Our guys came from the tree line dirty and heated. Berry was furious they had escaped. From the turret, I commended him for his John Wayne gunfighting skills, and he laughed a tired but appreciative laugh.

The clash over and the crowd forming, the convoy buttoned up and debated how to return to base. We had drawn attention to ourselves, and the enemy knew our routes to Rustamiyah. We had to gamble between staying on this side of the river and heading north or crossing the bridge and pressing through the outskirts of Jisr Diyala. The decision was made to cross the bridge, and we hammered on the last legs of our abused and battle-worn HMMWVs. We made it safe, but the truck's engine sounded injured and tired, just like us.

October 27, 2006 –

As luck would have it, we got a couple of days of no patrols thanks to the briefings and customs paperwork required for the big trip home. Stuff like this makes it hard to keep your head in the game, but we talked it over before we rolled out. We got a job to do.

We headed out on another mosque monitoring trip. The locals deserved to worship in safety, so we made our way to the area around the Wardiya mosque next to the fork in the road. We skirted Jisr Diyala, ripped through the market, and turned into Tuwaitha to ride the berm until we were within an ear-shot from the village.

We chilled there for a bit before deciding to move to where we would be more obtrusive but have a better response time. We found a better spot, and I tossed a couple of soccer balls into some lady's yard right next to us. Her kids lost their minds. Enjoy, kids. Soon, we are joined by some local elders who want to talk about kidnappings, murder, whatever.

We listened and relayed the information before heading out to the road along the Tigris. There is a small gun battle going on across the river, so we stopped to check it out. We couldn't see any dudes with guns, so we moved out. We looked hard for a fight but found not one person who wanted to play. We made it to the FOB to find our replacements have arrived. Things are looking pretty good.

Our squadron was to be relieved by our sister unit: 3rd Squadron, 61st Cavalry Regiment. They were a solid group of dudes, and many had spent the last deployment in Ramadi and Fallujah. Having fought to the west, they expected to use their experiences there in this area. We explained our methods of doing business, and they were incredulous.

It was not the Sunni insurgency that was the primary anti-Iraqi Force here. It was Shia militias, and they required a different approach. Counterinsurgency was a doctrine that was gaining traction throughout the bulk of the army. Pioneered in Al-Anbar, Tal Afar, and other territories of the country, we had taken it as our mantra, and it required a set of skills foreign to many soldiers on the battlefield but recognized by our leadership.

They brought their Bradley Fighting Vehicles, more HMMWVs, and a hundred more men who were a welcomed capability to the area we struggled to maintain with a fraction of the firepower and half the men. It was a bittersweet transition. We knew the region was going to hell. We knew that these guys had a tough road ahead.

With a new sense of duty, we handed over our area, showing them our victories, our defeats, and giving them tips on the areas we thought necessary. They will shoot at you from here, this road sees a lot of bombs, watch these guys were the sorts of tidbits we passed them. We knew they got the message. They were written in blood. Still, even if they understood the intricacies of the conflict, they were being handed a problematic fight. They could do everything right and still lose this war.

November 2, 2006 –

It was time. We went out on one last sightseeing adventure. We had a couple of the replacement guys with us. We jogged Pluto and turned towards Jisr Diyala. We drove towards the mosque—the Al-Huda Husseiniya. People were throwing shit at us, so we left before it got too wild. We are pretty much hated around these parts, so it was going to be a tough fight for the new guys to win over the crowd.

We weaved through the sewage-lined streets, hit the market, and made our way south towards Wardiya. It was quiet. The smoking skeletons of trucks remained, and the vacant charred homes stood, reminding us of what happened this year. We stopped at a spot alongside the Tigris to scope things out. The ancient river continued to carry its muddy water to the sea.

We edged over to Ja'ara. People closed doors and shied away. They didn't offer a final farewell chat. We continued north towards the FOB but not before spotting a nice new Mahdi roadside poster. I can't believe that was my last patrol—so much different than the first.

Crossing the small bridge from Route Pluto, we neared FOB Rustamiyah and the division placards that hung on the arch entrance. 'Old Abe' of the 101st Screaming Eagles sat adjacent to the 4th Infantry Division 'Ivy Leaf.' A sense of relief rushed over me as we zigzagged through the barriers intended to slow a would-be car bomber.

Our trucks idled in and dropped off the leaders at the squadron headquarters to hit the tactical operations center to do what leaders do. Everyone looked at each other in the eyes, but there was nary a smile as we drove away in our truck to park it at the motor pool. Pulling the M240 machine gun off the turret and handing it to Davis one last time, I asked if I thought we could make it to the chow hall. He was confident we could.

Our immediate priorities were food and a long shower. We had several days of work to do and indirect fire to avoid. Everyone made plans, but we were anxious about the certainty of our return to the greatest country on the planet. Rumors of stop-loss and a deployment extension circulated the smoke pits. Discussions were rife with scuttlebutt, including whispers we were staying into the spring. Many of us would not celebrate until we landed in the United States and the game was over. The only thing evident was that we wanted to end it, but if it came to overtime, we'd punish the other team for dragging it out.

The week of November 10th, 2006 –

Great news everyone! We get to go home! Bad news. Another unit from 1st Armored Division had its tour extended for a big push the top brass is putting together. They want to keep a set number of troops in the country into the spring. We are spared. Time to head to Kuwait. Our platoon made it through customs, hopped on a plane, and came home without an issue. It's one of the best feelings in the world.

Since we arrived earliest, the headquarters platoon was sent home first. We waited at the landing zone for our Chinook helicopter ride to Baghdad International Airport. Arriving at the airfield, we spent several hours waiting for our trip to Kuwait. A C-17 Globemaster loaded us up, strapped us into airline-style seats, and we flew south to a camp in the middle of the Kuwaiti desert. The loadmaster climbed into the internal structure of the airplane and hung an American flag from the ceiling of the aircraft. We cheered for a few minutes before falling fast asleep.

Once in Kuwait, we went through a customs station. Our baggage was searched for ammunition and other contraband. It was annoying, but our impatience added to the frustration. Before we knew it, though, we were aboard a commercial jet bound for Fort Campbell and the United States of America.

After many hours of flight and one pit stop, the pilot announced that we were due to land at Campbell Army Airfield. Once on the ground, we gathered our gear and filed down the stairs where the 101st Division Commander shook our hands, welcoming us home. I carried my rifle and my pack to an area outside a hangar arranged with a stage and backdrop to welcome us home.

Gathering in ragtag formation, we marched into the cheers of a crowd that had waited for hours to greet us—or maybe waited a year to be more accurate. The Division Commander gave a speech that none of the soldiers listened to, and we were released for fifteen minutes to find our families. We took thirty.

I chatted with my family about nothing important. I didn't know what appropriate post-combat deployment discussion topics would be, so I asked about the weather. We went to the company area and turned in our weapons. We were free men. I met my family, and we had lunch at my favorite restaurant before heading to a hotel room they had booked for me so I could sleep in a bed. I wasn't ready to relax.

As a 21-year-old long deprived of the forbidden fruit, I was determined to locate some beer. No vendor sold it on Sundays in Kentucky, so I drove a few minutes down the road to Tennessee. Everyone was going about their business without concern, enjoying a beautiful quiet afternoon. I was on a beer run. Except it was more than a beer run—it was my homecoming parade. I cheered to myself with the music turned up.

With a sixer of gas-station variety brew, I cruised to the hotel, climbed into the bed, and turned on the television. There was no programming on worth watching. I searched to see if I could find some news about the war. There was none. I drank a beer and fell asleep. It was around 4 o'clock in the afternoon. I slept for fourteen hours. I was home from war.

It was clear as we returned to the greatest nation on the planet that Iraq was in trouble. We had done what we could, and we did it better than most. In fact, a vignette of our operations made its way into Army doctrine. Our leaders made deals to develop rapport, manipulated the militias to try to secure a space for peace, and directed soldiers to knock the enemy off balance, denying sanctuary where possible. Soldiers dodged bombs, made tough choices, and aggressively engaged the enemy where they appeared. In the end, it was not enough to curb the sectarian violence and murder engulfing the nation that effectively undermined any effort to formulate a functioning government. The prospects for a free Iraqi future looked dim.

Two months later, on January 17th, the surge was announced to try to stymie the deterioration of Iraq. That evening, as I contemplated my future and questioned my past, I listened as President George W. Bush unveiled a new plan to halt Iraq's descent into a bloody civil war and debated what we'd been doing the last twelve months. I leaned forward on a worn couch I was thankful to have and glanced at a pile of papers from a year of memory, anxious to see what he had to say about America's future with Iraq. The President spoke,

"When I addressed you just over a year ago, nearly 12 million Iraqis had cast their ballots for a unified and democratic nation. The elections of 2005 were a stunning achievement. We thought that these elections would bring the Iraqis together and that as we trained Iraqi security forces, we could accomplish our mission with fewer American troops. But in 2006, the opposite happened. The violence in Iraq— particularly in Baghdad—overwhelmed the political gains the Iraqis had made. Al Qaeda terrorists and Sunni insurgents

recognized the mortal danger that Iraq's elections posed for their cause, and they responded with outrageous acts of murder aimed at innocent Iraqis. They blew up one of the holiest shrines in Shia Islam—the Golden Mosque of Samarra—in a calculated effort to provoke Iraq's Shia population to retaliate. Their strategy worked. Radical Shia elements, some supported by Iran, formed death squads. And the result was a vicious cycle of sectarian violence that continues today. The situation in Iraq is unacceptable to the American people—and it is unacceptable to me. Our troops in Iraq have fought bravely. They have done everything we have asked them to do. Where mistakes have been made, the responsibility rests with me. It is clear that we need to change our strategy in Iraq."

There is no turning back, changing the decisions made, or altering the consequences reaped. Only a surge. A surge, an increase, a burst, a movement onward, a motion forward. A surge to breathe life into a fledgling democratic government, a surge into a new life waiting. War will go on and so must we. Examine the past and use it to embrace the future. Like the debrief skills service members have long used to muscle meaning from tough scenarios, we reconstitute and find the redeeming value of harsh experiences to improve our resiliency and performance in any of life's challenges—both on and off the battlefield. And it looked like challenges were going to be abundant as the Commander-in-Chief continued.

"In our discussions, we all agreed that there is no magic formula for success in Iraq. And one message came through loud and clear: Failure in Iraq would be a disaster for the United States. The consequences of failure are clear: Radical

Islamic extremists would grow in strength and gain new recruits. They would be in a better position to topple moderate governments, create chaos in the region, and use oil revenues to fund their ambitions. Iran would be emboldened in its pursuit of nuclear weapons. Our enemies would have a safe haven from which to plan and launch attacks on the American people. On September the 11th, 2001, we saw what a refuge for extremists on the other side of the world could bring to the streets of our own cities. For the safety of our people, America must succeed in Iraq. The most urgent priority for success in Iraq is security, especially in Baghdad. Eighty percent of Iraq's sectarian violence occurs within 30 miles of the capital. This violence is splitting Baghdad into sectarian enclaves and shaking the confidence of all Iraqis. Only Iraqis can end the sectarian violence and secure their people. And their government has put forward an aggressive plan to do it. Our past efforts to secure Baghdad failed for two principal reasons: There were not enough Iraqi and American troops to secure neighborhoods that had been cleared of terrorists and insurgents. And there were too many restrictions on the troops we did have..."[†]

The fight was going to be demanding. We had tried to heal an open wound during our time in Iraq, but the bleeding wouldn't stop with a bandage. No, now it was time for a tourniquet. As the President declared in his speech, departing without a stable government and the rule of law in the country created a void from which uncontested enemies of freedom targeted an already frightened populace—both Iraqi and

---

[†] *George W. Bush, President's Address to the Nation, January 10th, 2007*

American. Extremism grows where the soil allows it to flourish. Eliminate the conditions, and it will wilt away. Our options were limited, and the terror of an emboldened insurgency was realized.

After being witness to the Iraqi people endure the horror of routine murder and chaos, there remained a tough decision to rid citizens of two nations from fear. It took me another ten years to make a choice a fraction of that magnitude—to share the journal and reflect on more than my actions in Iraq, but what the experience had meant to me, how it had shaped me, how I changed.

I needed to share and understand the story of Comanche Company for the guys to my left and right and for my own soul, fortunate to come out of the grinder unscathed. I owed it to our fallen who will remain a part of me. We carry forward their heroism unsung, ensuring their lives continue on inside us—a treasured bargain forged in the brotherhood of combat. To the end, for those free of fear, we shall forever march among ghosts.

Yet, sitting in the apartment that was as foreign as the nation I had just left, President Bush continued his speech. I understood the rest. I had lived it. I turned off the television and sat in quiet soberness. On the nicked and bruised coffee table lay a document with entries written after every patrol by a person experiencing events that had changed him though he didn't understand how. I asked myself that enigmatic question for the first time: what did it all mean? I became an adult in Iraq, and returning to the civilian world, I was meeting myself for the first time. I now understood a visceral level of humanity and had an appreciation for the sweetness of life gained from a series of patrols in a war zone.

I became determined to use those experiences in the way that served me best—post-traumatic growth if there was a thing. I had a whole life in front of me and, no matter the direction it took me, I had control over my outlook. I might not get closure, but I'd get peace. We were home from war, one that might not have gone the way we wanted, but it was going to be there, now as much a part of my spirit as the tribe with whom I had endured it.

Together, we mistakenly yearn for the smell of gunpowder, the dodging and thunder of exploding bombs, or the pounding pulse and knotted stomach of combat, but it was the brotherhood amongst the battle and that which it defended— each other—that we'd miss. The Comanches taught me so much in so little time, about myself and about the honor of those few that fight. Veterans possess a mutual understanding of one incomparable distinction—a solemn dignity is ours for when our nation called, we answered. It's what follows service that may lack clarity.

Though, in retrospect, while searching for a meaning insofar as how to live our postwar lives, we may admittedly fail to soldier forward and live it. I had a choice, and I chose to find redemption by remembering. I scanned the first page: November 2005. Our year in Iraq was, in many ways, a year set in motion before our arrival. However, its ending was not going to be mine. Our destinies are not tied. There is still much to be gained from wartime service to the nation.

Like the President, I was going to commit to the long-term and let the past be the past. I couldn't edit what happened or re-write my history, but I could grab a fresh sheet of paper and compose some thoughts for the future. In another decade, I'd share those quiet contemplations and grow older knowing I couldn't choose the outcome, but I could choose my outlook. After all, self-reflection sometimes happens in the muddiest of puddles, sometimes on the longest drives, sometimes in the silence of memories.

Those papers helped me make sense of it but it wasn't the way forward—only a framework for a life renewed and some lessons for the beginning of a new chapter. For me, it started with text messages one year in the making.

Ding. "Hey, it's Kat. Welcome home."

As for us, our days of combat are over. Our swords are rust. Our guns will thunder no more. The vultures that once wheeled over our heads must be buried with their prey. Whatever of glory must be won in the council or the closet, never again in the field. I do not repine. We have shared the incommunicable experience of war; we have felt, we still feel, the passion of life to its top.

-Oliver Wendell Holmes Jr.

ACKNOWLEDGEMENTS

An abundance of support was given to me for this project, and for that reason, I'd like to mention those who deserve more than simple recognition but my boundless gratitude. My wife, Kat, has long been the cornerstone to my life and provided countless words of advice to keep me inside my right and left limit. I'm indebted to her unmatched love and encouragement. My family at large; you all have shaped my way forward and listened while I droned on about this project. Thanks for your gracious and continued support. To my friends, especially B and M; thanks for entertaining my constant thinking out loud and mundane updates that kept me accountable. G, your eye for detail and prose improved this story beyond my potential. I'm optimistic you'll see your effort worthwhile. S & W, thanks for your directions and artistic visions. You have proven great soundboards to bounce my initial thoughts. M, thanks for your time. I will pay it forward.

Most importantly, I owe the Comanches. Not only do I owe them for their participation in the development of this story, but so much more. Without their bravery, feedback, and unyielding encouragement, these words would have never made it off the coffee table. I owe without reserve those Comanches mentioned here that steered me to publish the journal I shared at the ten-year reunion after our return from Iraq. You're all incredible people and I'm proud to have served by your side. I hope this book makes it to your shelf and you can hand it to those that want to know and say, "This is our story." I can't wait for the next rendezvous. Until then, Currahee.

ABOUT THE AUTHOR

Paul Endris lives outside Omaha, Nebraska with his wife, Kat, and their two young children. They have a dog named Wrigley after the greatest baseball stadium in the nation. Paul continues to passionately support Global War on Terror veterans and contemplate contemporary national security issues, a hobby he routinely uses to ruin date nights. This is his first book.

A NOTE FROM PAUL

There is much gained from reuniting with your fellow veterans. Sharing perspectives, discussing events, and even writing stories helps process and organize the unique experiences of combat. If you are a veteran, consider reaching out and starting your own *Operation Retrospect*.

Furthermore, as a self-published author, the challenges to spread the word about this book and more importantly, the sacrifices of those involved, is substantial. Reviews on Amazon.com or social media help overcome these barriers and acknowledge the fading memory of a war being forgotten.

If you liked this story, please provide a review so that others might enjoy it too. Cheers.

Visit OperationRetrospect.com
for exclusive content relating to this book.

Made in the USA
Columbia, SC
15 April 2019